William Torrey Harris

Introduction to the Study of Philosophy

Comprising Passages from his Writings

William Torrey Harris

Introduction to the Study of Philosophy
Comprising Passages from his Writings

ISBN/EAN: 9783744747103

Printed in Europe, USA, Canada, Australia, Japan

Cover: Foto ©Thomas Meinert / pixelio.de

More available books at **www.hansebooks.com**

INTRODUCTION

TO THE

STUDY OF PHILOSOPHY

BY
WILLIAM T. HARRIS

COMPRISING PASSAGES FROM HIS WRITINGS
SELECTED AND ARRANGED WITH COMMENTARY AND ILLUSTRATION
By MARIETTA KIES

Presented as a thesis in connection with work for the Master's Degree at the University of Michigan.

NEW YORK
D. APPLETON AND COMPANY
1890.

1889,
By D. APPLETON AND COMPANY.

PREFATORY NOTE.

The compiler and editor of this volume, Miss Kies, has my full consent to and approval of her selections and arrangement of such portions of my writings as she finds suitable for her purpose. I shall be very glad if this book proves helpful to her classes or to any persons who may use it.

WILLIAM T. HARRIS.

CONCORD, MASS., *July 25, 1889.*

PREFACE.

The present work of compiling and arranging some of the thoughts of Dr. Harris in a form convenient for class-use has been undertaken in order to bring together in a book widely scattered materials which the writer has found useful in presenting philosophy to her classes at Mt. Holyoke Seminary and College.

Philosophy as presented by Dr. Harris gives to the student an interpretation and explanation of the phases of existence which render even the ordinary affairs of life in accordance with reason; and for the higher or spiritual phases of life, his interpretations have the power of a great illumination; and many of the students are apparently awakened to an interest in philosophy, not only as a subject to be taken as a prescribed study, but also as a subject of fruitful interest for future years and as a key which unlocks many of the mysteries of other subjects pursued in a college course.

The "illustrations" given are such as have been used for several years at the Seminary. Such examples or illustrations have been found helpful in assisting students who have been accustomed to study the external aspects of the world to make the transition to a more thoughtful method, and thus to discover the fundamental principles of a world of things and events.

Those who have attempted to study the profound thoughts of Dr. Harris know how difficult it is to "get started." For the benefit of those students who have not yet found the philosophy of Dr. Harris "easy reading," a few suggestions as to the method used in teaching the subject at Mt. Holyoke may be in order.

The majority of the students who come to the study of the subject have never studied any form of mental philosophy. The phases of the subject are presented in the order given in this book. From six to eight weeks, four lessons each week, are taken for the first consideration of the subject, with lectures, explanations, etc. Very little is expected of the students in the way of recitation during their first time over the subject. About three fourths of the hour of each lesson is taken for explanation and comparison of views of other writers on the subject under consideration, the remaining one fourth of the hour for the Socratic method, questions and answers, the students presenting the questions. By this method the student is enabled to get at least a glimpse of the whole subject as a system, and then he is prepared to advance more rapidly.

But in attaining the first stages of philosophic knowing persistent effort as well as patient waiting is needed. After the first presentation of the subject, the same ground is gone over, taking the divisions of the subject in the same order, and giving nearly as many weeks to the work. This time over the subject the students, by means of recitation and papers prepared by them, are expected to do the greater part of the work.

The recitations and reading and discussion of the papers occupy three fourths of the hour, and one fourth is devoted to the views of the leading contemporary writers on the same questions, with occasional reference to the opinions of historic philosophers. This course is designed as a preparation for the study of the history of philosophy and as a means for interpreting the thoughts of the great philosophers of all centuries.

The strongest desire in preparing this book is that students will be led to study the thoughts of Dr. Harris in articles and books as originally presented by him, and to have a stronger desire to enter the fields of historic thought.

MARIETTA KIES.

SOUTH HADLEY, MASS., *June, 1889.*

CONTENTS.

CHAPTER I.
METHODS OF STUDY.

Introspection: Psychology—Physiological Psychology—Empirical Psychology—Comparative Psychology—Philosophy. . . . 1

CHAPTER II.
PRESUPPOSITIONS OF EXPERIENCE.

Nature of the Problems of Philosophy—The Starting-Point in Philosophical Investigation — Space, Time: Infinite — Effect, Cause, Causa sui, or Self-cause—Beings: Dependent, implies another, derived from another=World; Independent, whole, totality, self-determined=Creator 15

CHAPTER III.
PHILOSOPHY OF NATURE.

The World: Self-Activity shown in Inorganic Forms — Organic; Plants, Animals, Man 35

CHAPTER IV.
MAN: A SELF-ACTIVE INDIVIDUAL.

Man is Self-Activity, Self-Consciousness—Channels of Development of Activity: Feeling, or Sense-perception, Representation, Understanding, Reason, Emotions, Will 48

SECTION I.—SENSE-PERCEPTION.

Degree of Activity shown in Sense-perception: Touch, Taste, Smell, Hearing, Seeing 55

CONTENTS.

SECTION II.—REPRESENTATION.

Self-Activity shown in Representation: Recollection, Fancy, Imagination, Attention, Memory 59

SECTION III.

Significance of the Power to Use Language 71

SECTION IV.—REFLECTION.

"General Objects" of Memory, as Thought, become Judgments—Sense-perception: Sensuous Ideas perceive Objects; Identity, Difference—Understanding: Abstract Ideas investigate Object and Environment; Relations—The "General Objects" or "Universals" are possible because of Reason: Absolute Idea or Rational Insight knows Logical Conditions of Existence . . . 74

SECTION V.—THE SYLLOGISM.

The Mind Acts in the Modes of Syllogism: Sensuous Ideas use Second Figure, First Figure, Third Figure; Abstract Ideas use Third Figure, First Figure, Second Figure; Absolute Idea uses Third Figure 96

SECTION VI.—THE THIRD STAGE OF THINKING: THE ABSOLUTE IDEA, OR THE REASON.

Rational Insight knows: Causality, Self-cause—Space, Time—Quality, Quantity — Change, Self-activity — Life, Individuality, Absolute Personality—Absolute Thought; manifested in Truth, Beauty, Goodness 125

SECTION VII.—THE EMOTIONS.

Duplication of Self-Activity in Emotions: Sentient, Psychical, Rational 249

SECTION VIII.—THE WILL.

Stage of Knowing presupposed in Contemplation of Freedom—Substantial Will: Self-activity: Totality: Freedom—Formal Will: Action—Change sometimes regarded as produced only by Environment: External Conditions; Motives 263

CHAPTER V.

Immortality of Man 280

EXPLANATORY.

WHERE simply the abbreviation "vol." has been used, the reference is to the "Journal of Speculative Philosophy."

"ILL." has been used as an abbreviation of the word "illustration."

The intention has been to inclose in one set of quotation-marks a printed portion from the works of Dr. Harris, taken consecutively from one place, though in a few instances paragraphs have been transposed. Introductory words and parenthetical phrases have occasionally been changed, but the intention has been not in any instance to change the thought of the sentence. Below will be found a list of the names of articles and books used in the compilation; the pages are given in foot-notes.

ARTICLES AND BOOKS USED IN COMPILATION.

"Music as a Form of Art," Vol. I.
"Introduction to Philosophy," Vols. I and II.
"The Last Judgment," Vol. 3.
"The History of Philosophy in Outline," Vol. 10.
"The Relation of Religion to Art," Vol. 10.
"Michael Angelo's Fates, Vol. 11."
"Outlines of Educational Psychology," Vol. 14.
"The Philosophy of Religion," Vol. 15.
"Philosophy in Outline," Vol. 17.
"Immortality of the Individual," Vol. 19.
"Is Pantheism the Legitimate Outcome of Modern Science?" Vol. 19.

"Psychological Inquiry," "Education," Vol. VI.

"Philosophy of Education," International Education Series.

"The Mind of the Child," International Education Series.

"Philosophy made Simple," "The Chautauquan" (March, April, May, 1886).

"Religion in Art," "The Chautauquan" (January, February, March, 1886).

"Thoughts on Educational Psychology," "Illinois School Journal," series of articles beginning March, 1888.

"Reports of Lectures at Boston University," "The Journal of Education," December, 1888; January, 1889.

"Aristotle's Doctrine of Reason," "Journal of the American Akêdêmê," June, 1888.

"Historical Epochs of Art," "Concord Lectures," 1882.

"Results in Ontology," "Concord Lectures," 1887.

"Theory of the Syllogism," "Concord Lectures," 1887.

INTRODUCTION TO THE STUDY OF PHILOSOPHY.

CHAPTER I.

METHODS OF STUDY.

Introspection: Psychology — Physiological Psychology — Empirical Psychology — Comparative Psychology — Philosophy.

Introspection: Psychology.— "Introspection is internal observation—our consciousness of the activity of the mind itself. The subject who observes is the object observed. Consciousness is knowing of self. This seems to be the characteristic of mind and mental phenomena— there is always some degree of self-relation; there is self-feeling or self-knowledge. Even in mere life in the vegetative soul there is self-relation. This we shall study as our chief object of interest in psychology.

"We will note first the contrast between external and internal observation. Outward observation is objective perception or sense perception. It perceives things and environments. Things are always relative to their environment. Things are therefore dependent beings. They stand in causal relation to other things, and if moved are moved from without by external forces.

"Introspection, or internal observation, on the other

hand, perceives the activity of the mind, and this is self-activity, and not a movement caused by external forces. Feelings, thoughts, volitions, are phases of self-activity. This we shall consider more in detail. Let us note that a feeling, a thought, or a volition implies subject and object. Each is an activity and an activity of the self. External perception does not perceive any self. It perceives only what is extended in time and space and what is consequently multiple, what is moved by something else and not self-moved. If it beholds living objects it does not behold the self that animates the body, but only the body that is organically formed by the self. But introspection beholds the self. This is a very important distinction between the two orders of observation, external and internal. The former can perceive only phenomena, the latter can perceive noumena. The former can perceive only what is relative, and dependent on something else; the latter can perceive what is independent and self-determined, a primary cause and source of movement.

"To pass from the first order of observation, which perceives external things, to the second order of observation, which perceives self-activity, is to take a great step. We are dimly conscious of our entire mental activity, but we do not (until we have acquired psychologic skill) distinguish and separately identify its several phases. It is the same in the outer world—we know many things in ordinary consciousness, but only in science do we unite the items of our knowledge systematically so as to make each assist in the explanation of all. Common knowledge lacks unity and system. In the inner world, too, there is common introspection, unsystematized and devoid of unity—the light of our ordinary consciousness. But there is higher scientific introspection which discovers both unity and system." *

" This subject of introspection leads out to the end of the world and reappears underneath the method of modern natural science which studies all objects in their history—in their evolution. Strangely enough the scientists of the present day decry in psychology what they call the 'introspective method.' And just as in the case of the repudiation of teleology, they are bound to return to some other form of what they repudiate. Renounce teleology, and you find nothing but teleology in everything. Renounce introspection, and you are to find introspection the fundamental moving principle of all nature. All things have their explanation in a blind attempt on the part of nature to look at itself." †

ILL.—A botanist is able to study a plant only through acts of introspection. There are the unreflective acts of introspection by which he is able to know a plant as one of a class of objects, and the conscious reflective acts of introspection by which he is able to recognize a plant as belonging to a particular class and species; for in this study of the plant life, he learns the characteristics of the plant, the manner of growth, and the relations of this plant to the whole vegetable world and animal world, and in doing this he discriminates between the nature of the energy of the plant and that of the human mind.

Physiological Psychology.—" The so-called physiological psychology commences with the living organism,

---

* " Illinois School Journal," vol. vii, pp. 346, 347.   † Ibid., p. 349.

and investigates the correlation of psychic phenomena with corporeal changes, and seeks to find what psychic phenomena correspond to the several corporeal stimuli. Its chief industry may be said to be the search for an explanation of mental phenomena in bodily functions. These again it seeks to explain through environment." *

"It is evident that on the physiological basis psychological discovery is limited to bodily functions. The idea of life is as far as it can go without transcending what is physiological. A great service will be performed by those investigators who explore this field and demonstrate to science that thinking activity transcends physical functions, and refute physiologically the assertion of Moleschott, that 'thought is a secretion of the brain, just as bile is a secretion of the liver.' Then the limited form of self-activity, which is the principle of life, will be laid aside for the pure self-activity which we call *thought*.

"Physiological psychology, as we have stated, limits its investigations to discovering physical concomitants of mental actions. What portion of the body is affected to movement or change upon occasion of a given mental act? what kind of motion and its quantitative value? also, what mental action or response there is to various kinds of bodily stimuli? what part of the observation is external or objective experiment? and what part of it is introspective? are interesting questions. The presuppositions of the observation are: 1. a world of time and space in which the body is conditioned; 2. an internal perception or reflection that can observe what is

---

* "Education," vol. vi, p. 159.

within consciousness, to wit: a subjective world of feeling whose form is time and a world of thought whose form is neither space nor time; 3. concomitance or succession is all that can ever be observed in these fields; each series of facts requires observation by a different mental act—the physiological by the external senses, the feelings and thoughts by introspection of consciousness. You certainly can never perceive a feeling or a thought or a volition by touch, taste, smell, hearing, or seeing. You may only infer the existence of a thought, feeling, or volition by some external movement or change which you perceive by the senses.

"The scope of physiological psychology is logically limited at the outset. It can never catch a thought or feeling outside the internal self, and hence can never identify it with any external fact or object whatever, although it may fix an order of sequence or concomitance between the items of a series observed internally and a series observed externally.

"The legitimate conclusion here, therefore, is that in all psychology, physiological or otherwise, the scientist who observes must be able to reproduce within his own mind for himself the psychological phenomena that he perceives, for he can never perceive any psychological phenomena in any other being. The mental phenomena of children as well as of adults, of savages as well as of cultured people, can never be perceived as external phenomena, but only in one's self and inferred to exist in others as concomitant to certain external movements or changes which are perceived to exist externally. Here one comes to the paramount importance of insight into what we shall call pure psychology of thought in connection with physiology. If an investigator does not know how to discriminate thinking and reasoning on different planes, it is absurd to expect that he will recognize those different planes of thinking or reasoning in others. Even clear, human speech does not convey a generalization to the mind that is not cultured enough to make that generalization." *

"What is to be expected from researches in physiological psychology, limited as it is? To this we reply: Many and very great services, especially to family and school education. All of the provinces where the body acts as a means of expression to the external world, and all the provinces where the self-active mind uses the body as a means of exploring the world—all these provinces have, of course, a physiological factor which should be thoroughly understood qualitatively and quantitatively.

"All cases of insanity, idiocy; all matters of hereditary descent; all that pertains to the use and abuse of the five organs of sense; all that relates to food, clothing, and shelter, as favorable or unfavorable to the development of the soul; the questions of comparative psychology of nations—of the modifying influences of climate, age, sex, and occupation; and, finally, such phenomena as sleep, dreams, somnambulism, and the occurrences that are supposed to belong to the 'night-side of nature,' together with epidemics and superstitions—here is an immense field in which physiological psychology is bound to be of increasing service to man. But so long as it is cultivated apart from pure psychology, and

---

* "Education," vol. vi, pp. 159–161.

with a sort of persuasion that there is no self-active being that we are concerned with in psychology, it will be impossible to expect any first-class results." *

ILL.—Professor Ladd, after a careful consideration of the quality and quantity of sensations coming through the sense-organs and an enumeration and description of various experiments that noted physiological psychologists have made, concludes that " in general, it may be said that *every mental state has its value determined*, both as respects its quality and its so-called quantity, *by its relation to other states* "; or, in other words, his conclusion is that even the physiological psychologist is greatly dependent upon "introspection" for his results. †

Empirical Psychology.—" The good old-fashioned psychology laid chief stress on the 'faculties' of the mind. The weaker and more metaphysical (in the bad sense of the word 'metaphysical,' signifying analytical abstract thinking) adherents to this view of the mind went so far as to call these faculties 'organs' of mind, thus betraying the fact that they had unconsciously or purposely substituted the idea of life for that of mind. Life is organic being, and always reveals itself in organs. Mind does not thus manifest itself, but its so-called faculties are degrees of self-development which arise as the self-activity becomes complex by repeating its acts of reflection. Thus the metaphysical psychology, whose fundamental defect is that it regards the soul as a substance or thing instead of a self-activity, goes on to speak

---

* "Education," vol. vi, p. 162.
† Ladd's " Physiological Psychology," Part II, chaps. iii, iv, and v.

of the faculties of the mind as if they were properties of a mind-thing, instead of modes of activity of an essential spontaneity. In using the word 'organs' for 'faculties,' metaphysical psychology goes over to the ground of physiology or the science of living beings, and naturally enough becomes phrenology."*

ILL.—A large part of the text-books in common use furnish illustration of this kind of psychology. These writers vary in the standpoint taken from those who would examine and measure the "faculties" or "organs" of the mind according to the standard of a "common consciousness," thus virtually asserting that the thought of a Plato can be brought within the same limits as that of the most ordinary mind, to those who hold that the mind possesses the "lower faculties" which can be developed and improved, but the "higher faculties," or "innate ideas," are directly bestowed upon the mind, and that these ideas can be no further analyzed or understood, and only furnish a background for the development of the lower phases of the mind without themselves undergoing development.

Comparative Psychology.—"Experience, it is true, marshals its train of facts before us in an endless succession every day of our lives. But without scientific method one fact does much to obliterate all others by its presence. Out of sight, they are out of mind. Method converts unprofitable experience, wherein nothing abides except vague and uncertain surmise, into science. In science the present fact is deprived of its

---

* "Education," vol. vi, p. 158.

ostentatious and all-absorbing interest by the act of relating it to all other facts. We classify the particular with its fellow-particulars, and it takes its due rank. Such classification, moreover, eliminates from it the unessential elements." *

"The characteristics of accuracy and precision, which make science exact, are derived from quantity. Fix the order of succession, the date, the duration, the locality, the environment, the extent of the sphere of influence, the number of manifestations, and the number of cases of intermittence, and you have exact knowledge of a phenomenon. When stated in quantitative terms, your experience is useful to other observers. It is easy to verify it or to add an increment. By quantification, science grows and grows continually, without retrograde movements.

"One does not forget, of course, that there is something besides the quantitative and altogether above the quantitative. The object itself is more important than its quantitative relations. The soul, as a self-active essence, is the object in psychology. Science determines the quantitative of its phenomenal manifestation. In other words, science determines exactly the time when, the place where, the duration and frequency, the extent and degree of the manifestation of this self-activity in the body and through the body.

"The nature of feelings, volitions, and ideas in themselves is the object of introspective psychology and metaphysics. But all will concede that parents and

---

* "The Senses and the Will," Preyer, Editor's Preface, p. 5.

teachers are directly interested in the order of development of the soul from its lower functions into its higher ones, and are consequently concerned with these quantitative manifestations." *

"The supreme interest to us in these observations is the development from lower degrees of intelligence to higher ones. The immense interval that separates plant life from animal life, is almost paralleled by the interval between the animal and the human being. From mere nutrition to sensation is a great step; from mere sensation to the conscious employment of ethical ideas and the perception of logical necessity and universality is an equal step. Yet it is to be assumed that the transitions exist in all degrees, and that the step from any degree to the next one is not difficult when the natural means is discovered. It is this means that comparative psychology is discovering.

"The infant is contemplated in the process of gaining command over himself. His sense organs gradually become available for perception; his muscles become controllable by his will. Each new acquisition becomes in turn an instrument of further progress.

"Exact science determines when and where the animal phase leaves off and the purely human begins—where the organic phase ends and the individual begins. The discrimination of impulsive, reflective, and instinctive movements, all of them organic, throws light on the genesis of mind out of its lower antecedent. Imitation is the first manifestation of the transition from the organic to the strictly spiritual. In this connection it

---

* "The Senses and the Will," Preyer, Editor's Preface, p. 6.

is, before all, an important question, What is the significance of the relapse into unconscious instinct through the formation of habit? We do an act by great special effort of the will and intellect; we repeat it until it is done with ease. It gradually lapses into unconscious use and wont, and has become instinctive and organic." *

ILL. It is of interest that Prof. Preyer discovers among many other things, from his observations of children and animals, that an infant uses the sense of sight in the first day of his life; that indications of the use of the sense of hearing vary greatly in time, but appear as early as the fourth day of the child's life; and that a child can probably taste and smell soon after birth; and also that in the lower animals these senses are much more completely developed at birth than with children. And while the instinctive and reflex movements of the child are spontaneous, the imitative or voluntary movements, which indicate a development of the will, do not take place until after the forming of ideas, and that early in the mind of the child there is the "formation of concepts without language."

Philosophy.—" Philosophy is not a science of things in general, but a science that investigates the presuppositions of experience, and discovers the nature of the first principle. Philosophy does not set up the extravagant pretension to know all things. It does not 'take all knowledge for its province,' any more than geology or astronomy or logic does. Geology aspires to know the entire structure of this globe; astronomy to know all the stars; logic to know the structure of the reason-

---

* "The Senses and the Will," Preyer, Editor's Preface, pp. 6, 7.

ing process. Philosophy attempts to find the necessary *a priori* elements or factors in experience, and arrange them into a system by deducing them from a first principle. Not the forms of reasoning alone, but the forms of sense perception, of reflection, of speculative knowing, and the very forms which condition being, or existence itself, are to be investigated. The science of necessary forms is a very special science, because it does not concern itself with collecting and arranging the infinite multitude of particular objects in the world and identifying their species and genera, as the particular sciences do. It investigates the presupposed conditions and ascends to the one supreme condition. It therefore turns its back on the multitude of particular things, and seizes them in the unity of their 'ascent and cause,' as George Herbert names it. The particular sciences and departments of knowledge collect and classify and explain phenomena. Philosophy collects and classifies and explains their explanations. Its province is much more narrow and special than theirs. If to explain meant to find the many, the different, the particular examples or specimens, philosophy would have to take all knowledge for its province if it aspired to explain the explanations offered in the several sciences. But that is not its meaning. To explain means to find the common, the generic principle in the particular. This is just the opposite of that other process which would take all knowledge in its infinite details for its province. To explain all knowledge is not to know all things." *

---

* Vol. 17, pp. 296, 297.

"Philosophy is not religion, nor a substitute for religion, any more than it is art or a substitute for art. There is a distinction, also, between philosophy and theology, although philosophy is a necessary constituent of theology. While theology must necessarily contain a historical and biographical element, and endeavor to find in that element the manifestation of necessary and universal principles, philosophy, on the other hand, devotes itself exclusively to the consideration of those universal and necessary conditions of existence which are found to exist in experience, not as furnished by experience, but as logical, *a priori* conditions of experience itself." *

Ill.—Mathematics discovers and states as laws the position and action of bodies in space and time ; philosophy discovers the nature of time and space which condition the existence of things and events. The physical sciences take molecules and atoms as convenient " working hypotheses," and discover how these behave under different circumstances, and formulate laws for this behavior, and classify the various phenomena presented by their activity; philosophy discovers the nature of a thing, its activity, and sees the correlation of its energy with the different forms of force in the universe. The biological sciences investigate the phases of life—plant, animal, and that of man—the nature of cellular tissue and its structure, and the causes and conditions which produce its numerous variations in classes, genera, and species, and the characteristics and phenomena shown in the process of growth ; philosophy interprets the manifestations of life as manifestations of self-activity

---

* Vol. 17, p. 310.

in different degrees of completeness—plant life, animal life, and that of man. Psychology studies the mind or soul as a self-active, self-determined individual, and finds out how the individual develops in the channels of feeling, thought, and will, and classifies the phenomena presented in the phases of development; philosophy discovers not only motion—self-activity—but also discovers that self-determination is rendered possible because of God, freedom and immortality. The sciences which pertain to the relations of man with man investigate the conditions of the industrial, civil, social, and political relations of society, determine the causes which have produced the present conditions, and seek, by a study of past and present conditions, to determine how the institutions of society can assist in a better adjustment of these relations; moral philosophy considers the present condition of the individual, the family, society, state, and church in the light of what they ought to be, and compares the present life of each with its ideal life; philosophy considers the nature of the will which renders it possible and desirable for man to combine with man in the institutions of the family, civil society, state, and church, in order that the individual may reenforce society, and society the individual.

CHAPTER II.

PRESUPPOSITIONS OF EXPERIENCE.

Nature of the Problems of Philosophy—The Starting-Point in Philosophical Investigation—Space, Time: Infinite—Effect, Cause, Causa sui, or Self-cause—Beings: Dependent, implies another, derived from another = World; Independent, whole, totality, self-determined = Creator.

Nature of the Problems of Philosophy.—"The problems of philosophy are perennial. Each individual must solve them for himself when he comes to the age of reflection. No number of philosophers can ever settle philosophic questions so that it will not be necessary for each individual to think out solutions for himself. Questions of mere fact in nature can be settled by investigation, so that a mere statement suffices to convey the result to a school-boy. But it is not possible to 'settle' matters of insight just as we settle matters of fact. A truth that requires for its comprehension a certain degree of cultured power of thought can not, by any possibility, be taught as a matter of fact to a youth who has not yet arrived at the necessary stage of thinking.

"We recognize this quite readily in the acquirement of mathematical truth. Such truth can not be conveyed to minds that will not or can not grasp the elementary conceptions and make the combinations necessary. Only by intellectual energy can those truths be seen, and even mathematics has not 'settled' anything for people who have no insight into its demonstrations. Philosophic knowing is knowing of logical conditions of being and experience. It is, therefore, a special kind of knowing that arises from reflection. These logical conditions of existence are invisible to the one who does not specially reflect upon them. When one sees them at all, he sees that they are necessary elements of experience. It is a third stage of knowing, this knowing of logical presuppositions, and its insights can not be seen from the first or second stage of knowing. (The three stages of knowing are considered in chapter iv, section iv.)

"Truths that are 'settled' in philosophy may yet seem to be impossibilities to the one whose intellectual view is on the second stage of knowing." *

The Starting-Point. — "To illustrate philosophic knowing, and at the same time to enter its province and begin philosophizing, we shall take up at once a consideration of three ideas—space, time, and cause. Space and time—as the condition of nature or the world, as the necessary presuppositions of extension and multitude—will furnish us occasion to consider the infinite and the possibility of knowing it. The idea of cause will lead us to the fundamental insight on which true philosophy rests." †

Space.—" In all experience we deal with sensible objects and their changes. The universal condition of the existence of sensible objects is space. Each object is limited or finite, but the universal condition of the ex-

---

* Vol. 17, p. 342. † Vol. 17, p. 297.

istence of objects is self-limited or infinite. An object of the senses possesses extension and limits, and, consequently, has an environment. We find ourselves necessitated to think an environment in order to think the object as a limited object.

"Here we have, first the object, and second the environment as mutually limiting and excluding, and as correlatives. But the ground or condition of both object and its environment is space. Space makes both possible. Space is a necessary idea. We may think this particular object or not—it may exist or it may not. So, too, this particular environment may exist or not, although some environment is necessary. But space must exist, whether this particular object or environment exists or not. Here we have three steps toward absolute necessity: 1. The object which is not necessary, but may or may not exist—may exist now, but cease after an interval; 2. The environment which must exist in some form if the object exists—a hypothetical necessity; 3. The logical condition of the object and its environment, which must, as space, exist, whether the object exist or not.

"Again, note the fact that the object ceases where the environment begins. But space does not cease with the object nor with the environment; it is continued or affirmed by each. The space in which the object exists is continued by the space in which its environment exists. Space is infinite." *

Ill.—Suppose, for instance, one imagines a definite portion of space, say two feet each way, and then an-

---

* Vol. 17, pp. 297, 298.

other portion of equal dimensions about the former, and so on with successive additions without limit; the imagination soon discovers that it fails to grasp the extent of space pictured, and instead of a picture of the infinite the indefinite is the result. Then suppose that the mind with its thinking activity of reason sees that the one portion of space in limiting another portion really extends itself, and so the limitation is really a self-limitation, which is a continuation. Space in so limiting itself is infinite.

Time.—" The thought of space differs essentially from the thought of an object of experience because it is a thought of what is essentially infinite—infinite in its nature. Hence we arrive at this astonishing result— the knowledge of what is infinite underlies and makes possible our knowledge derived from experience, and the infinite makes possible the existence of what is finite. We may find all of these results by considering the nature of time. While space is the condition of the existence of things, time is the condition of the existence of all events or changes. If there is a change, it demands time for its existence; if there is an event, it demands time for its occurrence. Again, time is infinite; any finite time or duration presupposes other time to have existed before it and after it, and is thus continued by the very time that limits it. If we suppose all time to be finite, we see at once that it contradicts this hypothesis; because, if finite, it must have begun, and to begin implies a time before it in which it was not. Such a time before it, however, does not limit it, but affirms its existence beyond the boundary we have placed to it. Thus time is infinite, and yet it is the condition necessary to the existence of events and changes."*

Ill.—Suppose, for instance, a definite portion of time as an hour, and picture the hour preceding this hour and the hour which will succeed and so on with successive antecedent and subsequent times without limit and the picture will be only of an indefinite time; but when any one limited portion of time is considered as bounded by another portion it is seen that instead of one portion limiting another it really extends it or that the portions are self-limited "We can not picture to ourselves time any more than we can imagine space. We think it clearly as the condition of the existence of images and pictures, but not itself as a picture or image."

Cause and Effect, Self-Cause.—There is "another presupposition which is necessary to make experience possible, and which is an element far subtler and more potent than space and time, because it is their logical condition also. This deeper principle is Causality.

"1. We regard a thing or object as related to its environment as an external existing limit, in which case the ground or logical condition is space; or, 2. We regard the object as an event or process which consists of a series of successive moments with an environment of antecedent and subsequent moments; its ground or presupposition is time; or, 3. We may look upon an object as the recipient of influences from its environment, or as itself imparting influences to its environment. This is Causality.

"The environment and the object relate to each other

---

* "The Chautauquan," March, 1886, p. 324.

as effect or cause. The environment causes some change in the object, which change is its effect; or the object as cause reacts on the environment and produces some modification in that as its effect. The effect is a joint product of this interaction between the so-called active and passive factors or coefficients. For both are active, although one is relatively passive to the other." *

ILL.—A plant acts as cause upon its environment, the air, producing a change in the air, which change is the effect; the atmosphere in turn acts upon the plant, making changes in it; both are active, though one is relatively passive to the other.

"The principle of causality implies both time and space. In order that a cause shall send a stream of influence toward an effect, there must be time for the influence to pass from the one to the other. Also the idea of effect implies the existence of an object external to the cause, or the utterance of influence, and in this space is presupposed. Space and time are in a certain sense included in causality as a higher unity." †

ILL.—In order that the sun's rays may heat the surface of the ground and the atmosphere become of the right temperature that the plant may give off oxygen, there must be time; and the fact that the plant is acted upon by an external influence implies the existence of the plant, and the existence of the plant presupposes space.

"Now, if we examine causality, we shall see that it again presupposes a ground deeper than itself—deeper than itself as realized in a cause and effect separated into

---

* Vol. 17, pp. 302, 303. † Vol. 17, p. 303.

independent objects. This is the most essential insight to obtain in all philosophy.

"1. In order that a cause shall send a stream of influence over to an effect, it must first separate that portion of influence from itself.

"2. Self-separation is, then, the fundamental presupposition of the action of causality. Unless the cause is a self-separating energy, it can not be conceived as acting on another. The action of causality is based on self-activity." *

ILL.—If there is an effect, there must be a cause of that effect. If, for example, a person cut a rose from a rose-bush: in order that the act may take place, the person first separates by an activity of thought and will a portion of influence or energy, which is transmitted through the arm and hand and through the instrument to the rose-bush, and the result is seen, the rose is cut from the bush. If one imagines a cause or series of causes in the knife, hand, and arm, since there could be made an infinite number of divisions or steps in the process, the idea of a true cause is not helped but hindered, for the thought, the will, the self-activity, a pure energy is the cause which moves the arm, hand, knife, and cuts the flower.

"3. Self-activity is called *causa sui* to express the fact of its relation to causality. It is the infinite form of causality in which the cause is its own environment—just as space is the infinite condition underlying extended things, and time the infinite condition underlying events. Self-activity as *causa sui* has the form of

---

* Vol. 17, p. 304

self-relation, and it is self-relation that characterizes the affirmative form of the infinite. Self-relation is independence, while relation-to-others is dependence." *

ILL.—The person who cuts the rose, in the preceding illustration, in the origination of the thought to cut the rose knows that he could have created a thought not to cut the rose, and in this act of reflection thought is its own environment, and in this self-activity is the self-relation of thought and its independence; while the rose in its less degree of self-activity shows its dependence, its relation-to-others in a more marked way.

" *Causa sui,* or self-cause, is, properly speaking, the principle, *par excellence,* of philosophy. It is the principle of life, of thought, of mind—the idea of a creative activity, and hence also the basis of theology as well as of philosophy." † "Self-cause, or eternal energy, is the ultimate presupposition of all things and events. Here is the necessary ground of the idea of God. It is the presupposition of all experience and of all possible existence. By the study of the presuppositions of experience one becomes certain of the existence of One eternal Energy which creates and governs the world." ‡

" *Causa sui,* spontaneous origination of activity, or spontaneous energy, is the ultimate presupposition underlying all objects and each object of experience.

" We have before us three of the logical conditions or presuppositions of existence and experience:

" 1. Object, environment, space.
" 2. Event, environment, time.
" 3. Effect, cause, *causa sui.*" #

---

* Vol. 17, p 304.   ‡ Vol. 17, p. 306.
† Vol. 17, p. 304.   # Vol. 17, p. 304.

* ("Take the standpoint of materialistic philosophy, for example: matter is the ultimate, the whence and whither of all. Matter is thus posited as a universal which is the sole origin of all particular existences and also the final goal of the same; hence matter is active, giving rise to special existences, and also changing them into others with all the method and arrangement which we can see in natural laws. For matter must contain in it potentially all that comes from it. Hence matter is creative, causing to arise in its own general substance those particular limitations which constitute the differences and individuality of things. It is negative, or destroyer, in that it annuls the individuality of particular things, causing to vanish those limitations which separate or distinguish this thing from that other. Such a principle as this matter is assumed to be, which causes existences to arise from itself by its own activity upon itself and within itself, entirely unconditioned by any other existence or energy, is self-determination, and therefore analogous to that factor in sensuous knowing which was called the ego or self-consciousness—an activity which was universal and devoid of form, and yet incessantly productive of forms and destructive of the same. All this is implied in the theory of materialism, and exists there as separate ideas, only needing to be united by inferences." †

"The unity of space as the logical condition of matter, and of time as the logical condition of all change and manifestation, prove the unity of the world. The

---

* The portion inclosed in marks of parenthesis is not an integral part, but inserted to show the application of the preceding principles. † VoL 10, p. 228.

mathematical laws which formulate the nature of space and time condition the existence of all the phenomena in the world, and make them all parts of one system, and thus give us the right to speak of the aggregate of existence under such names as 'world' or 'universe.'

"This question of the existence of an absolute as Creator or as Ruler of the universe hinges on the question of the validity of such comprehensive unities as 'world' and 'universe.' If such ideas are derived from experience, it is argued that they are fictitious unities, and do not express positive knowledge, but only our ignorance, 'our failure to discover, invent, or conceive.' For we certainly have not made any complete inventory that we may call 'the universe.'

"Only because we are able to know the logical conditions of experience are we able to speak of the totality of all possible experience, and to name it 'world' and 'universe.' Finding unity in these logical conditions, we predicate it of all particular existence, being perfectly assured that nothing will ever exist which does not conform to these logical conditions. No extended objects will exist or change except according to the conditions of space and time. No relations between phenomena will arise except through causality, and all causality will originate in *causa sui*, or self-activity. . . .

"How does one know that things are not self-existent already, and therefore in no need of a Creator? If this question still remains in the mind, it must be answered again and again by referring to the necessary unity in the nature of the conditions of existence—space, time, and causal influence, based on self-cause.

The unity of space and the dependence of all matter upon it preclude the self-existence of any material body. Each is a part, and depends on all the rest. Presuppositions of experience can only be seen by reflection upon the conditions of experience. The feeble-minded, who can not analyze their experience nor give careful attention to its factors, can not see this necessity. Indeed, few strong minds can see these necessary presuppositions at first. But all, even the most feeble in intellect, have these presuppositions as an element of their experience, whether able to abstract them and see them as special objects or not." *)

Dependent and Independent Being.—" Let us vary the mode and manner of expressing this insight for the sake of additional clearness. First, let us ask what is the nature of self-existent being—of independent beings, whether there be one or more.

" 1. It is clear that all beings are dependent or independent, or else have, in some way, phases to which both predicates may apply." †

Ill.—Any material thing of the inorganic world is dependent and forms only a part of an aggregate. So, too, in the organic world a plant is dependent upon its surroundings for food-material, and also, as a plant, only becomes complete in the species. An animal has more independence than a plant, but only sufficient to have the power of reproducing the external world in an unconscious way, and preserving identity in species. In man there is independence in a more complete form. He presents the two phases—dependence upon his en-

---

* Vol. 17, pp. 305, 306.   † Vol. 17, p. 306, 307.

vironment and complete independence in the freedom of thought, of will.

"2. The dependent being is clearly not a whole or totality; it implies something else—some other being on which it depends. It can not depend on a dependent being, although it may stand in relation to another dependent being as another link of its dependence. All dependence implies the independent being as the source of support. Take away the independent being, and you remove the logical condition of the dependent being, because without something to depend upon there can be no dependent being. If one suggests a mutual relation of dependent beings, then still the whole is independent, and this independence furnishes the ground of the dependent parts." *

ILL.—Since inorganic things are determined by their environment in a greater degree than they are self-determined, they are only dependent parts of a system; man in the freedom of his thought and will transcends and modifies his environment and is independent.

"3. The dependent being, or links of being, no matter how numerous they are, make up one being with the being on which they depend and belong to it." †

ILL.—The earth shows dependence in all its parts—inorganic nature and organic are interdependent: the world manifesting and revealing thought and will, and the Creator, make an independent whole.

"4. All being is, therefore, either independent, or

---

* Vol. 17, p. 307. † Vol. 17, p. 307.

forms a part of an independent being. Dependent being can be explained only by the independent being from which it receives its nature." *

Ill.—The root, stem, or leaves of the rose-bush can only be explained by explaining the nature and office of the whole plant; the plant only by explaining the species; and the species only by comparison of the activity of the plant with other manifestations of self-activity. Man and the nature of finite thought can only be explained by an understanding and explanation of the nature of absolute thought.

"5. The nature or determinations of any being, its marks, properties, qualities, or attributes, arise through its own activity or through the activity of another being." †

Ill.—The nature, properties, or qualities of a crystal in the mineral world are to a degree determined by the temperature, moisture, pressure, etc. to which it is subjected, or "the qualities of crystals depend directly on the forces of the ultimate molecules or particles of matter"; thus a thing in inorganic nature is partly determined by activity without itself. Man, in the process of his growth and development, in contact with the external world of things, with other individuals, and with institutions of society, determines through his own activity his qualities or attributes; the qualities or attributes of God are completely determined by His own activity.

"6. If its nature is derived from another, it is a dependent being. The independent being is therefore

---

* Vol. 17, p. 307.   † Vol. 17, p. 307.

determined only through its own activity—it is self-determined."*

ILL.—Man only of all finite beings exercises conscious self-determination; Absolute Being in His complete self-activity is perfectly self-determined.

"7. The nature of self-existent beings, whether one or many, is therefore self-determination. This result we see is identical with that which we found in our investigation of the underlying presupposition of influence or causal relation. There must be self-separation, or else no influence can pass over to another object. The cause must first act in itself before its energy causes an effect in something else. It must therefore be essentially cause and effect in itself, or *causa sui*, meaning self-cause or self-effect." †

Being not Empty Form.—"We should note particularly that self-activity, or self-determination, which we have found as the original form of all beings is not a simple, empty form of existence, devoid of all particularity, but that it involves three important distinctions: Self-antithesis of determiner and determined, or of self-active and self-passive, or of self as subject of activity and self as object of activity. These distinctions may be otherwise expressed: (*a*) As the primordial form of all particularity; (*b*) the subject, or self-active, or determiner, regarded by itself is the possibility of any and all determination, and is thus the generic or universal and the primordial form of all that is general or universal; hence the presupposition of all classification; (*c*) the unity of these two phases of universality and partic-

---

* Vol. 17, p. 307.   † Vol. 17, p. 307.

ularity constitutes individuality, and is the primordial form of all individuality." *

Ill.—The thought of this paragraph can not be easily illustrated because in it is involved the process of creative thought. In Chapter V will be found an exposition of this process of creative thought.

An inadequate illustration may be taken from the thought and activity of every-day life of an individual, as, a man makes a journey; the self as subject originates the thought of making the journey; the self on the will side puts the thought into formal action and so renders the thought real in the will, or makes the self as object; and the thought, the universal, uniting with the particular through the specific act of the will, constitutes a phase of individuality.

("There is here an error of reflection very prevalent in our time, which does not identify these distinctions of universal, particular, and individual in the absolute existence, but calls this absolute or self-existent being 'the unconditioned.' It thinks it as entirely devoid of conditions, as simply the negation of the finite. Hence, it regards the absolute as entirely devoid of distinctions. Since there is nothing to think in that which has no distinctions, such an absolute is pronounced 'unthinkable,' inconceivable, or unknowable. The error in this form of reflection lies in the confusion which it makes between the environment and the underlying presupposition. It thinks the antithesis of object and environment, of object and cause, but fails to ascend to self-limit and *causa sui* as the ultimate

---

* Vol. 17, p. 308.

presupposition and logical condition of object and environment." *

"Any independent, or self-existent being is a self-distinguishing being, and not a mere empty 'unconditioned' without attributes or qualities. This is so much in favor of theism, and against pantheism. For theism sustains the doctrine of a 'living' (self-active) God against pantheism which holds to a transcendental unity that pervades all, and yet is nothing special, but only a void in which all characteristics are annulled, and hence is neither subject nor object, good nor evil, and is unconscious.

"It is, moreover, a presumption in favor of Christian theism, because the latter lays stress on the personality of God. Self-activity is self-distinction, and has many stages or degrees of realization. It may be life, as in the plant or animal; or feeling and locomotion, as in animals; or reason, as in man; or, finally, absolute personality, as in God. In the plant we have reaction against environment; the plant takes up its nourishment from without, and transmutes it into vegetable cells and adds them to its substance. In feeling, the animal exhibits a higher form of self-activity, inasmuch as it reproduces within itself an impression of its environment, while in locomotion it determines for itself its own space. In reason, man reaches a still higher form of self-activity—the pure internality which makes for itself an environment of ideas and institutions. But in these realms of experience we do not find pure self-activity in its complete development.

---

* Vol. 17, p. 308.

"Philosophy looks beyond for an ultimate presupposition, and finds the perfect self-activity presupposed as the personal God. Looking at the world in time and space we see that whatever has extension is co ordinate to other spatial existences and, therefore, limited by them. All things in space are, therefore, mutually interdependent to the degree that they are conditioned by space. Hence, they all presuppose one independent Being whose self-activity originates them.

"Moreover, in the phases of change, succession, or motion, all things in the world presuppose, as time-existences, the mutual dependence that reduces them to a unity dependent on a self-existent whose form is eternity. Thus the world in time and space presupposes as its origin a First Cause whose characteristics or attributes are such as follow as consequences from perfect self-activity. Perfect will, perfect knowing, perfect life, are implied in the perfect self-distinction of a First Cause. These implications, it is true, do not appear at first. Only after the thinking power has trained itself to look into the presuppositions of its experience does it begin to discover these wonderful conclusions. Then it grows in this power constantly by exercising its thoughts on divine themes.

"To the person who has never discovered the presuppositions that underlie experience, there is no necessary unity to the world and, consequently, no necessity for a God. He may, nevertheless, surrender his intellect to faith and adopt a belief in God. But if he persists in 'thinking for himself,' he will reach atheistic conclusions at this stage of thought. For ignoring the unity which time and space give to the dependent existences of the world, he will take for granted their independence. If objects in the world all possess self-existence just as they are, then, of course, they are independent beings, and do not presuppose one absolute independent Being. This is atheism. But it can not stand the test of reflection.

"Reflection discovers that extension in space and sequence in time involve mutual dependence throughout the universe. At this stage of thought he has left atheism and arrived at pantheism. For time and space are not forms of personality, but only of abstract unity and, hence, although they make atheism impossible they do not necessitate theism. The idea of causality followed out into the conception of self-activity and self-determination corrects the pantheistic result and arrives at theism." *)

Principle with which to examine the World.— "Every object of experience, then, involves as correlatives infinite space, infinite time, and self-cause, or spontaneous energy. These correlatives are necessarily thought as conditions which render the existence of the object of experience possible. If the object of experience possesses reality, those conditions possess reality, because it is their reality that this object manifests." †
"Each and every existence, then, is a self-determined being, or else some phase or phenomenon dependent on self-determined being. Here we have our principle with which to examine the world and judge concerning its beings. Whatever depends on space and time, and possesses external existence, in the form of an object con-

---

* "The Chautauquan," May, 1886, pp. 437, 438.   † Vol. 19, p. 197.

ditioned by environment, has not the form of self-existence, but is necessarily a phase or manifestation of the self-determination of some other being. If we are able to discover beings in the world that manifest self-activity, we shall know that they are in possession of independence, at least in a degree; or, in other words, that they manifest self-existence. When we have found the entire compass of any being in the world, we are certain that we have within it the form of self-activity as its essence." *

"The ground of Aristotle's identification of self-determination, or of energy which moves but is not moved, with reason or thinking being, becomes clear when we consider that this self-distinction which constitutes the nature of self-determination, or *causa sui*, is subject and its own object, and this in its perfect form must be self-consciousness, while any lower manifestation of self-activity will be recognized as life—that of the plant or of the animal. In the plant there is manifestation of life wherein the individual seed develops out of itself into a plant and arrives again at seeds, but not at the same seed—only at seeds of the same species. So the individual plant does not include self-determination, but only manifests it as the moving principle of the entire process. The mere animal, as brute animal, manifests self-determination more adequately than the plant; for he has feeling and locomotion, besides nutrition and reproduction. But as mere animal he does not make himself his own object, and hence the *causa sui* which is manifested in him is not included within his conscious-

---

* Vol. 17, pp. 307, 308.

ness, but is manifested only as species. Man can make his feeling in its entirety his object by becoming conscious, not only of time, space, and the other presuppositions, but especially of self-activity or original first-cause, and in this he arrives at the knowledge of the ego and becomes self-conscious. The presupposition of man as a developing individuality is the perfect individuality of the Absolute Reason, or God." *

---

* Vol. 17, pp. 309, 310.

CHAPTER III.

PHILOSOPHY OF NATURE.

The World: Self-Activity shown in Inorganic Forms—Organic; Plants, Animals, Man.

The World a Manifestation of Self-Activity, of Self-Determination, of the Creator.—In the preceding chapter "we have considered time and space as grounds of existence of material things. We have considered the principle of causality as the form in which all experience is rendered possible. Looking at its presupposition, we have seen that self-activity, or *causa sui*, alone makes possible any and all influence of one thing upon another. There must be self-separation of energy or influence as a condition of its transference from the environment to the object, or from any one object to another. This self-separation, or self-activity, is the basis of causality, and hence the basis of all things and phenomena in the world. . . .

"Being assured of the necessary existence of individuality or free self-determination as the form of all totalities,* we may now look for beings which manifest the Divine Self-Activity." †

---

* "Totality as here used does not mean quantitative totality, but qualitative—i. e., independent being."

† Vol. 17, pp. 343, 344, 345.

"The idea of self-activity is the source of our thought of God. If one lacked this idea of self-activity and could not attain it, all attempt to teach him divine truth would be futile. He could not form in his mind, if he could be said to have a mind, the essential characteristic idea of God; he could not think God as a Creator of the world, or as self-existent apart from the world. If the doctrine were revealed and taught to him, and he learned to repeat the words in which it is expressed, yet in his consciousness he would conceive only a limited effect, a dead result, and no living God. But the hypothesis of a consciousness without the idea of self-activity implicit in it as the presupposition of all its knowing, and especially of its self-consciousness, is a mere hypothesis, without possibility of being a fact." *

Inorganic Things.—" A general survey of the world discovers that there is interaction among its parts. This is the verdict of science, as the systematic form of human experience. In the form of gravitation we understand that each body depends upon every other body, and the annihilation of a particle of matter in a body would cause a change in that body which would affect every other body in the physical universe. Even gravitation, therefore, is a manifestation of the whole universe in each part of it, although it is not a manifestation which exists *for* that part, because the part does not know it. There are other forms wherein the whole manifests itself in each part of it, as, for example, in the phenomena of light, heat, and possibly in magnetism and electricity. These forms of manifestation of the exter-

---

* Vol. 17, pp. 310, 311.

nal world upon an individual object are destructive to the individuality of the object. If the nature of a thing is stamped upon it from without, it is an element only, and not a self; it is dependent, and belongs to that on which it depends. It does not possess itself, but belongs to that which *makes* it, and which gives evidence of ownership by continually modifying it." *

"Atoms, if atoms exist as they are conceived in the atomic theory, can not be true individuals, for they possess attraction and repulsion, and by either of these forces express their dependence on others, and thus submerge their individuality in the mass with which they are connected by attraction or sundered by repulsion. Distance in space changes the properties of the atom—its attraction and repulsion are conceived as depending on distance from other atoms, and its union with other atoms develops new qualities and conceals or changes the old qualities. Hence the environment is essential to the atomic individuality—and this means the denial of its individuality. If the environment is a factor, then the individuality is joint product, and the atom is not an individual, but only a constituent.

"Inorganic being does not possess individuality for itself. A mountain is not an individual in the sense that a tree is. It is an aggregate of substances, but not an organic unity. The unity of place gives certain peculiarities and idiosyncrasies, but the mountain is an aggregate of materials, and its conditions are an aggregate of widely differing temperatures, degrees of illumination, moisture, etc." †

---

* Vol. 14, p. 227. † Vol 19, p. 200.

Organisms.—" In an organism each part is reciprocally means and end to all the other parts—all parts are mediated through each.

"Mere aggregates are not individuals, but aggregates wherein the parts are at all times in mutual reaction with the other parts through and by means of the whole, are individuals. The individual stands in relation to other individuals and to the inorganic world. It is the manifestation of energy acting as conservative of its own individuality, and destructive of other individualities or inorganic aggregates that form its environment. It assimilates other beings to itself and digests them, or imposes its own form on them and makes them organic parts of itself—or, on the other hand, it eliminates portions from itself, returning to the inorganic what has been a part of itself.

"Individuality, therefore, is not a mere thing, but an energy manifesting itself in things. In the case of the plant there is this unity of energy, but the unity does not exist for itself in the form of feeling. The animal feels, and, in feeling, the organic energy exists for itself, all parts coming to a unity in this feeling, and realizing an individuality vastly superior to the individuality manifested in the plant." *

Individuality of Plants.—"The plant grows and realizes by its form or shape some phase or phases of the organic energy that constitutes the individuality of the plant. Roots, twigs, buds, blossoms, fruits, and seeds, all together manifest or express that organic energy, but they lack thorough mutual dependence, as

---

* Vol. 19, p. 201.

compared with the animal who feels his unity in each part or limb. The individuality of the plant is comparatively an aggregate of individualities, while the animal is a real unity in each part through feeling, and hence there is no such independence in the parts of the animal as in the plant." *

"Individuality begins with the power of reaction and modification of external surroundings. In the case of the plant, the reaction is *real*, but not also *ideal*. The plant acts upon its food and digests it, or assimilates it, and imposes its *form* on that which it draws within its organism. It does not, however, reproduce within itself the externality as that external exists for itself. It does not form within itself an idea, or even a feeling of that which is external to it. Its participation in the external world is only that of *real* modification *of* it or through it; either the plant digests the external, or the external limits it, and prevents its growth, so that where one begins the other ceases. Hence, it is that the elements—the matter of which the plant is composed, that which it has assimilated even—still retains a large degree of foreign power or force, a large degree of externality which the plant has not been able to annul or to digest. The plant-activity subdues its food, changes its shape and its place, subordinates it to its use; but what the matter brings with it, and still retains of the world beyond the plant, does not exist for the plant; the plant can not read or interpret the rest of the universe from that small portion of it which it has taken up within its own organism. And yet the history of the universe

---

* Vol. 19, p. 201.

is impressed on each particle of matter, as well within the plant as outside of it, and it could be understood were there capacities for recognizing it.

"The reaction of the life of the plant upon the external world is not sufficient to constitute a fixed abiding individuality. With each accretion there is some change of particular individuality. Every growth to a plant is by the sprouting out of new individuals— new plants—a ceaseless multiplication of individuals, and not the preservation of the same individual. The species is preserved, but not the particular individual. Each limb, each twig, even each leaf is a new individual, which grows out from the previous growth as the first sprout grew from the seed. Each part furnishes a soil for the next. When a plant no longer sends out new individuals we say it is dead. The life of the plant is only a life of nutrition. Nutrition is only an activity of preservation of the general form of new individuals; it is only the life of the species, and not the life of the permanent individual." *

ILL.—The phases of growth in the oak tree—the acorn, the little plant, the sapling, the full-grown oak— show the individuality of the tree; in all these phases, the activity of the tree manifests itself in modifying its surroundings and in assimilating them to a certain extent. Because, in the process of acting upon and taking in its external surroundings, the oak tree changes that portion of the external world which is impressed upon it, but does not know that change, the action of the external world upon the tree and the reaction of the

---

* Vol. 14, pp. 227, 228.

tree upon the surroundings is real but not ideal. The individuality of one oak tree is not permanent but consists of a series of changes, and even the one oak tree may die and a new one take its place. The extent of the activity of the oak is shown only in the species.

Individuality of Animals.—" Feeling, sense-perception, and locomotion characterize the individuality of the animal, although he retains the special powers which made the plant an organic being. The plant could assimilate or digest; that is to say, it could react on its environment and impress it with its own form, making the inorganic into vegetable cells and adding them to its own structure. Feeling, especially in the form of sense-perception, is the process of reproducing the environment within the organism in an ideal form.

"Sense-perception thus stands in contrast to the vegetative power of assimilation or nutrition, which is the highest form of energy in the plant. Nutrition is a subordinate energy in the animal, while it is the supreme energy of the plant. Nutrition relates to its environment only negatively and destructively in the act of assimilating it, or else it adds mechanically to the environment by separating and excreting from itself what has become inorganic. But feeling, even as it exists in the most elementary forms of sense-perception, can reproduce the environment ideally; it can form for itself, within, a modification corresponding to the energy of the objects that make up its environment.

"Sentient being stands in reciprocal action with its environment, but it seizes the impression received from without and adds to it by its own activity, so as to reconstruct for itself the external object. It receives an impression, and is so far passive to the action of its environment; but it reacts on this by forming within itself a counterpart to the impression out of its own energy. The animal individuality is an energy that can form limits within itself. On receiving an impression from the environment, it forms limits to its own energy commensurate with the impression it receives, and thus frames for itself a perception, or an internal copy of the object. It is not a copy so much as an estimate or measure effected by producing a limitation within itself similar to the impression it has received. Its own state, as thus limited to reproduce the impression, is its idea or perception of the external environment as acting upon it.

"The plant receives impressions from without, but its power of reaction is extremely limited, and does not rise to feeling. The beginnings of such reaction in plants as develops into feeling in animals are studied by intelligent biologists with the liveliest interest, for in this reaction we see the ascent of individuality through a discrete degree—the ascent from nutrition to feeling.

"Nutrition is a process of destruction of the individuality of the foreign substance taken up from the environment, and likewise a process of impressing on it a new individuality, that of the vegetative form, or the nutritive soul, as Aristotle calls it. Feeling is a process of reproducing within the individuality, by self-limitation or self-determination, a form that is like the external energy that has produced an impression upon it. The sentient being shapes itself into the impression, or reproduces the impression, and thus perceives the character of the external energy by the nature of its own effort required to reproduce the impression." *

Ill.—A dog, in common with the oak, has the power of assimilating a portion of his environment, but the dog has also feeling, sense-perception, and locomotion. With the dog, the reaction upon the external world is not only real, but also ideal; that is, the dog touches, tastes, smells, hears, and sees, and in these acts of sense-perception, he, by his own activity, reproduces that portion of the external world whose activity impressed his own activity; or, to be more specific, the dog sees a tree—an impression of the tree upon the activity of the dog through the physical organ, the eye, and the energy of the dog limits and measures within himself a copy of the tree, and in so doing he limits himself and sees an object external to himself. But in this act of sense-perception the dog sees the object as one particular object, and not as one of a class of objects.

Nutritive and Sentient Processes.—" In the two forms of the reaction of energy, or individuality, which have been discussed as nutrition and feeling, the former draws the object within itself and destroys its objective form, while in feeling the individuality recoils from the attack made on the organism, and reproduces its symbolic equivalent. Both of these forms find the occasion of action in the contact with the external. Without conjunction, without limitation of the individuality by the object, there arises neither nutrition nor feeling. This mutual limitation is the reduction of the two, the subject and object, to mutual dependence, and

---

* Vol. 19, pp. 201-203.

hence it is the destruction of individuality so far as this dependence exists. By the act of assimilation the vegetative energy reasserts its own independence and individuality by annulling the individuality of the object. The sentient process, on the other hand, reasserts its independence by escaping from the continuance of the impression from without, and by reproducing for itself a similar limitation through its own freedom or spontaneity. It elevates the real limit, by which it is made dependent on an external object, into an ideal limit that depends on its own free act. Thus both nutrition and feeling are manifestations of self-identity, in which the energy acts for the preservation of its individuality against submersion in another." *

"The difference between a nutritive process and a perceptive or sentient process is one of degree, but a discrete degree. Both processes are reactions on what is foreign; but the nutritive is a real process, destructive of the foreign object, while the sentient is an ideal or reproductive process that does not affect the foreign object. The nutritive is thus the opposite of the sentient; it destroys and assimilates, the latter reproduces. Perception is objective, a self-determination in the form of the object—it transforms the subject into the object; nutrition is subjective in that it transmutes the object into the subject and leaves no object. Perception preserves its own individuality while reproducing the individuality of the external, for it limits itself by its own energy in reproducing the form of the object.

"For the reason that feeling or perception measures

---

* Vol. 19, pp. 204, 205.

off, as it were, on its own organic energy—which exists for it in the feeling of self—the amount and kind of energy required to produce the impression made on it from without, it follows that sense-perception is not only a reception of impressions, but also an act of introspection. By introspection it interprets the cause or occasion of the impression that is felt. Feeling arises only when the impression made on the organism is reproduced again within the self—only when it recognizes the external cause by seeing in and through its own energy the energy that has limited it. The degree of objectivity (or the ability to perceive the reality of the external power) is measured by the degree of introspection or the degree of clearness in which it perceives the amount and limit of the internal energy required to reproduce the impression."*

Human Individuality.—" On this scale of degrees we rise from plant to animal, and from animal to man. The individuality of each lies in its energy. The energy of the plant is expended in assimilating the external; that of the animal in assimilating and reproducing; that of man in assimilating, reproducing, and self-producing or creating. The discrete degree that separates the plant from the animal is measured by the distance between destroying and reconstructing; the difference between the animal and the man is measured by the distance between reproducing and self-producing, or, in another form of statement, it is the difference in two kinds of perception—the perception of object as particular, and the perception of object as universal.

It is comparatively easy to recognize the difference

---

* Vol. 19, p. 203.

between nutrition and perception; indeed, one would say that the difficult part is the recognition of the essential identity of their energies. On the contrary, the identity of sense-perception and thought is readily acknowledged, but their profound difference is not seen without careful attention." *

ILL.—The life of the tree is shown in processes of absorption, assimilation, and preservation of the species; the dog has the added powers of feeling and locomotion and the perceiving of objects as individual particular objects. The man in seeing the same tree which the dog sees, not only sees the tree as a particular oak, but also at the same time sees that he belongs to one class of objects and the tree to another class; or, while the dog sees the particular the man sees the universal in the particular. The extent to which man consciously and reflectively recognizes different classes of objects and their nature and characteristics, depends upon the degree of culture to which he has attained. The perceptive-process and the thought-process of man are further considered in Chapter IV, Sections I, IV, V, and VI.

"These general or universal objects are not mere classes or abstractions, fictions of the mind for genera and species, but they stand for generic processes in the world—such processes in the world as abide while their products come into being and pass away. The oak before me is the product of a power that manifests itself in successive stages, as acorn, sapling, tree, and crop of acorns, etc., these stages being successive and partial,

---

* Vol. 19, pp. 203, 204.

while the energy is the unity whence proceed all of these phases through its action on the environment. The energy is a generic process, and whatever reality the particular existence may get from it is borrowed from its reality. The reality of this acorn is derived from the reality of organic energy of the oak on which it grew. The reality of that organic energy is at least equal to all the reality that has proceeded from it." *

---

* Vol. 19, p. 204.

CHAPTER IV.

MAN: A SELF-ACTIVE INDIVIDUAL.

Man is Self-Activity, Self-Consciousness—Channels of Development of Activity: Feeling, Sense-perception, Representation, Understanding, Reason, Emotions, Will.

CONSCIOUSNESS.

"The attempts to preserve individuality which we see in nutrition and feeling, do not succeed in obtaining perfect independence. Both these activities, as reaction upon the environment, depend on the continued presence of the environment. When the assimilation is complete the reaction ceases, and there must be new interaction with the environment before the process begins again. Hence, its individuality requires a permanent interaction with external conditions, and the plant and vegatative process is not a complete or perfect individuality. It is not entirely independent. Its process involves a correlative existence, an inorganic world for its food." *

"The defect in plant life was that there was neither identity of individualty in space nor identity in time. The growth of the plant destroyed the individuality of the seed, so that it was evanescent in time; it served only as the starting-point for new individualities, which

---

* Vol. 19, p. 205.

likewise, in turn, served again the same purpose; and so its growth in space was a departure from itself as individual." *

Ill.—In the growth of an oak tree no stage of its life is complete; in each succeeding period of time the oak, in each different aspect of growth, destroys the preceding appearance and size, and therefore the oak has not permanence as an individual—it lacks identity in time; also the oak produces new plants from itself, which again produce new oaks, and in this continuous growth of individuals from the oak the lack of permanence of the oak as regards space is seen.

"The animal is a preservation of individuality as regards space. He returns into himself in the form of feeling or sensibility; but as regards time, it is not so, feeling being limited to the present. Without a higher activity than feeling, there is no continuity of individuality in the animal any more than in the plant. Each new moment is a new beginning to a being that has feeling but not memory.

"Thus the individuality of mere feeling, although a far more perfect realization of individuality than that found in plant life, is yet, after all, not a continuous individuality for itself, but only for the species.

"In spite of the ideal self-activity which appertains to feeling, even in sense-perception, only the species lives in the animal, and the individual dies, unless there be higher forms of activity." †

Ill.—Since, through his power of feeling, a dog retains his unity and returns into himself, and since he

---

* Vol. 14, p. 231.   † Vol. 14, p. 231.

shows a degree of permanence under change, he preserves his individuality in space, but the life of the dog is limited to the present; he shows the power of representation and recollection to a degree, but not that of memory—true memory, the power which is known by the ability to use language, the power of mind which retains objects as classes.

"Memory," and its relation to the use of language, is further developed in Sections II and III of the present chapter.

"The being which perceives or feels is a self-activity in a higher sense than is manifested in plant life, but it is not its own object in the forms of mere feeling, or sense-perception, or recollection, or fancy. Individuality is persistence under change, self-preservation in the presence of alien forces, and self-objectivity. It is self-determination, or free causal energy—*causa sui*. To have an object, a particular, therefore, is not to be conscious of individuality, either of one's own or of another's. An individuality that does not exist for itself has no personal identity. When the self-activity in reproducing an impression perceives at the same time its own freedom or causal energy, then it becomes conscious of self." *

Ill.—While each — an oak and a dog — presents phases of individuality, in man is seen true individuality. In common with the dog, through the power of feeling, he preserves his unity of individuality in space; he also retains his individuality in time; through all changes and attacks of external forces the individuality

---

* Vol. 17, p. 353.

remains. Man, although conditioned by time and space, is not limited to the "here and now," but by the power of memory he can live in the centuries and ages that are past, and by the power of imagination and insight of the reason he can look into the future. Man can also look in upon his own mind and perceive how the mind acts and learn the nature of thought and see how the activity of thought is related to other phases of activity in the universe; in this power he shows his self-activity, his self-determination, his freedom in making the self as object of thought; and when the freely determined thought goes out in action, man is making himself real through his will, or man is a self-realizing being. The phase of individuality shown in the will is treated in Section VIII of the present chapter.

(*Real, Potential, Actual.*—"The immediate object before the senses undergoes change; the real becomes potential, and that which was potential becomes real. Without the potentiality we could have had no change. At first we are apt to consider the real as the entire existence, and to ignore the potential; but the potential will not be treated thus. Whatever a thing *can* become is as valid as what it is already. The properties of a thing by which it exists for us are its relations to other beings, and hence are rather its deficiencies than its being *per se*. The sharpness in the acid is the hunger of the same for alkali; the sharper it is the louder the call for alkali. Thus the very concreteness of a thing is rather the process of its potentialities. . . . In change, the real is being acted upon by the potential under the form of "outside influences." The pyramid is not air, but the air continually acts upon it, and the pyramid is in a continual process of decomposition; its potentiality is continually exhibiting its nature. We know by seeing a thing undergo change what its potentialities are. In the process of change is manifested the activity of the potentialities which are thus negative to it. If a thing had no negative it would not change. The real is nothing but the surface upon which the potential writes its nature; it is the field of strife between the potentialities. The real persists in existence through the potential which is in continual process with it. Thus we are led to regard the product of the two as constant. This we call actuality. . . .

"The highest aim is toward perfection; and this is pursued in the canceling of the finite, partial, or incomplete, by adding to it its other or complement—that which it lacks of the Total or Perfect. Since this complement is the *potential*, and since the potential is and can be the only agent that acts upon and modifies the real, it follows that all process is pursuant of the highest aim; and since the actual is the process itself, it follows that the actual is the realization of the best or of the rational." *)

"The sense-perception of the mere animal differs from that of the human being in this: The human being knows himself as subject that sees the object, but does not separate himself, as universal, from the special act of seeing. To know that I am I is to know the most general of objects. Consciousness, which is known by the ability to use language, and distinguishes the brute and human, begins when one can seize the pure

---

* Vol. 1, pp. 239, 240.

universal in the presence of immediate objects here and now." * "The so-called faculties of the mind rise in a scale, beginning with feeling. Each higher activity is distinguished from the one below it by the circumstance that it sees not only the object which was seen by the lower faculty, but also the *form* of the activity of that faculty. Each new faculty, therefore, is a new stage of self-consciousness." † "The degrees of consciousness are various, and differ through the completeness with which they grasp the determinations of the Ego." ‡ "Self-consciousness is therefore the basis of all knowledge; for all predication—from the emptiest assertion, 'this is now'—up to the richest statement involving the ultimate relation of the world to God." #

Ill.—As in the example in the preceding chapter, the dog in seeing the tree sees an object as a particular object, and he gives no evidence that he recognizes the tree as belonging to a different class of objects from himself; but the child, in learning the word tree in connection with the object, begins the process of recognition of classes of objects and perceives, though not at first in a conscious, reflective way, that the one word "tree" means any tree and that he himself is different from the tree. In this act of simultaneous recognition of the self, the universal, and of the object, self-consciousness begins.

Each successive addition of knowledge of objects of the external world and their relations, involving at the same time a greater knowledge of the universal through

---

* Vol. 14, p. 234. ‡ Vol. 10, p. 229.
† Vol. 19, p. 206. # Vol. 10, p. 227.

the powers of feeling, knowing, and willing, is a new stage of self-consciousness in the child, youth, and man. The degree of self-consciousness attained by the child, youth, or man depends upon the extent to which he can see the universal in whatever line he may be working and thinking; experience in the lines of physical industry, business, and professional life, and the growth and development obtained from the contact and relation of one mind with another and with absolute thought as interpreted in science, art, and religion are new stages of self-consciousness.

Care should be taken to avoid the thought of "doubleness" in reference to consciousness. Consciousness is not something apart and different (as "a light," "a witness," "a knowledge of the states of mind," "a power") from self-activity, from the mind, but is different stages or degrees of the one and the same activity.

Channels of Development of Consciousness.— "Experience is a complex affair, made up of two elements—one element being that furnished by the senses, and the other by the mind itself. Time and space, as conditions of all existence in the world and of all experience, can not be learned from experience. We can not obtain a knowledge of what is universal and necessary from experience, because experience can inform us only that something is, but not that it must be." *

The two elements of experience unite in various ways and have different names for the different stages of development: Feeling, known by various names—sensation, sensibility, sensitivity, sense-perception, intuition,

---

* Vol. 17, p. 299.

and others; Representation, in the forms of recollection, fancy, imagination, attention, and memory; Understanding in the planes of sensuous ideas and abstract ideas; Reason, with its absolute idea, or knowledge of totality; Emotions in the grades of sensuous, psychical, and rational; and the Will, or free energy.

Section I.—Sense-Perception.

Degree of Activity shown in Sense-Perception: Touch, Taste, Smell, Hearing, Seeing.

The specializations of sense—touch, taste, smell, hearing, and seeing—in man have greater significance than in the animal, for these are instrumental in gaining a knowledge of the outer world, and this process and the knowledge thus gained furnishes occasion for the higher activity of mind. " Hence, man's act of cognition is more complex than that of mere sense-perception, which he shares with the animal. . . . The energy presupposed in the act of feeling and sense-perception is a self-activity, but one that manifests itself in reproducing its environment ideally. It presupposes an organic energy of nutrition in which it has assimilated portions of the environment and constructed for itself a body. In the body it has organized stages of feeling, constituting the ascending scale of sense-perception.

"(*a*) First there is the sense of touch—containing all higher senses in potentiality. When the higher senses have not developed, or after they have been destroyed by accident, the sense of touch may become sufficiently delicate to perceive not only contact with bodies, but also the slighter modifications involved in the effects of taste and smell, and even in the vibrations of sound and light." *

Ill.—The sense of touch " contains all the higher senses in potentiality." Also the sense of touch may be subdivided into those of pressure, temperature, etc. By these subdivisions, knowledge of the nature and action of the organs of touch—nerve-fibers, corpuscles, "tactile-cells," etc.—may be rendered more specific, but little is gained as to the significance of the power of sense-perception. Introspection, in considering the nature of the activity of sense-perception, presupposes a being, "an organic energy of nutrition" and assimilation which has constructed a body having the organs necessary for an act of sense-perception.

The celebrated case of Laura Bridgman furnishes an illustration of the extent to which the power of touch can be developed.

"(b) The lowest form of special sense is taste, which is closely allied to nutrition. Taste perceives the phase of assimilation of the object which is commencing within the mouth. The individuality of the object is attacked and it gives way, its organic product or inorganic aggregate suffering dissolution—taste perceives the dissolution. Substances that do not yield to the attack have no taste. Glass and gold have little taste compared with salt and sugar. The sense of taste differs from the process of nutrition in the fact that it does not assimilate the body tasted, but reproduces ideally the energy that makes the impression on the sense-organ of taste. Even taste is an ideal activity, although it is present

---

* Vol. 19, p. 206.

MAN: A SELF-ACTIVE INDIVIDUAL. 57

only when the nutritive energy is assimilating—it perceives the object in a state of dissolution." *

Ill.—In the commencement of the process of assimilation of salt, the energy of the saliva of the mouth attacks the energy with which the particles of salt are held together, and the sense of taste, or the mind in a phase of its activity, perceives the dissolution of the salt, or the mind " reproduces ideally the energy that makes the impression on the sense-organ of taste."

"(c) Smell is another specialization which perceives dissolution of objects in a more general form than taste. Both smell and taste perceive chemical changes that involve dissolution of the object." †

Ill.—The oxygen of the air attacks the connective energy of the vegetable tissue of the rose, and the sense of smell perceives the fragrance, the dissolution of the object.

"(d) Hearing is a far more ideal sense, and notes a manifestation of resistance to dissolution. The cohesion of the body is attacked and it resists the attack, and resistance takes the form of vibration ; and the vibration is perceived by the special sense of hearing. Taste and smell perceive the dissolution of the object, while hearing perceives the defense or successful reaction of an object in presence of an attack. Without reaction of cohesion there would be no vibration and no sound." ‡

Ill.—A rock is struck with a hammer. The cohesion of the rock resists the force represented by the hammer. Vibrations are the result of the attack. These are communicated by the means of the air, the compli-

---

* Vol. 19, pp. 206, 207.   † Vol. 19, p. 207.   ‡ *Ibid.*

cated arrangement of the ear, the nerves, and the brain; the mind perceives the resistance to the attack. The kind of vibrations and intensity, and cultivation of the activity of mind shown in the power of hearing, determines the character of the sound, varying from the harshest noise to the most beautiful music.

"(*e*). The sense of sight perceives the individuality of the object not in a state of dissolution before an attack, as in the case of taste and smell, or as engaged in active resistance to attack, as in case of hearing, but in its independence. Sight is, therefore, the most ideal sense, inasmuch as it is furthest removed from perception by means of the real process of assimilation, in which one energy destroys the product of another energy and extends its sway over it." *

ILL.—The rays of light which are reflected to the eye from a neighboring church-steeple do not cause a dissolution of the object, neither is there an active resistance to the impinging rays, but the eye and organs of sight receive the reflected rays and the sense of sight perceives the steeple in its independence. The self-activity, or energy which reproduces this object, the steeple, does not destroy the product of another energy.

Extent of self-activity shown in feeling.—" Sense-perception as the developed realization of the activity of feeling belongs to the animal creation, including man as an animal." † "Mere feeling alone is the perception of the external within the being, hence an ideal reproduction of the external world. In feeling, the animal exists not only within himself, but also passes over his

---

* Vol. 19, p. 207. † Vol. 14, p. 230.

limit, and has for object the reality of the external world that limits him. Hence it is the perception of his finiteness—his limits are his defects, his needs, wants, inadequateness—his separation from the world as a whole. In feeling, the animal perceives the separation from the rest of the world, and also his union with it. Feeling expands into desire when the external world, or some portion of it, is seen as ideally belonging to the limited unity of the animal being. It is beyond the limit and ought to be assimilated within the limited individuality of the animal. Mere *feeling*, when attentively considered, is found to contain these wonderful features of self-activity: it reproduces for itself the external world that limits it; it makes for itself an ideal object, which includes its own self and its not-self at the same time." *

Remark.—In each of the above phases of sense-perception we have seen that the point of especial interest in the study of the human mind is that each act of sense-perception of the individual is a process in which the self limits and determines himself at the same time that he reproduces ideally a portion of the external world in himself. In desire, a "counterpart of feeling," self-activity goes out in the form of will and therefore becomes an emotion. See Section VII.

Section II.—Representation.

Self-Activity shown in Representation: Recollection, Fancy, Imagination, Attention, Memory.

"All forms of sensibility are limited and special; they refer only to the *present*, in its forms of *here* and

---

* Vol. 14, p. 229.

now. The animal can not feel what is not here and now. Even seeing is limited to what is present before it." *

"The activity of mere feeling or sense-perception is aroused by external impressions, and is conditioned by them. If there is no object then there is no act of perception. Every occasion given for the self-activity involved in perception is an occasion for the manifestation of self-activity, but a self-activity that acts only on external incitation is not yet separable from the body." †

"While mere sensation, as such, acts only in the presence of the object, reproducing (ideally, it is true) the external object, the faculty of representation is a higher form of self-activity (or of reaction against surrounding conditions), because it can recall, at its own pleasure, the ideal object. Here is the beginning of emancipation from the limitations of time.

"The self-activity of representation can summon before it the object that is no longer present to it. Hence its activity is now a double one, for it can seize not only what is now and here immediately before it, but it can compare this present object with the past, and identify or distinguish between the two. Thus recollection or representation may become *memory*." ‡

The distinctness of the image in a reproduced sense-perception varies as the activity of the will in Attention enters the process, and these degrees are shown in Recollection, Fancy, Imagination, and Memory.

Remark.—The idea that first one "faculty" of the

---

* Vol. 14, pp. 230, 231.   ‡ Vol. 14, pp. 231, 232.
† Vol. 19, p. 205.

mind and then another begins the process of development, should be guarded against. The truth is, that, although at different periods in the life of an individual some power of the mind is shown in a greater degree than others, the mind in its development is one, and there is no reason why, for instance, the simple "good faith" of the child in the reality of things is not the same power as the "reason" which, at a later period of life, consciously sees the reality of things. And the fact that the "feelings are made over" by new thoughts, and that the will early appears in attention and in desire, shows that no point of time can be assigned for the beginning of the development of one power of the mind over another.

But for the sake of clearness in studying the development of the mind, each phase will be considered by itself, with the purpose to show how the "lower phases" blend with or develop into the highest phase, or that of "rational insight."

Recollection.—"Representation is reproduction without the presence of the sense-object; recollection and memory are forms of this. In the form of recollection the individual energy reproduces the activity of a past perception. The impression on the sense-organ is absent, and the freedom of the individual is manifested in this reproduction without the occasion which is furnished by the impression on the organism from without. The freedom to reproduce the image of the object that has been once perceived leads by easy steps to the perception of general notions." * "As memory, the mind

---

* Vol. 19, p. 207.

achieves a form of activity far above that of sense-perception or mere recollection. It must be noted carefully that mere recollection or representation, although it holds fast the perception in time (making it permanent), does not necessarily constitute an activity completely emancipated from time, nor indeed very advanced toward it. It is only the beginning of such emancipation. For mere recollection stands in the presence of the special object of sense-perception; although the object is no longer present to the senses (or to mere feeling), yet the image is present to the representative perception, and is just as much a particular here and now as the object of sense-perception. There intervenes a new activity on the part of the soul before it arrives at memory. Recollection is not memory, but it is the activity which grows into it by the aid of the activity of attention." *

ILL.—For instance, in the previous illustration of the sense of sight, there was an ideal reproduction of the steeple by the beholder. The steeple may be no longer present to the beholder; the activity of the mind freely and spontaneously brings up an image or picture of the steeple. The mind, in its representative power, has before it the one steeple, and the beholder is limited to the presence of the one image. This power which spontaneously brings up the image of an object does not show the conscious use of the will in attention which intervenes before the power of mind seen in the ability to represent the steeple, becomes memory, or the activity which perceives the general class or type of objects.

---

* Vol. 14, p. 222.

Fancy.—Representation repeats itself promiscuously, and makes new combinations, and forms, from images arising from sense-perception, an indefinite number of pictures. Tendencies and circumstances may to a degree influence the working of Fancy, yet the essential characteristic is that it acts without the directive power of the will.

Ill.—Dreams, reverie, etc., are examples of fancy. The mental life of children is largely that of fancy, and also of those grown-up people who have never exercised the will in attention sufficiently to direct the activity of the mind into the planes of thinking. Writers of fairy tales and stories of improbable wonders and doings recognize this activity of the child-mind. The workings of fancy have also been made the foundation of suggestive poems and prose works, as Burns's "Tam O'Shanter," Drake's "Culprit Fay," Wordsworth's "To a Skylark," Poe's "The Raven," etc., and "Arabian Nights," stories of Jules Verne, "Alice in Wonderland," etc.

"We may here distinguish between the imagination and the fancy. The imagination follows the lines of Nature. Its creations take their place with her works. It brings to light what is hidden in Nature, or what she is striving to accomplish. The fancy works more independently. It forsakes the intent of Nature and adopts ends of its own. It combines the elements of Nature arbitrarily and artificially. Thus the fancy brings together parts of the man and of the horse, and creates the centaur; the imagination creates the Apollo. Fancy creates the dainty Ariel; imagination creates Miranda with her sweet and innocent wonder. The world of fancy may be beautiful and fascinating, full of airy and delicate shapes; we find in it enjoyment and refreshment, but it is a world apart from the real world. The world of imagination may be more natural than that of nature itself." *

Imagination.—" Fancy and imagination are next higher than recollection, because the mind not only recalls images, but makes new combinations of them, or creates them altogether." †

" Creative imagination sees the correspondence of the lower to the highest order of being, and hence is a revealer of the nature of the absolute." ‡

Ill.—In the lower planes of thought, the work of the imagination is mechanical and the combinations deviate but little from the patterns furnished by memory; but in the higher or creative planes, the imagination invests the commonplace and familiar with a new light, and from the infinite realms unknown to ordinary minds reveals wonderful glimpses of truth and beauty.

The housekeeper, in the arrangement of her home, and the farmer, by the vision of rich harvest fields, are assisted and encouraged in the daily tasks. An imaginative view of their completed work spurs on a Watts, Stephenson, or Edison to attempt remarkable utilizations of the forces of Nature. A Darwin sees the species of plants and animals arranged in an orderly manner in a process of development even before he starts out on his voyages of discovery and verification. Washington is moved to persistent and heroic deeds because his

---

* C. C. Everett, "Poetry, Comedy, and Duty," pp. 4, 5.
† Vol. 14, p. 231.   ‡ Dictation.

imaginative insight shows him a nation united under a federal constitution while as yet not one word of the nation's constitution had been written.

And the world's master-minds in their creative power: Beethoven, Mendelssohn, convey their thoughts and feelings in music ; Phidias sees the possible dignity and nobility and beauty and grace of the human mind and represents them in the human form ; through painting, Raphael and Micheal Angelo give to the world their marvelous interpretations of the divine ; Homer, Dante, Goethe, Shakespeare, by the means of poetry, disclose the nature of spirit, and portray the unnumbered awful conflicts of good and evil in the human soul. This creative power sees totalities, and therefore comes into harmony with rational insight. See Section VI, " Beauty."

Attention.—" The activity by which the mind ascends from sense-perception to memory is the activity of attention. Here we have the appearance of the will in intellectual activity. Attention is the control of perception by means of the will. The senses shall no longer passively receive and report what is before them, but they shall choose some definite point of observation, and neglect all the rest. Here in the act of attention we find abstraction, and the greater attainment of freedom by the mind. The mind abstracts its view from the many things before it, and concentrates on one point.

" Attention abstracts from some things before it, and concentrates on others. Through attention grows the capacity to discriminate between the special, particular object and its general type. Generalization arises, but not what is usually called generalization—only a more elementary form of it." *

"For when the mind notices its mode of activity by which the former perception is reproduced or represented, it perceives, of course, its power of repeating the process, and notes that the same energy can produce an indefinite series of different images resembling one another. It is by this action of representation that the idea of the universal arises. It is a reflection on the conditions of recalling a former perception. The energy that can produce within itself the conditions of a former perception at pleasure, without the presence of the original object of perception, is an energy that is generic—that is, an energy that can produce the particular and repeat it to any extent. The universal or generic power can produce a class." †

ILL.—"Educators have for many ages noted that the habit of attention is the first step in intellectual education. With it is found the point of separation between the animal intellect and the human. Not attention simply—like that with which a cat watches by the hole of a mouse—but attention which arrives at results of abstraction is the distinguishing characteristic of educative beings." ‡

"Some writers would have us suppose that we do not arrive at general notions except by the process of classification and abstraction in the mechanical manner that they lay down for this purpose. The fact is that the mind has arrived at these general ideas in the pro-

---

* Vol. 14, p. 232, 233.   ‡ Vol. 14, pp. 232, 233.
† Vol. 19, pp. 207, 208.

cess of learning language. In infancy, most children have learned such words as is, existence, being, nothing, motion, cause, change, I, you, he, etc." *

For instance, the process by which the perception of an apple becomes a conception, is not by separating the apple into its qualities, as the color, size, sweetness, sourness, the number, size, and arrangement of seeds etc., and then from the various parts building up the apple in a mechanical way, but the concept apple arises through the activity of attention to the object in the very process of learning the word apple.

The child shows that the concept arises thus spontaneously by the fact that he can recognize and identify the same object under different circumstances, another apple of different size and color, and the picture of an apple even before he is able to enumerate the various qualities necessary to make an apple.

This "concept" apple is not the same as the image which arose through the representative power from the reproduced object of sense-perception, but this image has become the concept through the activity of the will in attention, or by means of an act of reflection. This concept apple does not stand for any particular apple, as the image apple did, but stands for any apple of the whole class of apples, and this concept arose in the process of learning the word apple. The concept apple is not the result of conscious reflective acts, but these concepts are the preparation for thought, the objects of memory, the "general objects" which thought uses.

"Memory and the phenomena of language are not

---

* Vol 14, pp 234, 235

recognized by psychologists generally as being the first manifestation of the self-conscious individuality."

Memory.—Recollection or representation may become memory. "The special characteristics of objects of the senses are allowed to drop away, in so far as they are unessential and merely circumstantial, and gradually there arises in the mind the type—the *general form*—of the object perceived. This general form is the object of memory. Memory deals therefore with what is general and a type, rather than with what is directly recollected or perceived." *

"With this consciousness of a generic energy manifested in the power of representation, arises the recognition of a generic energy manifested in the external world as the producer of the particular objects perceived, and each object is seen in its producing energy as one of an indefinite number produced by the continued existence of that energy. The consciousness of freedom of the ego in this restricted form of freedom of representing or recalling former sense-perceptions lies thus at the basis of the perception of objects as specimens of classes; hence, representation or recollection, which is special and individual, leads to the act of reflection, by which the energy is perceived and its generic character, and with it the perception of the necessary generic character of the energy at the foundation of every impression upon our senses, or at the foundation of every object perceived.

"At this point the activity of perception becomes conception, or the perception of the general in the par-

---

* Vol. 14, p. 232.

ticular. The 'this oak' is perceived as 'an oak,' or a specimen of the class oak. The class oak is conceived as an indefinite number of individual oaks, all produced by an energy which manifests itself in an organic process of assimilation and elimination, in which appear the stadia of acorn, sapling, tree, and crop of acorns—a continuous circle of reproduction of the species oak, a transformation of the one into the many—the one acorn becoming a crop of acorns, and then a forest of oaks.

"The rise of self-consciousness, or the perception of self-activity, and the perception of the general object in the external world are thus contemporaneous. With the perception of the general energy the psychological activity has outgrown representation and become conception. With conception the energy or soul begins to be an individuality for itself—a conscious individuality. It recognizes itself as a free energy. The stage of mere perception does not recognize itself, but merely sees its own energy as the objective energy, because it acts wholly as occasioned by the external object. In the recognition of the object as an individual of a class the soul recognizes its own freedom and independent activity. Recollection (*Erinnerung*) relates to individuals, recalling the special presentation or impression, and representing the object as it was before perceived. Memory (like the German word *Gedächtniss*) may be distinguished as the activity which reproduces the object as one of a class, and therefore as the form of representation that perceives universals. With memory arises language." *

---

* Vol. 19, pp. 208, 209.

"Such a stage we call memory, in the special and higher sense of the word, as corresponding to not ἀνάμνησις, but μνημοσύνη or μνήμη—not *Erinnerung*, but *Gedächtniss*—not the memory that recollects, but the memory that recalls by the aid of universal ideas. (Such memory is creative as it goes from the general to the particular.) These general ideas are mnemonic aids—pigeon-holes, as it were, in the mind—whereby the soul conquers the endless multiplicity of details in the world. It refers to its species, and saves the species under a name—then is able to recall by the name a vast number of special instances." * . . . "In thinking of such faculties in the lives of great men of science—like Agassiz, Cuvier, Lyell, Von Humboldt, Darwin, and Goethe—we see what this means. It is the first or crudest stage of mental culture that depends chiefly on sense-perception and recollection. After the general has been discovered, the mind uses it more and more, and the information of the senses becomes a smaller and smaller part of the knowledge. Agassiz in a single scale saw the whole fish, so that the scale was all that was required to suggest the whole; Lyell could see the whole history of its origin in a pebble; Cuvier could see the entire animal skeleton in one of its bones. The memory, which holds types, processes, and universals, the condensed form of all human experience, the total aggregate of all sense-perception of the universe and all reflection on it, this constitutes the chief faculty of the scientific man, and sense-perception and mere recollection play the most insignificant part. This points to

---

* Vol. 19, p. 211.

the complete independence of the soul as a far-off idea. When the soul can think the creative thought, the theoretic vision of the world—ἡ θεωρία, as Aristotle calls it—then it comes to perfect insight, for it sees the whole in each part, and does not require any longer the mechanical memory, because it has a higher form of intellect that sees immediately in the individual thing its history, just as Lyell or Agassiz saw the history of a pebble or a fish, or Asa Gray sees all botany in a single plant. Mechanical memory is thus taken up into a higher 'faculty,' and its function being absorbed, it gradually perishes. But it never perishes until its function is provided for in a more complete manner." *

Section III.

Significance of the Power to use Language.— "There is no language until the mind can perceive general types of existence; mere proper names nor mere exclamations or cries do not constitute language. All words that belong to language are significative—they 'express' or 'mean' something—hence they are conventional symbols, and not mere individual designations. Language arises only through common consent, and is not an invention of one individual. It is a product of individuals acting together as a community, and hence implies the ascent of the individual into the species. Unless an individual could ascend into the species he could not *understand* language. To know words and their meaning is an activity of divine significance; it denotes the formation of universals in the mind—the

---

* Vol. 19, p. 212, 213.

ascent above the here and now of the senses, and above the representation of mere images, to the activity which grasps together the general conception of objects and thus reaches beyond what is transient and variable." *

"Language fixes the knowledge of objects in universals. Each word represents an indefinite number of particular objects, actions, or relations. The word *oak* stands for all oaks—present, past, or future. No being can use language, much less create language, unless it has learned to conceive as well as perceive—learned to see all objects as individuals belonging to classes, and incidentally recognized its own individuality. All human beings possess language. Even deaf and dumb human beings invent and use gestures with as definite meaning as words, each gesture denoting a class with a possible infinite number of special applications." †

"Language is the sign by which we can recognize the arrival of the soul at this stage of development into complete self-activity. Hence language is the criterion of immortal individuality. In order to use language it must be able not only to act for itself, but to act wholly upon itself. It must not only perceive things by the senses, but accompany its perceiving by an inner perception of the act of perceiving (and thus be its own environment). This perception of the act and process of perceiving is the recognition of classes, species, and genera—the universal processes underlying the existence of the particular.

"Language in this sense involves conventional signs,

---

* Vol. 14, pp. 233, 234. † Vol. 19, p. 209.

and is not an immediate expression of feeling like the cries of animals. The immediate expression of feeling (which is only a reaction) does not become language, even when it accompanies recollection or the free reproduction—nor until it accompanies memory or the seeing of the particular in the general. When it can be shown that a species of animals use conventional signs in communication with each other, we shall be able to infer their immortality, because we shall have evidence of their freedom from sense-perception and environment sufficient to create for themselves their own occasion for activity. They would then be shown to react not merely against their environment, but against their own action—hence they would involve both action and reaction, self and environment. They would, in that case, have selves, and their selves exist for themselves, and hence they would have self-identity." *

"Language is the means of distinguishing between the brute and the human—between the animal soul, which has continuity only in the species (which pervades its being in the form of *instinct*), and the *human* soul, which is immortal, and possessed of a capacity to be educated. . . .

"Doubtless the nobler species of animals possess not only sense-perception, but a considerable degree of the power of representation. They are not only able to recollect, but to imagine or fancy to some extent, as is evidenced by their dreams. But that animals do not generalize sufficiently to form for themselves a new objective world of types and general concepts we have a

---

* Vol. 19, p. 212.

sufficient evidence in the fact that they do not use words, or invent conventional symbols. With the activity of the symbol-making form of representation, which we have named memory, and whose evidence is the invention and use of language, the true form of individuality is attained, and each individual human being, as mind, may be said to be the entire species. Inasmuch as he can form universals in his mind, he can realize the most abstract thought; and he is conscious. . . .

"It should be carefully noted that this activity of generalization which produces language and characterizes the human from the brute is not the generalization of the activity of thought so called. It is the preparation for thought. These general types of things are the things which thought deals with. Thought does not deal with mere immediate objects of the senses; it deals rather with the objects which are indicated by words, i. e., general objects." *

Section IV.—Reflection.

"General Objects" of Memory, as Thought, become Judgments—Sense-perception: Sensuous Ideas perceive Objects; Identity, Difference—Understanding: Abstract Ideas investigate Object and Environment; Relations—The "General Objects" or "Universals" are possible because of Reason: Absolute Idea or Rational Insight knows Logical Conditions of Existence.

A Conception is not a Mental Picture.—"Perceptions relate to individual objects; conceptions relate to general classes or to abstractions—such is the current doctrine of psychology. Let us now take up the in-

---

* Vol. 14, pp. 233, 234.

quiry, What constitutes a general notion or conception? To this we may reply that it is not a mental image but a definition. The general notion *tree* should include all trees of whatever description, and it is expressed by a definition. But no sooner do I attempt to conceive the notion tree than I form a mental image. The image, however, is not general enough to suit the notion. I image a particular specimen of tree—an oak, for example. If I image it vividly it is an individual just as much as the oak that I may see before me in the forest. My conception of tree in general recognizes the inadequacy of the image and dismisses it or permits it to be replaced by another image which presents a different specimen. Perhaps we have never noticed this relation of images to the conception. We are conscious of only a few phases of our mental activity until we have cultivated our powers of introspection. Notice carefully the act of realizing any general conception (or "concept," if one wishes technically to distinguish the product from the process itself). We shall discover that our definition is a sort of rule for the formation of images, rather than an image. What conception do we form of bird? We think of a flying animal—of feathers, wings, bill, claws, and various appurtenances which we unite in the idea of bird. We call up images and dismiss them as we go over the elements of our definition, for we recognize the images to be too special or particular to correspond to the conception. In the rudest and least developed intellects, whether of savages or children, the same process is repeated. Is this a bird? Yes; it has a bill, claws, feathers, wings, etc. But it does not have either of these in general. Its bill is a particular specimen of bill, having one of the many shapes or colors or magnitudes possible to a bill. So, too, of its feathers, wings, claws, etc. The image of our bird was not of a bird in general, but of a hawk or duck, a hen or pigeon, or of some other species of birds. Nor was the image that of a hawk or a duck, etc., *in general*, but of a particular variety and not even of a variety in general, but finally of a possible or remembered individual specimen of a variety. So, too, the features of the bird are only individual specimens or examples that fall under the general conceptions of claws, feathers, bills, wings, etc.

"The definition which we have formed for ourselves serves as a rule by which we form an image that will illustrate it. This difference between the conception and the specimen is known to the child and the savage, though it is not consciously reflected upon.

"Take up a different class of conceptions. Take the abstractions of color, taste, smell, sound, or touch; for example—redness, sourness, fragrance, loudness, hardness, etc. Our conception includes infinite degrees of possible intensity, while our image or recalled experience is of some definite degree and does not correspond to the general notion.

"We have considered objects and classes of objects that admit of images as illustrations. These images, if vague, seem to approximate conceptions; if vivid, to depart from them. But no image can be so vague as to correspond to any conception. Let us take more general notions, such as force, matter, quality, being. For force, image, if one can, some action of gravitation or of heat. If some image or experience can be called up it is felt to be a special example that covers only a very small part of the province of force in general. But an image, strictly considered, can not be made of force at all nor of any special example of force. We can image some object that is acted upon by a force—we can image it before it is acted upon and after it is acted upon. That is to say, we can image the results of the force, but not the force itself. We can think of force, but not image it.

"If we conceive existence, and image some existent thing; if we conceive quantity in general and image a series of things that can be numbered, or an extension or degree that may be measured; if we conceive relation in general and try to illustrate it by imaging particular objects between which there is a relation—in all these and similar cases we can hardly help being conscious of the vast difference between the image and the conception. In realizing the conception of relation, as in that of force or energy, we do not image even an example or specimen of a relation or force, but we image only the conditions or termini of a specimen relation; but the relation itself must be thought, just as any force must be thought but can not be imaged. We can think relations, but not image them.

"Just here we notice that we have a lurking conviction that these general ideas or conceptions are not so valid and true to reality as our images are or as our immediate perceptions are. Conceptions, we should think, are vague and faint impressions of sensation. 'Ideas are the faint images of sense-impressions' said Hume.

"Nominalism says that there is nothing in reality corresponding to our general conceptions, and that such conceptions are mere devices of ours for convenience in knowing and reasoning. If so, our images are truer than our conceptions. Herbert Spencer says (in his 'First Principles') that our conceptions are mere symbols of objects too great or too multitudinous to be mentally represented.

"If the views of Hume and Herbert Spencer are true in regard to our general notions, psychology would have a very different lesson in it—very different from that which we propose to find. To us the images are far less true than our conceptions. The images stand for fleeting or evanescent forms, while the conceptions state the eternal and abiding laws, the causal energies that constitute the essence of all phenomena." *

"As sense-perception has before it a world of present objects, so thought has before it a world of general concepts, which language has defined and fixed.

"It is true that few persons are aware that language stands for a world of general ideas and that reflection has to do with this world of universals." †

"It is usual, however, to account for the reproduction of these universal ideas by supposing that the mind first collects many individuals and then abstracts so as to omit the differences and preserve the likeness or resemblance, and thus forms the conception of class. It therefore makes reflection responsible, not only for the recognition of the universal, but for its creation. But the act of reflection only discovers what had already been elaborated in the lower faculty of the mind. Self-

---

* "Illinois School Journal," vol. vii, pp. 494–496, July, 1888.
† Vol. 14, p. 236.

consciousness is not the cause of universal ideas, but the universal rises with it as its condition (the perception of the universal being perception of the self). Both appear at the same time as essential phases of the same act. The soul uses universals in language long before it recognizes the same as universal (its first recognition of the universal being only self-recognition). Reflection discovers that these ideas are general—but it has used them ever since human beings became human. After reflection has dawned, however, a new series of universal terms begin to come into use, which denote not merely universal classes or generic energies, but the pure energy in its self-activity, as producing inward distinctions which do not reach external particular things as results. Here begins conscious independence of the world of sense-perception." *

"The first stage of knowing concentrates its attention upon the object, the second upon its relations, and the third on the necessary and infinite conditions of its existence. The first stage of knowing belongs to the surface of experience, and is very shallow. It regards things as isolated and independent of each other. The second stage of experience is much deeper, and takes note of the essential dependence of things. They are seen to exist only in relation to others upon which they depend. This second stage of experience discovers unity and unities in discovering dependence of one upon another. The third stage of experience discovers independence and self-relation underlying all dependence

---

* Vol. 19, p. 210.

and relativity. The infinite, or the self-related, underlies the finite and relative or dependent. These three stages of knowing, found in considering the relation of experience to time and space-object, environment, and logical condition—these elements are in every act of experience, although the environment is not a very clear and distinct element in the least cultured knowing, and space and time are still more obscure." *

Sense-perception: Sensuous ideas.—" As a human process, the knowing is always a knowing by universals—a recognition, and not simple apprehension, such as the animals, or such as beings have that to do not use language. The process of development of stages of thought begins with sensuous ideas which perceive mere individual, concrete, real objects, as it supposes. In conceiving these, it uses language and thinks general ideas, but it does not know it, nor is it conscious of the relation involved in such objects. This is the first stage of reflection. The world exists for it as an innumerable congeries of things, each one independent of the other, and possessing self-existence. It is the standpoint from which atomism would be adopted as the philosophic system. Ask it what the ultimate principle of existence is, and it would reply, ' Atoms.' " †

"In the most rudimentary form of knowing, i. e., in sense-perception, there is a synthesis of the two extremes of cognition: 1, the immediately conditioned content, which is the particular object as here and now perceived; 2, the accompanying perception of the self or ego which perceives, that is, the activity of self-

---

* Vol. 17, pp. 300, 301. † Vol. 14, p. 236.

consciousness—the knowledge that it is I who am subject in this particular act of perception. Hence, in sense-perception, two objects are necessarily combined: (*a*) the particular object here and now presented; (*b*) the universal subject of all activity of perceiving. . . . Such a thing as the perception of the permanent, or a relation of any sort (for example, the one of identity, or of difference, the most elementary and fundamental ones) can not take place without attention on the part of the subject who perceives, to the perception of self, or to one of the universal factors which are present in perception. This act of attention to self is reflection—self-perception entering all perception." *

"This lowest stage of thinking is least able to discriminate distinctions and differences. The most immature mind thinks all objects as having being. All objects to it are co-ordinate and of equal validity in this respect. The moment the mind begins to observe relation, this co-ordination vanishes, and we make the terms of experience unequal. This object depends upon that object in some respect, and therefore is not co-ordinate, but subordinate to it. This belongs to that, and is only a manifestation of that object's energy or sphere of influence." †

"The lowest stage of thinking supposes that its objects are all independent one of another. Each thing is self-existent, and a 'solid reality'; to be sure, it thinks relations between things, but it places no special value on relations. Things exist apart from relations, and relations are for the most part the arbitrary product of

---

* Vol. 10, p. 226. † Vol. 17, p. 338.

thought or reflection. Things, it is true, are composite and divisible into smaller things, and smaller things are divisible again. All things are composed of smallest things or atoms. This lowest stage of thinking, it appears, explains all by the two categories of 'thing' and 'composition.' All differences accordingly arise through combination or composition. But since differences include all that needs explanation, it follows that this stage of thinking deceives itself in supposing that *things* are the essential elements in its view of the world and that *relations* are the unessential. A little development of the power of thought produces for us the consciousness that some *relations*, at least, are the essential elements of our experience." *

ILL.—The *process* in sense-perception has already been described. It has been found helpful in class to consider how the different stages of thinking regard the same object. To the plane of sensuous ideas, a tree exists in the correct external adjustment of the parts— root, stem, and leaves. One tree differs from another in its size, shape, kind of leaves, flowers, wood, etc. The uses of the tree for shade, timber, etc. are apparent. An oak, birch, beech, maple, etc. each exists in its independence.

Wordsworth's Peter Bell, to whom—

<blockquote>
A primrose by a river's brim,
A yellow primrose was to him,
And it was nothing more,
</blockquote>

lived in this plane of thought nearest allied to sense-perception, or the plane of sensuous ideas.

---

* "Illinois School Journal," vol. vii, p. 442.

Understanding: Abstract Ideas.—" But this view (from the plane of sensuous ideas) of the world is a very unstable one, and requires very little reflection to overturn it and bring one to the next basis—that of abstract ideas. When the mind looks carefully at the world of things, it finds that there is dependence and interdependence. Each object is related to something else, and changes when that changes. Each object is a part of a process that is going on. The process produced it, and the process will destroy it, nay, it is destroying it now, while we look at it. We find, therefore, that things are not the true beings which we thought them to be, but processes *are* the reality. Science takes this attitude, and studies out the history of each thing in its rise and its disappearance, and it calls this history the truth. This stage of thinking does not believe in atoms or in *things;* it believes in *forces* and *processes*—'abstract'—because they are negative, and can not be seen by the senses. This is the dynamic standpoint in philosophy." *

"Sense-perception increases in richness of knowledge in proportion as the power of synthesis or of combining the successive elements of perception increases. And this power of combining such separate elements is contingent on the power of reflection or of attention to the self-activity in perception. Such reflection is the condition of all generalization. The minimum of this power of reflection admits barely the possibility of combining the perceptions of time-moments that are slightly separated, and hence its results are the mere perception of

---

* Vol. 14, pp. 236, 237.

identity or difference without quantity or quality thereof." *

"That first stage of thinking, nearest allied to sense-perception, supposes that *things* are the essential elements of all being. The second stage, which we may call the *understanding*, knows better what is essential. By relations it does not mean arbitrary comparisons or the result of idle reflections. It has made the discovery of truly essential relations. It deals with the category of relativity, in short, and goes so far as to affirm that if a grain of sand were to be destroyed, all beings in space would be changed more or less. Each thing is relative to every other, and there is reciprocal or mutual dependence.

"Isaac Newton's thought of universal gravitation deserves all the fame it has got, because it sets up in modern thinking this category of relativity, and all thinking in our day is being gradually trained into its use by the application constantly made of it. Isaac Newton is a perpetual schoolmaster to the race.

"Herbert Spencer owes his reputation to his faithful adherence to the thought of relativity in his expositions. Our knowledge is all relative, says he (with the exception of that very important knowledge—the knowledge of the principle of relativity itself—we add, *sotto voce*), and things, too, are all relative, he continues. Essential relativity means dependence. A is dependent on B, so that the being of B is also the being of A. Such is the law of relativity. Moreover, it refuses to think an ultimate principle as origin of all. It say, A depends on

---

* Vol. 10, pp. 226, 227.

B, B, again, on C, C on D, and so on, in infinite progression. Relativity, as a supreme principle, is pantheistic. It makes all being dependent on something beyond it. Hence it denies ultimate individuality. All individuality is a transient result of some underlying abstract principle, a 'persistent force,' for example. Individual things are the transient products (static equilibria) of forces. Forces, again, are modes of manifestation of some persistent energy into which they all vanish.

"This second stage of thinking attains its most perfect form in the doctrine of correlation of forces, and is the ancient skepticism of Pyrrho and Sextus Empiricus. It underlies, too, the Buddhist religion and all pantheistic theories of the world. Nothing is so common among men of science in our day as theories based on absolute relativity. It is often set up by those who still hold the non-relational theory of the lower plane of thought, though if held with logical strictness it is incompatible with the preceding stage.

"The first stage explains by the category of things, or independent non-relational beings, while the second stage explains by the category of *force* or essential relation. Take notice that force does not need a nucleus of things as a basis of efficacy; for things are themselves only systems of forces held in equilibria by force." *

("Modern natural science sets up the doctrine of the correlation of forces and the 'persistence of force.' In the case of individual forces—heat, light, electricity,

---

* "Illinois School Journal," vol. vii, pp. 442, 443.

magnetism, attraction of gravitation, and cohesion—there is finitude, each force manifesting itself only when in process of transition into another form of force. But there is a ground to all these forces, which is an energy. The 'persistent force' is the energy of each force without the particular quality of each force. But it is that which originates each special force, and that which likewise causes it to lose its individuality and pass over into another force. The 'persistent force' is not a special force, like light, heat, etc., for the special forces are in a state of tension against each other, or are merely names for different stages of the same energy. The 'persistent force' is an energy that acts, not on another, but only on itself. In all changes and loss of individuality on the part of particular forces the 'persistent force' abides the same, continually emerging from its successive disguises under the mask of particular forces.

"Persistent force can not, like a special force, act on something else, because it is the totality of all forces. All things are mere equilibria of forces, and hence things, too, are manifestations of the self-activity of 'persistent force.' Thus natural science does not find itself able to avoid thinking self-activity as the ground of things and forces." *

"A logical investigation of the principle of 'persistent force' would prove that the principle of Personal Being is presupposed as its true form. Since the 'persistent force' is the sole and ultimate reality, it originates all other reality only by self-activity, and thus is

---

* Vol. 17, pp. 338, 339.

self-determined. Self-determination implies self-consciousness as the true form of its existence." *)

ILL.—In its conscious independence of the objects of sense-perception, the mind in the plane of abstract ideas freely makes universals from the universals, or concepts, or general objects of memory, or thoughts in the sensuous plane; in doing this the mind not only recognizes these universals, but also at the same time notices the mind's own activity in forming these, and thus in the sphere of the understanding the mind "looks upon the image-making process."

This stage of thought considers both the object and its environment. A tree no longer exists in its independence. The transformation of water, air, and earthy materials into oxygen, hydrogen, nitrogen, carbon, etc. is of far greater interest. The difficulty with which these combinations are made and broken up in the laboratory, and the ease with which the tree does this work are plainly evident to this plane of thought. And again, what seemed so stable in the tree is again changed, and a handful of ashes remains in the place of the growing tree. Notwithstanding these changes, this plane of thought sees that the changes have not been a process of destruction, but that the elements which before made the tree have assumed new forms and that the plant-energy bears a relation to other kinds of energy and correlates with the whole.

Reason: Absolute Idea.—"Relativity presupposes self-relation. Self-relation is the category of the reason,

---

* Vol. 14, p. 238.

just as relativity is the category of the understanding or non-relativity the category of sense-perception. Dependence implies transference of energy, else how could energy be borrowed? That which originates energy is independent being. Reflection discovers relativity or dependence, and hence unites beings into systems. Deepest reflection discovers total systems and the self-determining principles which originate systems of dependent being. The reason looks for complete, independent, or total beings. Hence the reason finds the self-active or its results everywhere.

"Sense-perception is atheistic; it finds each thing sufficient for itself, that is to say, self-existent. The understanding is pantheistic; it finds everything finite and relative and dependent on an absolute that transcends all qualities and attributes—'an unknown and unknowable' 'persistent force,' which is the negative of all particular forces. The reason is theistic because it finds self-activity or self-determination, and identifies these with mind. *Mind* is self-activity in a perfect form, while *life* is the same in a less developed stage. Every whole is an independent being, and hence self-determined or self-active. If not self-determined it has no determinations (qualities, marks, or attributes), and is pure nothing; or, having determinations, it must originate them itself or else receive them from outside itself. But in case it receives its determinations from outside it is a dependent being. Reason sees this disjunctive syllogism. While Buddhism and Brahmanism are religions of the understanding, Christianity is essentially a religion of the reason and furnishes a sort of universal education for the mind in habits of thinking according to reason. It teaches by authority the view-of-the-world that reason thinks." *

"The final standpoint of the intellect is that in which it perceives the highest principle to be a self-determining or self-active Being, self-conscious, and creator of a world which manifests him." †

"Each step upward in ideas arrives at a more adequate idea of the true reality. *Force* is more real than *thing;* persistent force than particular forces; Absolute Person is more real than the force or forces which he creates. This final form of thinking is the only form which is consistent with the theory of education. Each individual should ascend by education into participation —conscious participation—in the life of the species. Institutions—family, society, state, church—all are instrumentalities by which the humble individual may avail himself of the help of the race, and live over in himself its life. The highest stage of thinking is the stage of insight. It sees the world as explained by the principle of Absolute Person. It finds the world of institutions a world in harmony with such a principle." ‡

ILL.—The third stage of thought not only renders the other stages possible and sees what can be known in those planes of thought, but has an insight into the nature of the universe as a whole; and this rational insight can not be obtained from the first or second stage of thought. What to the lowest stage of thinking had been "dead results," fixed objects, to the second had been mere "processes," to the third becomes a living

---

* "Illinois School Journal," vol. vii, pp. 443, 444.
† Vol. 14, p. 238. ‡ Vol 14, p. 239.

energy. The nature of change or activity is seen. The life of the tree, the extent of self-activity manifested in the tree—that this life, this self-activity, is an organic energy appearing in the various stages of growth of a single plant, of the species, and of the whole class; that the organic energy differs in its power and manifestations in plant and in animal life; and that the organic energy of man shows still another phase of life, in that when the self is not only able to act, but to act upon itself, it becomes self-producing, and then self-activity becomes true individuality. Therefore, the insight into the nature or life of a tree includes not only an insight into the conditions of the existence of the tree, the external phases of growth, the processes, the nature of these processes, the difference between these processes and other organic processes, or the difference between activity of life in its lower phases and the activity of thought, the nature of thought in its phases of limitation and self-determination, and the nature of Absolute Thought or complete self-determination.

The Three Stages of Thought.—" It has appeared that each of the three stages of thinking is a view-of-the-world, and that it is not a theory of things worn for ornament, so to speak, or only on holidays, but a silent presupposition that tinges all one's thinking.

" A person may wear his religion on Sabbath-days and put it off on week-days possibly; but his view-of-the-world shows itself in all that he does. All things take on a different appearance when viewed by the light of the reason. For reason is insight; it sees all things in God, as Malebranche expressed it; for it looks at each thing to discover in it the purpose of the whole universe. To see the whole in the part is justly esteemed characteristic of divine intelligence.

"The oft-asserted ability of great men of science—that of Cuvier to see the whole animal in a single bone of its skeleton; that of Lyell to read the history of the glacial period in a pebble; that of Agassiz to recognize the whole fish by one of its scales; that of Asa Gray to see all botany in a single plant—these are indications of the arrival at the third stage of knowing on the part of scientific men within their departments. Goethe's 'Homunculus' in the second part of 'Faust,' symbolizes this power of insight which within a limited sphere (its bottle!), is able to recognize the whole in each fragment. The spirit of specialization in our time aims to exhaust one by one the provinces of investigation, with a view to acquire this power to see totalities. Plato described this third stage of thinking as a power of knowing-by-wholes (totalities).

"Learn to comprehend each thing in its entire history. This is the maxim of science guided by the reason. Always bear in mind that self-activity is the ultimate reality; all dependent being is a fragment; the totality is self-active. The things of the world all have their explanation in the manifestation of self-activity in its development. All is for the development of individuality and ultimate free union of souls in the kingdom of God.

"To sum up; the lowest thinking activity inventories things, but neglects relations; the middle stage of thinking inventories relations, forces, and processes, and sees things in their essences, but neglects self-relation or totality; the highest stage of thinking knows that all independent being has the form of life or mind, and that the Absolute is a person, and it studies all things to discern traces of the creative energy which is the form of the totality.

"The theory of evolution, comprehended as the movement of all things in time and space toward the development of individuality—that is to say, toward a more perfect manifestation or reflection of the Creator, who is above time and space—this theory is (properly understood) the theory of the reason. The theory of gravitation, as a world-view, on the other hand, is that of the understanding." *

(" Within philosophy itself arises a fourth stage. The attention of the mind in its fourth intention is directed not merely to the relation of the ultimate principle to the world (regarded under the phases of particular and general existences), but to the method by which the relation is traced from one to the other. Each higher intention of the mind has for its object the previous intention of the mind, and its relation to those (if any) preceding it. Thus, the second intention (ordinary generalization) notes the relation between sensuous perceptions by attending to its own activity in perception. The third stage of the mind notes the relation of all objects of the mind, whether general (of the second stage) or special (of the first stage) to one principle (of course selected from the objects of second intention), and it does this by attending to its own activity in the act of second intention. The fourth intention notes the activity of the mind in its third intention,

---

* " Illinois School Journal," vol. vii, pp. 444, 445.

and hence recognizes the form under which the many are related to the one—it notes the *method* of the philosophical system.")*

(" The science of formal logic states three laws of thought which correspond to these three stages of consciousness, although they may be looked upon as three statements of the same principle. These are the so-called principles of identity, contradiction, and excluded middle. *A is A, or an object is self-identical,* is the formula for the principle of identity, and it is very clear that it expresses the point of view of the category of being, or of the first stage of consciousness. It ignores all distinction, all relation, and hence all environment.

"The principle of contradiction states the environment explicitly. Its formula is, Not-A is not identical with A, or it is impossible that the same thing can at once be and not be, or what is contradictory is unthinkable. Here we add in thought to the concept of A its contradictory, not-A. We distinguish them, but make one of them the limit of the other. We moreover assert mutual exclusion, hence the finitude of both. Not-A is the formula for the relative or dependent, because it is expressed only in terms of something else, something else limited or negated. Change A, and you change the extent or compass of not-A. In the principle of identity the finitude of the object is not expressed, but in the principle of contradiction two mutually limiting spheres of being are defined.

" The formula for the principle of excluded middle

---

* Vol. 10, p. 230.

tells us that A either is or is not, or that of two mutual contradictories we can affirm existence of only one.

"This principle adds the concept of totality to that of identity and contradiction, and therefore relates to the idea of ground or logical condition, the third stage of consciousness. Looking upon the total sphere, we can reason from the existence or non-existence of a part to the existence or non-existence of the other parts. It is the principle of the disjunctive judgment. The principle of sufficient reason, which is added as a fourth law of thought to the three already named, if admitted to this rank of laws of thought, expresses not only a ground of knowledge, but also a ground of being. It means not only that we must have a ground for affirming the existence of any being, but that there must be a real ground or reason for the existence of any being. Understood in this sense it is the positive statement of the principle by which we cognize the logical condition underlying object and environment. 'Excluded middle' is the *negative* statement of this principle, while 'sufficient reason' is the positive statement of it. The former states that 'either, or' is true, while the latter states that the one is through the other, or that the totality is one unity. By it we perceive the necessity of *causa sui*, or self-activity, as the sufficient reason for any causal action whatever. By it we affirm the truth that all being is grounded in energy, or that dynamic existence is the basis of static existence.*

"We observe in these principles the importance of the idea of the negative as the basis of the idea of rela-

---

* C. C. Everett's "Science of Thought," p. 236.

tion. We can call the second stage of consciousness the negative stage, because it makes so much of the relative. The environment is the negative of the object, and its formula is not-A. It is of the utmost importance in philosophy to recognize the negative in all forms that it assumes. It is the principle of limit, of speciality and particularity, hence of all distinction and difference; it is likewise the principle of all contrariety, and hence of essence, force, cause, potentiality, and substance. What is most wonderful is that it is the principle of life and thinking, only that in these realms it appears as self-related. It sounds absurd, or at least pedantic, to hear one speak of self-negativity as the principle of mind. But really there is no insight possible into self-activity, and the logical conditions of experience, without some recognition of the self-negative. Self-distinction, as self-negation, is also affirmative, because it is identity as well as distinction.

"We must see that the categories of experience and the world are not based on being, or even on essence, but that being and essence are based on this negative process of self-relation, which we recognize as pure energy, *causa sui*, or personality. This alone is the root of individuality, independence, and freedom. The idea of God is the unfolding of its complete, positive import." *)

---

* Vol. 17, pp. 339-341.

Section V.—The Syllogism.

The Mind Acts in the Modes of Syllogism: Sensuous Ideas use Second Figure, First Figure, Third Figure; Abstract Ideas use Third Figure, First Figure, Second Figure; Absolute Idea uses Third Figure.

"*The Logic of Sense-Perception.**—Sense-perception is not a simple act that can be no further analyzed. In its most elementary forms one may readily find the entire structure of reason. The difference between the higher and lower forms of intelligence consists not in the presence or absence of phases of thought, but in the consciousness of them—the whole is present but is not consciously perceived to be present.

"Perhaps one will reply to this: 'The absence of consciousness is a lack of the essential structure of reason with a vengeance.' Let us, however, reassert that the whole structure of reason functions not only in every act of mind, no matter how low in the scale, say even in the animal intelligence—nay, more, in the life of the plant which has not yet reached the plane of intellect—yes, even in the movement of inorganic matter; in the laws of celestial gravitation there is manifested the structural framework of reason. 'The Hand that made us is divine.' The advance of human intellect, therefore, consists not in realizing more of the logical structure of reason, but in attaining a more adequate consciousness of its entire scope.

---

* This section as far as "Abstract Ideas" is taken from the "Illinois School Journal," vol. vii, No. 4, pp. 162-166, No. 5, pp. 213-217, No. 6, pp. 262-267, and "develops some new insight into the nature of sense-perception," which Dr. Harris "has recently discovered after many years' study on the subject."

"Let us imagine, for illustration, an entire circle, and liken the self-activity to it. (Self-determination is a movement of return to itself like the circle). The lowest form of life is not conscious of the smallest arc of this circle; but the animal with the smallest amount of sensation is conscious of points or small arcs of it. The lowest human intelligence knows at least half a circle. The discovery of ethical laws, of philosophic principles, of religious truths, gradually brings the remaining arc of the entire circle under the focus of consciousness.

"What is more wonderful is this: there are degrees of higher consciousness. The lower consciousness may be a mere feeling or emotion—much smoke and little flame of intellect. There are, in fact, degrees of emotional consciousness covering the entire scale. First, the small arcs or points; next, the half-circle; finally, the whole. Think of emotions that concern only selfish wants; next, of emotions that are æsthetic, relating to art; next, of emotions that are ethical and altruistic; then, of religious emotions relating to the vision of the whole and perfect. Next above the purely emotional (all smoke and no flame of abstract intellect), think of the long course of human history in which man becomes conscious of his nature in more abstract forms, and finally reaches science. The progress is from object to subject, and finally to the method that unites both. We act and then become conscious of our action, and finally see its method.

"The entire structure of reason is revealed in logic. Logic is thus a portion of psychology—it is 'rational psychology.'

"Let us examine sense-perception and see what logical forms make themselves manifest. Take the most ordinary act of seeing; what is the operation involved there? Is it not the recognition of something? We make out the object first as something in space before us; then as something limited in space; then as something colored; then as something of a definite shape; and thus on until we recognize in it a definite object of a kind familiar to us. The perception of an object is thus a series of recognitions—a series of acts of predication or judgment: 'This is an object before me in space; it is colored gray; it looms through the fog like a tree; no, it is pointed like a steeple; I see what looks like a belfry; I make out the cross on the top of the spire; I recognize it to be a church spire.' Or, again: 'Something appears in the distance; it is moving; it moves its limbs; it is not a quadruped; it is a biped; it is a boy walking this way; he has a basket on his arm; it is James.'

"First we recognize a sense-impression, and through that impression an object; then the nature of the object; its identities with well-known kinds of objects; its individual differences from those well-known kinds of objects. But the differences are recognized as identical with well-known kinds of difference. It is the combination of different classes or kinds of attributes that enables us to recognize the individuality of this object. It is like all others and different from all others.

"Let us notice what logical forms we have used. First, the act of recognition uses the second figure of the syllogism. The second figure says S is M; P is M; hence S is P; or, in the case of sense-perception (*a*) this object (the logical subject) has a cross on the summit of its spire—or is a cross-crowned spire; (*b*) church spires are cross-crowned; (*c*) hence this object is a church spire.

"We notice that the syllogism is not necessarily true. It may be true, but it is not logically certain to be true. This uncertainty attaches to sense-perception. Its first act is to recognize, and this takes place in the second figure of the syllogism which has "valid modes" (or necessary conclusions) only in the negative. But sense-perception uses *in-valid* modes, i. e., syllogisms which do not furnish correct inferences. Sense-perception, using a *valid* mode of the second figure (the mode called 'Camestres'), might have said:

"This object is cross-crowned.

"No natural tree is cross-crowned.

"Hence this object can not be a natural tree.

"(S is M; no P is M; hence S is not P.)

"The structure of reason as revealed in logic shows us always universal, particular, and individual ideas united in the form of inference or a syllogism.

"Grammar shows us the logical structure of language. Language is the instrument of, and reveals the structure of reason. Grammar finds that all speech has the form of a judgment. A is B—something is something. All sense-perception is a recognition of this sort: Something (an object before me) is something (an attribute or class which I have known before). But this recognition takes place through some common mark or property that belongs to the object and to the well-known class—this mark or property being the middle term. Hence the judgment is grounded on other judgments, and the whole act of sense-perception is a syllogism. The mind acts in the form of a syllogism, but is dimly conscious or quite unconscious of the form in which it acts when it is engaged in sense-perception. I perceive that this is a church steeple. But I do not reflect on the form of mental activity by which I have recognized it. If asked 'How do you know that it is a church steeple?' then I elevate into consciousness some of the steps of the process and say, 'Because I saw its cross-crowned summit.' This implies the syllogism in the second figure: (*a*) Church spires have cross-crowned summits; (*b*) this object has a cross-crowned summit; (*c*) hence it is a church spire. But this is not a necessary conclusion—it is not a 'valid mode' of the second figure. The mind knows this, but is not conscious of it at the time. An objection may be raised which will at once draw into consciousness a valid mode. Let it be objected, 'The object that you see is a monument in the cemetery.' The reply is, 'Monuments do not have belfries, but this object has a belfry.' Here sense-perception has noted a further attribute—the belfry. Its conclusion is simply negative: 'It is not a monument, because it has a belfry,' and it concludes this in a 'valid mode' of the second figure. (*a*) No monuments have belfries; (*b*) this object has a belfry; (*c*) hence it is not a monument. If the premises (*a* and *b*) are correct, the conclusion necessarily follows.

"In the first act of recognition the second figure is used. The characteristic of the second figure is this: Its middle term is the predicate in both propositions (the **major** proposition or premise, and the **minor** proposition or premise). There are four 'modes' in this figure which are valid; that is to say, four modes in which necessary truth may be inferred. The conclusions of these are all negative, and run as follows:

"1. No S is P (this is the 'mode' called 'Cesare'): (*a*) no P is M, (*b*) all S is M, (*c*) hence no S is P; or, (*a*) all P is M, (*b*) no S is M, (*c*) hence no S is P.

"2. Some S is not P (this is the 'mode' called 'Festinö'): (*a*) no P is M, (*b*) some S is M, (*c*) hence some S is not P; or, (the 'mode' called 'Baroco'), (*a*) all P is M, (*b*) some S is not M, (*c*) hence some S is not P.*

"In the *first figure* the middle term is subject of the major premise and predicate of the minor premise, thus: (*a*) M is P; (*b*) S is M; (*c*)hence S is P.†

"In the *second figure* (as already shown) the middle term is the predicate of both premises, thus: (*a*) P is M; (*b*) S is M; (*c*) hence S is P.

"In the *third figure* the middle term is the subject

---

* "Let the reader not familiar with logic who desires to learn more of it than is explained here read the first eight chapters of Aristotle's 'Prior Analytics,' and he will see the subject as presented by its first discoverer. Or, any ordinary compend of logic will give the essential details. For this psychological purpose note in particular the nature of the three figures which are distinguished by the way in which they employ the middle term (the term which unites or divides the subject and predicate of the conclusion)."

† "S is used to denote the word subject; M to denote the word middle (term); P is used to denote the word predicate. S and P are respectively subject and predicate of the proposition that expresses the conclusion or inference. M is the middle term that brings together S and P, as it is subject or predicate to either term. S and P are called 'terms,' and the two first propositions are called, respectively, 'major' and 'minor' premise."

of both premises, thus: (*a*) M is P; (*b*) M is S; (*c*) hence S is P.

"In the *first figure* we unite the subject (S) to the predicate (P) because of a middle term (M) that contains the subject, but which is itself contained in the predicate: All men are mortal; Socrates is a man; hence Socrates is mortal. Here man is the middle term (M) which contains Socrates, the subject (S), and is contained in the more general class of mortal beings, the predicate (P).

"In the *second figure* we unite the subject to the predicate, because of a middle term that *includes* both; that is to say, is *predicate* of both (because the predicate includes its subject). All men are language-using beings; no monkeys are language-using beings; hence no monkeys are men. Here monkeys are discriminated from men by the middle term, 'language-using,' which includes all men and excludes all monkeys.

"In the *third figure* we unite the subject to the predicate because of a middle term which is included in both, i. e., is subject of both (because the subject is included in the predicate). All men are animals; all men are rational; hence some animals are rational. Here animals (the subject) is united with rational (the predicate) through the middle term, man.

"We have now called attention to the use of the second figure as the primary form of sense-perception. We shall next show how the first figure comes to the aid of the second figure in perceiving.

"*How Sense-Perception uses the First Figure of the Syllogism to re-enforce its First Act, which takes place in the Second Figure.*—We have asserted that sense-perception uses the second figure of the syllogism in its first act. The proof of this may be found in the fact that the object can not be perceived except in so far as it is recognized or identified. Identification takes place in the second figure of the syllogism. Before one can notice the differences of a thing one must identify it as an object. And he must identify it as a sensation before he can identify the sensation as a sensation of an object. One may not be able to take account of differences, except in so far as he has a basis of identity as a ground to go upon. The primary form of seizing the object—the form of 'presentation,' as certain psychologists call it —is that of the second figure. But immediately after its presentation in the second figure begins the activity of the first figure.

"No sooner have I recognized and classified the object by one of its marks than I begin to look after the other marks which I have learned in my previous experience to belong to objects of its class. I recognize the object to be a church steeple by its cross-crowned summit, and begin at once to look for other characteristics of a church steeple, such as a belfry, for example. I also look for the well-known outlines of a spire, for the roof of the church to which it is united, and so on.

"If the first step of the process of sense-perception is in the form of the second figure, the second step is in the form of the first figure. By the second figure I have identified the object as a church spire. To classify is to refer the new object to what is well known. It is possible now to re-enforce the present perception by bringing to it all the stored-up treasures of experience. I begin at once to draw out of the treasure house of the general class a series of inferences: If it is a church spire it is likely to have a belfry—possibly a clock, a steep slope above, shingled with slate or wood, joined below to the body of the church at the ridge of the roof or else at the corner of the edifice, etc. Hence I look again and again; being now helped by my previous experience, I collect much information in a very short interval of time. The form of this second activity in the first figure is (*a*) M is P; (*b*) S is M; (*c*) S is P.

"'This object is a church steeple' is the conclusion of the second figure or first act of perception. Then by the first figure I conclude: (some) church steeples have belfrys; this is a church steeple; hence it has (or may have) a belfry.

"And I continue to look for characteristics which the first figure infers to be present in a steeple. I see a dark opening at the bottom of the steeple and I infer the existence of a belfry by the second figure, thus: (*a*) belfries have the appearances of a dark opening at the base of the steeple; (*b*) this object has that appearance; (*c*) hence it is a belfry.

"Thus to and fro moves the syllogizing without coming to consciousness. The mind acts without reflecting on the form of its acts. The classification of the object being effected by the second figure, I go on to infer by the first figure what I may expect to find there, namely, a bell, and I look for it and see a portion of a wheel in the dark opening. I infer a bell from this. The steps are very complex; I recognized the wheel by some characteristic appearance that belongs to a wheel. Thus we have a series of middle terms, each one of which has been used first as predicate in a syllogism of the second figure and then as middle term in one of the first figure.

"The modes of the syllogism ordinarily used by sense-perception are not the so-called valid modes. That is, they deduce only possible or probable knowledge at best. The cross-crowned object may be something else than a steeple; the dark space below may be something else than a belfry; the wheel may be there with no bell attached to the axle; the axle may not be there; the appearance of the wheel may be deceptive. Sense-perception abounds in deception. The second figure, of identification, is corrected by the use of the first figure, of deduction, which offers a number of additional marks for verification. By verification we decrease the possibility of error by the law of probabilities. Every additional mark verified increases the probability immensely.

"The first figure acts in very subtle ways in the first stages of a given observation. I look out through the fog in a given direction and see some object so dimly that I should not be able to say what it is. But I know where I am and that in the direction where I am looking there is a village. In a village church steeples are wont to be seen, and hence I am led to expect that the most prominent object will be such a steeple. Here the first figure acts to suggest what I may expect to see. It acts in a not-valid mood, thus: (*a*) Some villages have churches with steeples; (*b*) this is a village; (*c*) it has (or may have) a steeple. And, again (second figure): (*a*) Steeples are prominent objects; (*b*) you behold a prominent object; (*c*) it is (or may be) a steeple.

"The identification of the present place (the 'here') and the present time (the 'now') leads to a number of anticipations of perception by the aid of the first figure. And these lead to verification by means of the second figure.

"Besides these very general anticipations there are more abstract ones, and even *a priori* anticipations which guide our sense-perception. The general idea of space as a major premise suggests externality and the anticipation that the object is limited on all sides; and sense-perception is directed to look for boundaries.

"Next, the idea of time suggests movement, and the object is examined for changes.

"Then the idea of causality suggests functions, and these, too, are anticipated, and the object is observed to find its relations to other things. These 'anticipations of perception' are not conscious ordinarily, although they may become so, in case doubt suggests investigation and verification.

"The educational significance of these facts of sense-perception is obvious. The school labors to give the pupil the results of human experience. This stored-up material furnishes anticipations of experience to each so that he may know what to look for when the object is presented to him. In a brief time he verifies all that experience has recorded of an object. By the first figure of the syllogism the individual re-enforces his present vision by all his past experience. More than this, he re-enforces it by the experience of the race. This makes human progress possible, and by accumulation develops civilization.

"To teach powers of quick perception it is not necessary simply to use one's senses (although a false psychology often tells us so). It is necessary to store up, in the form of scientific generalizations, the observations of the race, and then (for this is not all) learn to verify these observations and critically test them so as not passively to mimic the former observers and repeat their errors. To master the results of the past sharpens one's observation by setting up in the mind a myriad anticipations of experience which test and cross-question observation at every turn, and make the alert and critical observer. One learns how to eliminate the personal coefficient from his observations. This personal coefficient is due to the individual peculiarity of the observer—to his defects and weaknesses. As no two persons are likely to have the same defects of sense-perception, it is possible for each one to correct the errors due to his own personal coefficient by the aid of the observations of others.

"Formal logic has fallen into great contempt in modern times. This contempt is not deserved. The study of logic as an industry by which we are to learn the art of reasoning—this perhaps deserves all the contempt it has received; but as a science of the spiritual structure of cognition—a science of the forms of perception—it is not contemptible.

"Formal logic, as the exposition of the structure of mind—the forms of its functions—is the most important part of psychology, and a key to all the unconscious activities of the mind. Treatises on logic usually hold the doctrine that logic is the form of reflection, and of conscious reflection alone. Hence they suppose that sense-perception and emotion are not syllogistic in their structure. Hegel was the first to show explicitly that every form of life has a syllogistic structure, and that even the inorganic world is dominated by the same form. He did not, it is true, make this analysis of sense-perception which I have here given, but he pointed out the dependence of the first figure on the third and likewise that of the second on the first, for the proof of its major premise. Many years ago, when engaged on Aristotle's 'Prior Analytics,' I was struck with the doctrine of the three figures and inquired: What significance have these in psychology? Do they not mark important distinctions in the functions of mind? I was not successful in finding the subject treated in the literature of logic. Hegel alone seemed to have looked to the distinction of figures as having a profound significance. The major premise of each figure needs proof; that of the first figure is proved by the third; that of the third by the second figure; and finally the major premise of the second figure requires the first figure for its proof. Hence Hegel changed the order that Aristotle gave for the second and third figures. In the psychology of sense-perception, as we have expounded it here, we should change the order of the use of the figures to the following: second, first, third.

"Next, we must inquire what function, if any, the third figure has in sense-perception. We shall answer this question by attempting to show that it is the form by which the mind generates its universals—arrives at classes, genera, species—in short, the major premise of the first figure.*

---

* "A POSTSCRIPT FURTHER EXPLANATORY OF THE FIRST FIGURE.— There are four valid moods in the first figure—four moods in which a conclusion may be deduced with absolute certainty from the prem-

"*How General Concepts arise. How Sense-Perception uses the Third Figure of the Syllogism to store up its Experience in General Terms.*—The activity of the second figure gives occasion to that of the first figure. The stored-up experience leads to a number of anticipations of perception, which are verified or tested. But, by what process do classes, species, genera, and all the universals which furnish the major premise of the first figure arise? The answer to this brings us to the consideration of the third figure.

---

ises given. That is to say, if the premises are true in these four moods the conclusion must be true. These are as follows:

"1. (*a*) All M are P; (*b*) all S are M; (*c*) hence all S are P. Illustrating this symbolism, (*a*) all men are mortal (all M are P, or all of the middle term, men, are mortal, mortal being the predicate of the conclusion); (*b*) all Indians are men (all S are M, or all of the subject of the conclusion, Indians, are men, the middle term); (*c*) hence all Indians are mortal (all S are P, all of the subject, Indians, are mortal, the predicate). This mode is called *Barbara*.

"2. (*a*) No M are P; (*b*) all S are M; (*c*) hence no S are P. This mode is called *Celarent*.

"3. (*a*) All M are P; (*b*) some S are M; (*c*) hence some S are P. This is called *Darii*.

"4. (*a*) No M are P; (*b*) some S are M; (*c*) hence some S are not P. This is called *Ferio*.

"There are sixty-four 'moods' possible in each figure, as one may see by calculating the permutations possible in three terms, each one of which has four possible forms. Each term, S, M, P, may be universal affirmative—all are (indicated in logic by the letter *a*); universal negation—none are (indicated by the letter *e*); particular affirmative—some are (indicated by the letter *i*); particular negative—some are not (indicated by the letter *o*). But of the sixty-four possible moods in each figure only a few are valid or draw necessary conclusions. There are only four valid moods in the first figure; the same in the second figure; and six valid moods in the third figure."

"The third figure necessarily comes into activity after the second and first figures. This will be obvious when we consider its nature. Its schema is:

"M is P.
"M is S.
"Hence S is P.
"Man is a biped.
"Man is rational.
"Hence (some) rational being is a biped.

"Here man is the middle term, and it is the subject in both premises.

"In the third figure, as used in sense-perception, the middle term is the object perceived, and the two extremes are connected to each other by the fact that they both belong to the same object.

"Now, since the middle term is subsumed under both extremes, it follows that only particular affirmative conclusions can be made in it—we can only say *some* S is P and not all S is P. *Some* rational beings are bipeds.

"There are six valid moods in this figure—three particular affirmative and three particular negative conclusions. These valid moods, however—useful as they are in deducing necessary conclusions—like the valid moods of the second and first figures, are, nevertheless, not of much use in sense-perception. Certainty in experience comes from repetition and verification, rather than from single necessary conclusions.

"The third figure follows the first and second figures, and can not precede their activity because each of its premises presupposes the action of identifying. The object M is S (S is recognized in the object). The object M is P (P is now recognized). Thus there are two identifications, one for each premise (both using the second figure of the syllogism), before the third figure can begin to function.

"Now it acts and connects the two phases of the object (S P) making a new predication which may serve for a new major premise of the first figure. Hereafter we may say: Such objects as those (M) are S P, and when we see one of this kind we may recognize it in the second figure at once.

"Let us suppose that our object before had been a black eagle, a well-known object. Now we recognize eagle and white head by two acts of the second figure; white-headed (bald-headed) eagle makes a new class, derived by the third figure. Hereafter an object may be recognized as white-headed (or bald-headed) eagle by the second figure, and all its other peculiarities stored up in observation deduced by the first figure.

"The second figure identifies in sense-perception; the first figure anticipates further identification; but it is the third figure that distinguishes, divides, and determines, and, by making a new synthesis of already familiar marks, defines new classes. The new class arises by adding a special new attribute to an old class. Every new combination of marks discovered in an object is potentially a new class. All other specimens discovered like it are recognized, and their peculiarities, stored up by experience, may be deduced by the first figure so as to abridge the act of perception and make it swift and compendious.

"The third figure notices the striking characteristics of an object, and unites them through this middle term of the object itself—these are characteristics of one and the same object and distinguish it from other objects, making it belong to the S-P class.

"Inasmuch as the characteristics S and P exist together in the same object, there is some deeper unity to be sought for them. This leads to the application of the principle of causality. S and P are related in some way causally. They are means, or ends, or agents, or results, in the same process. The *a priori* principle of causality here acts as an "anticipation of perception" and sets mental activity in the third figure to looking for a synthesis of causality between the attributes discovered in the same object.

"The causal relation has many phases; these fall under two classes—(*a*) subjective and (*b*) objective. (*a*) as relating to manifestation to sense—color, noise (especially), taste, touch, smell; the object may be obtrusive on our attention—conspicuous, attractive, monpolizing attention. Here the causative energy is subjective in the sense that its effect is chiefly upon our senses and not an essential element in the process of the object itself.

"(*b*) The causal relation is that of self-activity for the object's own sake. The activity of limbs in locomotion—legs, fins, wings, or in prehension as arms, hands, claws, jaws, or in growth implying assimilation, as of trees, etc. The object is a producer of effects on its environment.

"The activity of the syllogism thus far treated is supposed to be unconscious in various degrees; but the activity in the third figure comes nearest to being a conscious one because it notes what is new and announces the results of synthesis in a new definition.

"It would seem from this study of the third figure in sense-perception that the formation of general terms is not conducted after the manner supposed in ordinary treatises on psychology. We do not proceed by abstraction, comparison, generalization, etc., to classification. We make a synthesis of traits, and, although we have only one case before us, this synthesis is a definition of a possible class. If we observe a second, like the first, we use this synthetic concept (S P) and subsume the object under it. We recognize by the second figure any other specimen of the same.

"Thus each synthesis performed by the third figure becomes a class definition under which an indefinite amount of experience may be stored up by the second and first figures. Should no new examples occur the synthetic characteristic S P drops into the background and remains an individual mark, or it may get lost altogether and forgotten.

"The lower use of the third figure notes the obtrusive characteristics—those which strike the senses first—and usually not the characteristics important to the object itself. Its means of self-preservation are most important to the object; its means of procuring subsistence and defending itself—what it uses as a means of survival in its struggle for existence.

"Herein is objective causality manifest, and our general terms get something objective to correspond to them. In the case of subjective characteristics which are prolific in giving names to the lower varieties, we do not have an objective universal named but only a subjective—a constant for the form of obtrusion on the sense. For example, shade-tail for squirrel (*skia-oura*, *skiourus, skia*—shadow from *ska*, to cover, and *oura*, a tail. See Skeat's 'Etymology'). The striking characteristic of the squirrel is his bushy, upturned tail. The animal seated on his haunches struck the Greek imagination as an animal sitting in the shadow of his tail; or his tail appeared as a materialized shadow of him. The name falcon is from its curved beak; here the name indicates the objective causal process—its instrument of action. So rodent is a gnawer, an example of objective causal process. Cow, and the many words for kine, come from *gu*, to low, to bellow (old Indo-European root—see Fick I, 577); just as Bos, *Bous* in the Greek and Latin come from the root *Bu*, to low, to bellow, (see Fick IV, 178). The most important thing about the use of the third figure is this apprehension of causality—this formation of concepts based on the causal connection between two attributes belonging to the object. This is an explaining process—the reaching of a universal that is universal because it is a process that begets many examples—the self-producing power of life.

"The action of the third figure, as we have seen, produces a definition because it unites two characteristics in one object. The third figure is that of definition or determination. The definition may or may not be valid for many subsequent specimens. The test is the further experience which stamps the definition with currency or leaves it an exceptional case.

"Says Aristotle: 'When one thing without difference invariably prevails, there is then first a universal in the soul; for the singular is indeed perceived by the sense, but sense is of the universal—as of man, but not the man Callias.' It perceives individually, but it is the universal, or potentially universal, that sense perceives in the individual.

"For further illustration here are a few examples of the action of sense-perception in the third figure, by which two attributes are united by a causal idea: Tree, evergreen, resinous sap (resisting the action of cold). Bird, hooked beak, for tearing its prey. Bird, sharp talons, clutches living prey. Beast, chews cud, extra stomach. Beast, chews cud, divided hoofs, (this contrast to the former is a mere subjective class, no causality being obvious). Beast, large pupil to eye, prowls at night. Desert plant, dew-absorbing, no rain.

"The second figure classifies, using a property as its middle term. The first figure adds to the present observation the results of past observation, using the class as a middle term. The third figure, using the object as a middle term, perceives a new property and adds it to the class, making a new definition of a possible subclass of which the object before it is an example.

"There are three terms in sense perception, the object, its class, its properties. The object is middle term in the third figure, the class in the first figure, and a property in the second.

"We have seen that a conception is not a mental picture, but a definition. Here we have found the process by which the definition arises.

"The ultimate consequences of this principle in psychology are important as touching the doctrine of categories of the mind. Sense-perception uses these categories unconsciously. Reflection subsequently discovers their existence and finally their genesis. The fundamental act of mind, as self-determining, discriminates self from the special modification in which the self finds itself. The self is the general capacity for feeling, willing, knowing; but it is at a given moment determined as one of these, if not exclusively, at least predominantly. Every act of perception begins with identification (second figure). This is an act of removal of the special limitation from the object—a dissolving of it in the general self as a capacity for any and all sensation, volition, or thought. It is this first act that gives rise to the category of being, and the category of negation born with it is next perceived. All other categories arise from division of this most general of categories (*summun genus*). The third figure shows how these arise by progressive definition. The categories, in so far as they do not imply in their definition any properties derived from sense-perception, are called categories of pure thought or logic. Hegel undertakes to show the process of progressive definition by which these arise, in his logic ('Wissenschaft der Logik').

"There are six valid moods in the third figure, named, respectively:

"*Darapti*—all M is P; all M is S; hence some S is P.

"*Disamis*—some M is P; all M is S; hence some S is P.

"*Datisi*—all M is P; some M is S; hence some S is P.

"*Felapton*—no M is P; all M is S; hence some S is not P.

"*Bocardo*—some M is not P; all M is S; hence some S is not P.

"*Ferison*—no M is P; some M is S; hence some S is not P."

Abstract Ideas use the Syllogism.—" The middle term in this syllogism (third figure), as used in sense-perception, is commonly individual or singular, and not a universal. It is always in the form of, this object is thus and so, and again thus and so. For example: This individual is web-footed, it swims in the water; the synthesis has to find some causal relation between web-footed and swimming. Unconscious syllogizing forms the warp and woof of human experience, and deposits, as a result, the larger of general terms in language, and especially the words expressing classes, species, and genera. Any coincidence that it notices, whether accidental or essential, gets from related into a general class through this syllogistic process, and is handed over to the first figure, which keeps charge of the deductive first figure. From this it is handed to the second figure of immediate perception for verification or refutation. If the generalization has been rash, it gets quickly eliminated; but if it arose from a real insight into a causal relation it gets confirmed and established. One more very wonderful thing; the causal idea it is that carries one over from the particular individual to the general. The causal activity reaches results as examples, but is not exhausted thereby. One, therefore, can make many things, and all will belong to one family—all will bear the marks of the force which is a universal. All true classification presupposes the identity of generic power lying back of the immediate phenomena, which are only results of its activity." *

Absolute Idea uses the Third Figure.—" It is energy that changes quality into quantity. Energy produces a first result—as a first, it is simply different from all others. Such difference is simply and solely quality. Let the same energy continue to act, and it repeats its result indefinitely, and thus arises a class of similar terms, and extension and quantity come to exist. In quantity has banished the qualitative, and a new species of difference has arisen; difference of real being remains, the second is independent of the first and a different real being from the first, but qualitatively it may be the same, possessing all the attributes of the first. In fact, so far as it belongs to the same class, it would be the same qualitatively.

"But qualitatively there can be no such thing as difference of individuality; for qualitative difference is always and everywhere a dependence on, and correlation with another, and it takes both to make up an individual. The whole qualitative sphere must be in the individual, at least in the form of first entelechy; that is to say, in a form dependent upon the self-activity of the individual to realize it, or else there is no true individuation, but only difference as a manifestation of dependence, partiality, and phenomenality of being. Whence the strange fact of the use of the third figure in sense-perception, and of its generation of universals from singulars. Such generation is the product of the

---

* From a lecture given at Concord, July, 1887: "The Syllogism of Aristotle, as compared with that of Hegel."

reason, unconsciously furnishing to some the idea of causal activity or energy—its highest form being self-activity as reason or thought.

"In each of the figures of the syllogism is furnished a fundamental category of the reason as the principal of its activity. For the lowest and first there is given the category of reality, which can be first or second; that is to say, immediate or self-mediated, but never mediate, or, in other words, never the predicate of anything. It must be a real as basis of all that sense perceives. It must be a real as the general which energizes to produce any and every object of sense-perception or any higher real being. Real being is the first of the primordial ideas given in the constitution of all intelligence, even the animals being governed by it theoretically and practically. It governs perception in the syllogistic process of the second figure. The principle presiding over the second figure of the syllogism is that of the formal cause producing and resolving under the universal the entire realm of difference and particularity. The principle presiding over the third figure of the syllogism is that of energy as creative causality. It seeks the unity or synthesis of difference in causal energy, and furnishes the principles for the first figure in so far as they are derived from experience.

"The third figure, moreover, represents the form of the deepest and most subtle insights of the rational soul. One might affirm, indeed, that it is the essential form of the theoretical activity of the Reason itself in its immediate perception of principle. For a principle as energy involves the production of distinction or difference, the procession of the one to the many, a primordial self-separation, and all true principles are of this kind. But such principles involve the unfolding of difference or distinction upon a real being that eternally abides the same, even in the activity of distinction or self-distinction, if we may so call the knowing which as subject knows itself as object. It is a supreme synthesis of distinction in its highest and most complete form —the root and source of all difference in the universe.

"This sharpest difference appears, too, as an identity of real being, so that both the subject and the object are real and one in their distinctions. This is the transfigured third figure which unites two distinctions through energy that it finds united in one single individual as middle term. The third figure is essentially the figure which is transfigured in the divine theoretical activity. We must, on the other hand, hold that the first figure, when transfigured, is that of the divine creative will—a deductive syllogism that gives by the middle term of particularity to determine individuals in their activity. The second figure gives us the æsthetic of mind in its poetic activity, a symbol-making, correspondence-discovering, creation-imitating activity, which identifies the particular of sense-perception with its universal archetype." *

ILL.—It is not hoped to make the thought clearer by adding another illustration, but it may be helpful to give an illustration in something the same manner as given in class. As the students are becoming familiar with the subject and can give their own illustrations,

---

* From a lecture given at Concord, July, 1887; "Theory of the Syllogism."

the different points are taken up and explained. As a person is coming up the walk, something white upon the grass attracts his attention. He knows already what a real object is, and that it exists independent of his body in space. He recognizes the grass, the walk, and surrounding objects. The color white is also known to him. Since these are familiar, the process of identification is rapid, but the object is unknown. Cotton-cloth, with which he is familiar, is white, and he unconsciously reasons: This object is white; a piece of cotton-cloth is white; therefore, this may be a piece of cotton-cloth.

The middle term of his reasoning is the attribute white. The unknown object is white. A familiar object, cotton-cloth, is white, and he identifies the object and perceives a piece of white cloth. The middle term white is predicate in both premises. A necessary conclusion is not drawn. But how is this conclusion rendered more sure? By continuing the process and verifying the conclusion, or by correcting it. He approaches the object. He recognizes the warp and woof, the texture of the cotton, and confirms his perception, or he finds that the object has properties which do not correspond with the familiar object cotton-cloth. But whatever he perceives is by the same process of recognition and identification. Identification proceeds by the invalid modes of the second figure. But if some one else had called his attention to the white object on the grass and asked him to perceive snow, he would have reasoned in a valid mode of the second figure: as, snow never lies on the ground in warm weather; this object lies on the ground in warm weather; therefore, this object is not snow.

Joined with the act of recognition in the second figure of the syllogism, is the activity of the first figure of the syllogism. All the person's previous knowledge of cotton-cloth comes to the surface and he unconsciously syllogizes: All cotton-cloth has threads which cross each other and has a fine, soft texture; this object is cotton-cloth; therefore, this object will have these properties. Then continues the process of identification, and at a single glance a series of qualities appear, the identification being made through the syllogistic process of the second figure. In the first figure cotton-cloth is the middle term and is subject of the major premise and predicate of the minor.

Or perhaps the object could not be recognized as cotton-cloth. Other familiar white objects come before the mind, and through the repetition of the former syllogistic processes of the second and the first figures, the granular structure is noticed, the small white particles are seen as crystals, the saline quality is perceived by the taste and the object identified with a familiar object, salt.

Now begins the syllogistic activity in the third figure, the object itself being the middle term. This object is observed to be white, to be made up of small particles, to have a saline taste, to remain scattered on the green grass of the lawn and other properties identified by the former processes. We have then a "series of premises furnished by perception and suggested by experience all relating to the middle term, the object," as

This is salt.

It has a saline taste.

It is made up of crystals.

It is scattered loosely over the grass.

Now take any one of these premises and add another relating to the same middle term, the object, and a conclusion may be drawn which adds in some degree a new element to experience; as, this is salt; it lies scattered on the grass; salt gets spilled by careless grocer boys. Or, this is salt; it has a saline taste; salt mixed with other ingredients renders those saline. For the peculiarity of the third figure of the syllogism is that it perceives causal activity. By connecting one attribute with another the causal activity is discerned. No causal activity as such is seen by the senses, but the object is seen in one state and then in another and the mind makes the synthesis which furnishes the new ideas of experience. This process is through the activity of the third figure of the syllogism.

To continue the illustration for the plane of conscious reflection or that of abstract ideas. The chemist or investigator in studying and analyzing salt proceeds first by the third figure of the syllogism, because in the plane of thought involving processes and relations, the perception of causal activity by which new elements of knowledge are obtained is of chief interest. He proceeds: This object crystallizes according to the cubical order; this object has received this shape through the action of heat and water; therefore, crystallization in the form of cubes is caused by the action of heat and water. This synthesis, as a conclusion, remains in experience summed up in the first figure of the syllogism, as: All crystallization in the shape of cubes is formed by the action of heat and water; salt has crystallization in the form of cubes;

therefore, salt has received the action of heat and water. Or, again, in the third figure, the chemist sees that salt with other substances when subjected to heat in the laboratory presents a new appearance, and he reasons: This salt has been subjected to heat; this salt has been changed into substances having different appearance; therefore, the action of heat causes chemical change. And by means of the first figure he embodies this result, sure to the extent of one experiment, in his experience, and keeps it as a working hypothesis. Chemical change is caused by the action of heat; salt has undergone chemical change; therefore salt has been subjected to the action of heat. This is the stored-up knowledge for finding new properties of the same object, or for identifying and classifying a new object. For instance, in the second figure, a new property of the same object; this object has now a disagreeable odor; chlorine has a disagreeable odor; therefore, this may be chlorine. Or, the investigator finds another object; he identifies the crystallization as that of the cubical order and proceeds by the second figure: This object has crystallization in cubes, a familiar object of silver-gray color, namely, iron pyrites has such crystallization; therefore, this may be iron pyrites. Through this process of analysis and identification of one property after another he classifies this new object and hands it over to the first figure again as a result of past experience.

Thought in the plane of the absolute idea uses the third figure of the syllogism, for this stage of thinking is concerned with the perception of causal activity in all its phases. As in the preceding example: This object crystallizes according to the cubical order; this object has received its shape through the action of heat and water; therefore, crystallization in the form of cubes is caused by the action of heat and water. But the perception of causal activity from this third stage of thinking includes not only the modification through the environment, but also sees that the mode of crystallization is due likewise to the nature of the activity in the object itself and that the environment only assists, but does not produce the nature of the energy of the object.

This phase of thinking does not need the first figure of the syllogism as a medium for stored-up knowledge, for, by the same mind, the perception of the nature of this activity will always be the same and true at all times; nor does it need the second figure of identification, for the identification was included in the one act of rational insight. In this power of the reason we see the nature of creative thought.

SECTION VI.—THE THIRD STAGE OF THINKING: THE ABSOLUTE IDEA, OR THE REASON.

Rational Insight knows: Causality, Self-cause—Space, Time—Quality, Quantity—Change, Self-activity—Life, Individuality, Absolute Personality—Absolute Thought; manifested in Truth, Beauty, Goodness.

"Space and time have been considered as the presuppositions or preconditions in all experience. Three grades of knowing have been found by analyzing experience. First, there was knowledge of the object; second, of the environment; and, third, of the ground or logical condition, which rendered the object and its environment possible. There was the thing in space;

second, its relation to an environment of things in space; and third, there was space. There was likewise the event, and its environment of antecedent and subsequent events; and then the underlying logical condition of time." *

"Philosophy, as a higher, special form of reflection, investigates the presuppositions or logical conditions of the objects and environments of our experience and makes the third stage of experience clear and distinct— far more clear and distinct than the first or second stages, because they relate to contingent and changeable objects, while the insight into the unchanging nature of time and space sees the necessary and universal conditions of the existence of all phenomena. The third element of experience, which furnishes these logical conditions is the basis of universal, necessary, and exhaustive cognitions.

"The most rudimentary form of human experience, as it is to be found in the case of the child or the savage, contains these logical presuppostions, although not as a distinct object of attention. Even the lowest human consciousness contains all the elements which the philosopher, by special attention, develops and systemizes into a body of absolute truth.

"Every act of experience contains within it not only a knowledge of what is limited and definite, but also a cognition of the total possible, or the exhaustive conditions implied or presupposed by the finite object. Hence those vast ideas which we name world, nature, universe, eternity, and the like, instead of being mere

---

* Vol. 17, p. 300.

artificial ideas, or 'factitious' ideas, as they have been called, are positive and adequate ideas in so far as they relate to the general structure of the whole. We know, or may know, the logical conditions of the existence of the world far better than we know its details.

"All our general ideas, all our concepts, with which we group together the multitude of phenomena and cognize them, arise from this third stage of experience. It is the partial consciousness of the logical conditions of phenomena which enters as conditions of our experience that enables us to rise out of the details of the world and grasp them together, and preserve them in bundles or unities, which we know as classes, species, genera, processes, and relations. These classes and processes we name by words. Language is impossible to an animal that can not analyze the complex of his experience so far as to become to some degree conscious of the third element in his experience—the *a priori* element of logical conditions.

"Another most important point to notice is that these *a priori* conditions of experience are both subjective and objective—both conditions of experience, and likewise conditions of the existence of phenomena. The due consideration of this astonishing fact leads us to see that, whatever be the things and processes of the world, we know that mind as revealed in its *a priori* nature is related to the world as the condition of its existence. All conscious beings in the possession of the conditions of experience—in being rational, in short—participate in the principle that gives existence to the world, and that principle is reason. Time and space condition the existence of the world; time and space we find *a priori* in the constitution of mind or reason. This surprising insight, which comes upon us as we consider time and and space, is confirmed by all our philosophical studies. In our study of causality, we find confirmation of this insight." *

Causality and Self-Cause.—" Without using the idea of causality the mind can not recognize itself as the producer of its deeds, nor can it recognize anything objectively existing as the producer of its sense-impressions. All sense-impressions are mere feelings and are subjective. How do we ever come to recognize objects as the causes of our sense-impressions? We can see that it is impossible for us to derive the idea of cause from experience, because we have to use that idea in order to begin experience. The perception of the objective is possible only by the act of passing beyond our subjective sensations and referring them to external objects as causes of them. Whether I refer the cause of my sensations to objects and thereby perceive, or whether I trace the impressions to my own organism and detect an illusion of my senses in place of a real perception—in both cases I use the idea of causality. The object is a cause, or else I am the sole cause.

" 'When we are aware of something that begins to be, we are, by the necessity of our intelligence, constrained to believe that it has a cause,' says Sir William Hamilton. The idea of causality contains the idea of energy or self-activity (or self-determination), we should say, and it is not a mere impotence of the mind, but a positive idea that reveals to us, more than any other,

---

* Vol. 17, pp. 301, 302.

the transcendence of mind. Hamilton (Metaph., pp. 533, 555) refers causality to 'a negative impotence' of the mind. 'We can not conceive any new existence to commence; therefore all that now is seen to arise under a new appearance had previously an existence under a prior form.' This is his analysis of causality: What exists now must have existed somehow before. 'There is conceived an absolute tautology between the effect and its cause. . . . We necessarily deny in thought that the object which appears to begin to be really so begins, and we necessarily identify its present with its past existence.' Here we see the defect of Hamilton's analysis. He eliminates the idea of cause altogether, and has left only one of its factors—that of continuity or continuous existence. The element of difference or distinction is omitted and ignored. (Hume reduced the idea of cause to that of invariable sequence.)

"In our idea of causality we conceive something as producing something different from itself, or as originating a distinction, a difference. Change involves the origination of something new, something that did not exist before. This is one of its elements. On the other hand, causality involves the identification of this new determination with what existed before. But this is not all. The difference and identity are united in a deeper idea—the idea of cause contains the unity of difference and identity in a deeper idea, the idea of energy. Energy is deeper than existence because it is the originator of existence. We think the cause as an energy that gives rise to changes. It gives rise to new distinctions and differences—something, through the action of a cause, becomes different from what it was before. The action of the energy is the essential element in the idea of cause, and Hamilton's analysis omits just this, and reduces the idea of an activity to a sequence of existences.

"Experience would be utterly impossible with such an idea as Hamilton's or Hume's in place of the causal idea. We should say, as Hamilton does say, in fact, *ex nihilo nihil;* that is to say, there can be no origination, but only a persistence of being.

"The idea of causality involves this: An existence which is an energy shall by its activity originate a distinction within itself, and by the same activity transfer this distinction to something else, thus producing a change.

"A cause sends a stream of influence to an effect. It must, therefore, separate this stream from itself. Self-separation is, therefore, the fundamental idea in causality. Unless the cause is a self-separating energy it can not be conceived as acting on something else. The action of causality is based on self-activity.

"The attempt to form a mental image of causality is futile. We can imagine existences, but not the origination of them. We can not imagine time and space as we conceive them. We can not imagine causality as we conceive and think it.

"It is, in fact, the most repugnant idea to a mind that clings to mental pictures as the only form of thinking. Such a mind fails to discriminate clearly between efficient cause and transmitting links or agents. By doing this it produces an infinite regress of causes which are at the same time effects. In this way it succeeds in losing the idea of efficient cause altogether.

(This is done in the third antinomy of Kant's 'Critique of Pure Reason.') For example: a change, A, is caused by B, another change; B is caused by C, a third change; C by D; and D by E, and so on, *ad infinitum.* Here we have a change A, which, being an effect, must have a cause. We look first for the cause in B, but, upon examination, we see that B is only a transmitter of the cause—it is an instrument or agent through which the causal energy passes on its way from beyond. We successively trace it through C, D, E, etc. The imagination says, 'so on forever.' This, of course, means that a true cause is not to be found at all in the series. But if this is so, it follows, likewise, that there are no effects in the series, for there is no effect without a cause. Here we see that there is a fallacy in the idea of infinite progress (or regress) in causes. The infinite regress can not be in the cause, but in the effect. For A, B, C, D, E, etc., are all effects. But just as sure as we see that these are effects, so sure are we that there is an efficient cause to produce them. The infinite series of links or transmitting members of the series change by reason of the activity of a true cause. If any one denies this, he denies that the changes are effects.

"To deny that a change is an effect does not escape the law of causality, but it asserts that the change is self-caused or spontaneous. But this is only to come to the same result that one finds if he asserts that the change is caused by something else.

"A real cause is an originator of changes or new forms of existence. It is not something that demands another cause behind it, for it is self-active. The chain of relativity ends in a true cause and can not be conceived without it.

"The true cause is an absolute, inasmuch as it is independent. That which receives its form from another is dependent and relative. That which is self-active or a true cause, gives form to itself or to others, and is itself independent of others. That which can supply itself does not need others to supply it.

"Our idea of cause, therefore, is the nucleus of our idea of an absolute. It is the basis of our idea of freedom, of moral responsibility, of self-hood, of immortality, and, finally, of God.

"All things that exist owe their qualities, marks, and attributes either to causes outside themselves or to their own causality. If the former—that is, if they are what they are through others—they are dependent beings, and can not be free or responsible or immortal. If the latter—if they are what they are through their own causality—they are free and morally responsible, immortal selves, and they are in the image of God, the Creator of all things, who has endowed them with causal energy, that is to say, with the power to build themselves, and he has not built them or furnished them ready-made. The causal existence may be perfect as God, or it may be partially realized and partially potential, as in the case of man. ('Partially potential'—that is to say, man has not fully realized himself, although he has the power thus to realize himself.)

"The idea of a whole or complete being is realized in our minds solely through the idea of cause. Any dependent being is relative to another and involved with it, so that it can not be detached from it and exist by itself. It is no center of formation and transformation.

"Our idea of life or living being also has this causal idea as its basis.

"When one does not confound the idea of causality with the application of it to this or that case, but looks in the face of it, and sees the absolute certainty which he possesses that there can be no change without an efficient cause—and the like certainty that the true cause is an originator of movement and of new forms—when he sees that experience can not furnish the idea because it can not begin without it, and because the external senses can never perceive a true cause at all—he will see how important this investigation is in psychology." *

Space and Time.—"Previous to the formation of general ideas, sense-perception is merely the ceaseless flow of individual impressions without observed connection with one another. In fact, we do not perceive at all, strictly speaking, until we bring general ideas to the aid of our sense-impressions. For we do not perceive *things* except by combining our different sense-impressions—that is to say, by uniting them by means of the ideas of time, space, and causality.

"These three ideas are not derived from experience —in other words, they are not externally perceived as objects, or learned by contact with them as individual examples. We know that this is so by considering their nature, and especially by noting that they are necessary as conditions for each and every act of experience. We

---

* "Illinois School Journal," vol viii, pp. 57–60, *October*, 1888.

10

do not mean, of course, that we must be conscious of these ideas of time, space, and causality before any act of experience; nor would we deny that we become conscious of those ideas by analyzing experience—what we deny is that they were furnished by sense-impressions; what we affirm is that they were furnished by the mind in its unconscious acts of appropriating the sense-impressions and converting them into perception. The mind's self-activity is the source of such ideas.

"We find these ideas *in* experience, but as furnished by the self-activity of the mind itself, and not as derived from sense-impressions. We may each and all convince ourselves of the impossibility of deriving these ideas from sense-impressions by giving attention to the peculiar nature of these ideas. We shall see, in fact, that no act of experience can be completed without these ideas. Immanuel Kant called them 'forms of the mind'— they may be said to belong to the constitution of the mind itself because it uses these ideas in the first act of experience, and in all acts of experience.

"Why could not these ideas be furnished by experience like ideas of trees and animals, of earth and sky? The answer is: Because the ideas of time and space involve infinitude, and the idea of causality involves absoluteness; and neither of these ideas could by any possibility be received through the senses. And it is not correct to say that we derive even ideas of trees and animals, earth and sky, from sense-impressions, because sense-impressions can not become ideas until they are thought under the forms of time, space, and causality. Before this they are merely sensations; after this they are ideas of possible or real objects existing in the world.

"Let the psychologist who believes that all ideas are derived from sense-impressions explain how we could receive by such means the idea of what is infinite and absolute. Is not any sense-perception limited to what is here and now? How can we perceive by the senses what is everywhere and eternal?

"The materialist will answer, perhaps: We can not, it is true, perceive what is infinite and eternal by means of the senses; nor can we conceive or think such ideas by any means whatever. In fact, we do not have such ideas. Time and space and causality do not imply conceptions of infinitude or absoluteness. All supposed conceptions of the infinite and absolute are merely negative ideas, which express our incapacity to conceive the infinite rather than our positive comprehension of it.

"The issue being fairly presented we may test the matter for ourselves. Do we think space to be infinite, or simply as indefinite? Do we not think space as having such a nature that it can only be limited by itself? In other words, would not any limited space or spaces imply space beyond them and thus be *continued* rather than limited? Let any one try this thought and see if he does not find it necessary to think space as infinite, for the very reason that all spatial limitation implies space beyond the limit. Space, as such, can not be limited—the limitation must belong always to that which is *within* space. An attempt to conceive space itself as limited results in thinking the limited space as within a larger space. Space is of such a nature that it can only be thought as self-continuous, for its very limitations continue it. A limited portion of space is bounded only by another space. The limited portion of space is continuous with its environment of space.

"This is a positive idea, and not a negative one. The idea would be a negative idea if our thinking of it could not transcend the limit—that is to say, if we could not think space beyond the limit. But as our thought of space is not thus conditioned (we are, in fact, obliged to think a continuous space under all spatial limitations) space is a positive or affirmative idea. We see that the mind thinks a positive infinite space under any idea of a thing extended in space.

"Let us state this in another way: We perceive or think things as having environments—each thing as being related to something else or to other things surrounding it. This is the thought of relativity. But we think both things and environments as contained in pure space—and pure space is not limited or finite, because all limitation implies space beyond.

"The difficulty in this psychological question arises through a confusion of imagination with conception or thinking. While we conceive infinite space positively, and are unable to think space otherwise than infinite or self-continued—yet, on the other hand, we can not image, or envisage, or form a mental picture of infinite space. This inability to imagine infinite space has been supposed by Sir William Hamilton (see his 'Lectures on Metaphysics,' page 527 of the American edition) to contradict our thought of infinite space. His doctrine was adopted by Mansell and Lewes, and also by Herbert Spencer, who made it the foundation thought of his 'unknowable' ('First Principles,' Part I, chap. i).

"Now, a little reflection (and introspection) will

convince us that this incapacity of imagination to picture infinite space is not a proof that we can not conceive or think that idea, but the contrary. Our incapacity to imagine infinite space is another proof of the infinitude of space!

"When we form a mental picture of space, why do we know that that picture does not represent all space? Simply because we are conscious that our thought of the mental picture finds boundaries to that picture, and that these boundaries imply space beyond them; hence the limited picture (and all images and pictures must be limited) includes a portion of space, but not all of space. Thus it is our thought of space as infinite, or self-continued, that makes us conscious of the inadequacy of the mental picture. If we *could* form a mental picture of all space, then it would follow of necessity that the whole of space is finite. In that case imagination would contradict thinking or conceiving. As it is, however, imagination confirms conception. Thinking says that space is infinite because it is of such a nature that all limitations posit space beyond them, and thus only continue space instead of bound it. Imagination tries to picture space as a limited whole, but finds it impossible because all its limitations fall *within* space, and do not include space as a bounded whole. Thus both mental operations agree. The one is a negative confirmation of the other. Thinking reason sees positively that space is infinite, while imagination sees that it can not be imaged as finite.

"Time is also infinite. Any beginning presupposes a time previous to it. Posit a beginning to time itself and we merely posit a time previous to time itself.

Time can be limited by time only. The now is limited by time past and by time future; no, it is not correct to say that it is *limited*, for it is *continued* by them. Time did not begin; nor will it end.

"But one can not perceive an event without thinking it under the idea of time. No sensation that man may have had could be construed as a change or event happening in the world except by the idea of time. But it is impossible to derive the idea of time, such as we have it from sense impressions, for any one, or any series of such impressions could not furnish an infinite time nor the idea of a necessary condition.

"Nor could the experience of any limited extension give us the idea of infinite space or of the necessity of space as a condition of that experience." *

Causality conditions Space and Time.—"The principle of causality is so deep a logical condition of experience that it conditions even space and time themselves. For the externality of the parts of space or the moments of time are conditioned upon mutual exclusion. Each now excludes all other nows, and is excluded by them. Each part of space excludes all other parts of space, and is excluded by them. Any portion of space is composed of parts of space, and it is the mutual exclusion of these parts that produces and measures the including whole. Suppose, for instance, that one of the parts of space allowed another part to become identical with it, penetrate it, and did not exclude it; then, at once, the portion of space to which these two parts belonged would shrink by just that amount of space,

---

* "Illinois School Journal," vol. viii, pp. 7–11.

which had admitted the other. The portion of space and all portions of space, are what they are through this exclusion, and this exclusion is a pure form of causality, or an utterance of influence upon an environment. Time itself is another example of the same exclusion. The present excludes the past, and is excluded by it. Both present and past exclude the future, and are excluded by it. Suppose one of these to include the other, then time is destroyed; but, as time is the condition of all manifestation and expression, the thought of such mutual inclusion of moments of time is impossible. The same implication of causality is found in time as in space." *

"The true infinite is freedom. An infinite is defined as that which is its own other or environment. But if this separation of self from environment is static or passive, the unity is imperfect, and must be supplemented by another. Space is supplemented by time, because its unity is imperfect, a unity in kind, or species, of all parts of space, but not a unity of energy in which each part is the whole.

"In freedom the self is its own other or environment, infinitely continued or affirmed by itself. Its other, too, is activity or energy, and is free, and hence infinite. Therefore it exists for itself. But a part of space, although continued by its environment, exists not for itself, but for the unity of all space, which alone is infinite. Space is infinite, but it does not consist of parts that are also self-existent and infinite. Hence the unity of all space is not perfect, as before stated." †

---

* Vol. 17, pp. 303, 304. † Vol. 17, p. 341.

"The skepticism in vogue, called 'agnosticism,' rests on the denial of the capacity of the mind to conceive the infinite; and, strange to say, this very example of the infinite, which we find in space and time, is brought forward to support the doctrine. 'I can conceive only finite spaces and times, but not space or time as a whole, because as wholes they contain all finite spaces and times.' But agnosticism bases its very doctrine on a true knowledge of the infinity of time and space. For, unless it knew that the environing space was necessarily a repetition of the same space over and over again forever, how could it affirm the impossibility of completing it by successive additions of the environment to the limited space. It says, in effect: 'We can not know space, because (we know that) its nature implies infinite extent, and can not be reached by successive syntheses.'" *

"The attitude of modern science against philosophy—the attitude of positivism against metaphysics—the attitude of mysticism and 'theosophy' against Christianity—in short, all agnosticism and pantheism branches out at the point treated in this chapter ('Space and Time'). Most of it starts professedly from Sir William Hamilton's supposed proof that the idea of the infinite is merely a negative idea—an incapacity instead of a real insight. From the psychological doctrine of the negativity of our ideas of the infinite and absolute (first applied by Hamilton in his famous critique of Cousin) it is easy to establish the world-view of pantheism, and to deny the doctrine of the personality of God." †

---

* Vol. 17, p. 300.   † "Illinois School Journal," vol. viii, p. 11.

Quality and Quantity.—" The general form under which we behold objects in sense-perception is that of thing and environment. This is called the category of quality. To the question that asks what kind, or after the qualities, we answer by describing the difference of the thing from its environment. We mention its boundaries, its contrasts, and its reciprocal relations. In the category of quality there is (*a*) affirmation (of the thing), (*b*) negation (of the environment), and (*c*) limitation (of the thing by the environment). We have already seen by this category of quality, or by external perception, which invariably uses this category in all its knowing, that it is impossible ever to perceive self-activity. All this, we thus perceive has the form of external limitation and dependence; and limitation and dependence make an object finite. In contrast to this is the category of internal perception, which beholds some example or specimen of self-activity—a feeling, an idea, or a volition. We have called the objects of external perception phenomena, and the objects of internal perception noumena. A phenomenon depends on another being for its origin and present existence, but a noumenon is sufficient for itself; it is an original cause, a source of energy, an essence that manifests its own nature in what it produces. It is a self-activity. Introspection perceives self-activity as feeling, willing, and thinking.

" There is a realm lying between these two existences —the realm of the quantitative. Quantity is a very important category, because it lies midway between the form of the external perception and the internal perception, and participates in both. The idea of quantity is one of the chief problems in psychology. It is an instrument by which man becomes lord of Nature. Man divides and conquers. He moves mountains and fills up valleys by first estimating the number of cubic yards (or tip-cart loads) it is necessary to transport, and marshals against this quantity of earth the quantity of hands and machines necessary to produce the result in the quantum of time required. All science of Nature is, in the first place, an effort to get behind the qualitative aspects of external things to the quantitative conditions. To obtain exact knowledge of a phenomenon, you must fix the order of succession, the date, the duration, the locality, the environment, the extent of the sphere of influence, its degree of intensity, the number of manifestations, and the number of cases of intermittence. It is easy to perceive what is already known, and to note new differences, and by this add an increment to the sum of knowledge. By quantification, science grows continually without retrograde movements.

"We all have experience, but few attain to scientific method. Every day of our lives marshals its train of facts before us in endless succession. But without scientific method each fact does much to obliterate all others by its presence. Like the fabled Saturn, such experience devours its own offspring. Out of sight, they are out of mind. In science, the present fact is deprived of its ostentatious and all-absorbing interest by the act of relating it to all other facts. To study the nature of quantity can not fail to give us some insight into a great part of intellectual education. Mathematics deals directly with the separation of the quantitative elements from the qualitative and the fixing their universal value by comparison with a given unit. The science of inorganic nature and of molecular physics—including chemistry, heat, light, and electricity—are little else but the application of mathematics. The sciences of organic nature use mathematics in order to fix exact results.

"Quantity is opposed to quality and to self-activity, but it presupposes and participates in both. In quality, each thing is limited by an environment different in kind from itself. In quantity, the environment of each unit of number, extension, or degree, has an environment of the same kind. Its other is like itself; whereas in quality everything is regarded as different from the others. The thought of quantity is a double. It first thinks quality, and then negates it or takes it away. In other words, it abstracts from quality. It first thinks quality, or thing and environment, and then thinks both as the same in kind, or as repetitions of the same. A thing becomes a unit when it is repeated so that it is within an environment of duplicates of itself. In quantity we have repetitions of the same unit, and then again the sum or the whole is a unit because all is homogeneous. Quantity is, in fact, the ratio of these two units, the constituent units, and the whole, or sum, which they make. The difficulties in mathematics increase just in proportion to the explicitness of this ratio—that is to say, the higher mathematics deal more with the ratio and less with the terms of the ratio; while elementary mathematics deals more with the terms of the ratio. The ratio between the unity of the sum and the elemental unit is not explicit in elemental arithmetic, but it is made explicit in common fractions by expressing the quantity by means of two numbers. The child finds it requires a double act of the mind to think quantity at all, for he has to start with quality and to abstract from it. But he has to double this mental act again to think a fraction. Decimal fractions involve one step of difficulty higher than common fractions. They have the same elements of ratio with the added difficulty that the denomination, instead of being expressed by a simple number, is itself a ratio, and must be calculated mentally by the pupil from the number of decimal places occupied in expressing the numerator. Arithmetic rises into difficulties through making the ratio of the two orders of units involved in all quantity, its object. Algebra drops out the definite expression of the two orders of units between which the ratio exists, and deals with ratios altogether. The complexity of such mathematical thought is obvious. The expression of this ratio becomes still more explicit, and finally explicit in fluxions and the differential calculus." *

"Consider the nature of quality, and you will see an idea that could not be an object of experience at all. Under the idea of the finite lies the idea of the infinite, not as a negative idea, an unlimited or unconditioned, but as a self-limited or self-conditioned. For, if each object depends upon another, and is conditioned by it, it makes up a part of one totality where the conditioning is mutual and the process of one being. Hence, self-conditioning is the form of the whole—the form of that which is its own other—the infinite. All true

---

* "Journal of Education," vol. xxix, p. 25, Jan. 10, 1889.

being is self-conditioned. Only as seen in fragments by experience are qualitative or dependent beings seen.

"There is in the nature of the objects of experience a presupposition of quantity. There is externality, and hence extension. There is repetition of the same, and hence number and succession. All mathematics furnish to us *a priori* knowledge of the quantitative constitution of objects as forming a world of experience. If objects are to exist, or if they are to move, they must exist and move according to quantitative laws, as defined in mathematics. A triangle will always have the sum of its three angles equal to two right angles. If acted upon by a constant force, an object will move with accelerated velocity, into whose measure enters the square of the time interval as a factor. Our knowledge of quantity is a knowledge of what is universal and necessary, and hence it is not derived from experience. Causality is, in fact, presupposed by quality and quantity. It makes possible the inter-relation of things, and the existence of repetition, which lies at the basis of quantity, as extensive or intensive. It explains all influence of one object upon another. Without the idea of causality we should see differences, but no movements or changes. We should see only contradiction—a thing first in one state and then in another; the blossom and then the apple, without the idea of change and action to explain how one object may be both A and B." *

Change and Self-Activity.—"What is the great central fact to be kept in view in the study of the mind? To this question there is only one answer: It is self-

---

* "Results in Ontology," Concord Lectures, July, 1887.

activity. But the answer is likely to be a Sphinx riddle to the beginner. Who has not heard it often repeated that the end and aim of education is to arouse self-activity in the pupil? And yet who means anything by that word? The moment that one calls attention to its true implications, he is met by the objection: It is impossible to conceive the origination of activity; it is impossible to frame a concept of what is both subject and object at the same time; self-activity and self-consciousness are inconceivable. 'The words exist, it is true, but the mind is unable to realize in thought what is signified by them.' Herbert Spencer ('First Principles,' page 65 of first edition), says of self-consciousness: 'Clearly a true cognition of self implies a state in which the knowing and known are one, in which the subject and object are identified; and this Mr. Mansell rightly holds to be the annihilation of both.'

"Just the difficulty found in the conception of self-consciousness is found in that of self-activity. We can not form a mental picture of self-activity, nor of self-consciousness. We can not picture an activity in which the origin is also the point of return. But this does not surprise us so much when we learn that we can not form a mental picture of any activity of any kind whatever. We can not picture even a movement in space although we may picture the two places between which the motion occurs. So, too, becoming and change can not be pictured in the mind, although we may picture the states of being before and after the transition. We may picture an object as here or there, but not as moving. The ancient skeptics expressed this fact by denying motion altogether. 'A thing,' said they, 'can not move where it is, because it is there already, and of course it can not move where it is not; hence it can not move at all.'

"The unwary listener who supposes that he is thinking the elements of the problem when he merely exercises his imagination, finds himself drawn into a logical conclusion that contradicts all his experience. To deny motion, in fact, makes experience impossible. Take all motion out of the world and there could be no experience; for experience involves motion in the subject that perceives, or in the object perceived, or in both. And yet we can not form a mental picture of motion or change. We picture different states or conditions of an object that is undergoing change and different positions occupied by a moving thing. But the element of change and motion we do not picture.

"Hence it is not surprising that we can not form for ourselves a mental picture of self activity, since we are unable to picture in our minds any sort of activity, movement, or change. And yet the thought of motion, change, and activity, is necessary to explain the world of experience—nay, even to perceive or observe it. So, too, the thought of self-activity is necessary in order to explain motion, change, and activity.

"To make this clear, consider the following: (*a*) That which moves, moves either because it is impelled to move by another, or because it impels itself to move. (*b*) In the latter case, that of self-impulsion, we have self-activity at once. (*c*) In the former case, that of impulsion through another, we have self-activity implied as origin of the motion. Either the other which moves it is directly self-active, or else it receives and transmits the energy causing motion (without originating it). (*d*) Were there no originating source of movement it is obvious that there could be no motion to transmit. Suppose, for once, that all things received and transmitted and yet none originated energy. Then all phenomena of movement would be derived, but from no source; all would be effects, but effected by no cause. The chain of transmitting links may be infinite in extent, but it is only an infinite effect without a cause. Here we contradict ourselves. If there is no self-active cause from which the energy proceeds, and from which it is received by the infinite transmitting series, then that series does not derive its energy, but originates it and is self-active.

"Hence, self-activity must be either within the series or outside it, and in any case self-activity is the essential idea presupposed as the logical condition of any thought of motion whatever. . . .

"What phenomena are attributed to self-activity? In the first place we recognize it in plants. All human observation, whether of civilized or of savage peoples, takes note of self-activity in the phenomena of vegetation.

"The plant grows, puts out new buds, leaves, branches, blossoms, fruit; adds layers to its thickness, extends its roots. It does this by its own activity, and its growth is not the effect of some outside being, although outside conditions must be favorable or else the energy of the plant is not able to overcome the obstacles.

"The plant must grow by adding to itself matter that it takes up from its environment—water, salts, carbon, etc. Notice that the plant-energy attacks its surroundings of air, moisture, and earth, and appropriates to itself its environment, after transforming it. One may admit that the environment acts on the plant, but he must contend for the essential fact that the plant reacts on its environment, originating motion itself, and meeting and modifying external influences. The plant builds its structure according to an ideal model, not a conscious model, of course. Its shape and size, its roots and branches, its leaves and flowers, and fruit resemble the ideal (model or type) of its kind or species, and not the ideal of some other species. The self-activity of the plant is manifested in action upon its environment, which results in building up its own individuality. It not only acts, but acts for itself; it is self-related.

"Again, notice that the plant acts destructively on other things, and strips off the individuality that transforms their substance into its own tissue, making it into vegetable cells.

"The self-activity of the plant is then a formative power that can conquer other forms and impose its own form upon them.

"In the next place, consider the kind of energy that we call the self-activity in animals. The individual animal is also a formative energy, destroying other forms, eating up plants, for example, and consuming the oxygen of the air, and making over the matter into animal cells.

"But the animal shows self-activity in other ways. It not only appropriates and assimilates, but it moves its limbs and feels. In the plant there is movement of circulation and growth, and this is also found in the animal. But locomotion is a new feature of self-activity. It enables the animal to change his environment. The animal can use some part of itself as an instrument for providing food, or as a lever by which to move its whole body.

"Self-activity is manifested in locomotion, and especially in its conformity to design or purpose. The animal moves in order to realize a purpose. With purpose or design we have reached internality.

"Purpose or design implies a distinction between what is and what is not. The lowest and blindest feeling that exists deals with this discrimination. Pleasure and pain, comfort and discomfort, appetite and aversion, all imply discrimination between one's organism and the environment, as well as between the organism as it is and the organism as it should be. There is in all feeling a discrimination of limit, and a passing beyond limit. This transcending of the limit to the organism by the self-activity constitutes sensibility.

"Feeling is an activity; it is a self-activity; it is like assimilation or digestion, a reaction against an environment. The environment negates or limits the organism; feeling perceives the limitation, or discriminates itself as organism from its not-self as environment. Feeling, therefore, transcends its organism, and unites two factors—organic self and environment. The self moves in order to relieve itself of the pain or discomfort attending this negative action of the environment. Hunger and cold, all varieties of appetite and desire, have this elemental discrimination between organism and environment, and a further discrimination between the being of the self and the non-being of the self, so that something not yet existent (some ideal state) is discriminated. This discrimination of the ideal is the essential element in desire and sensation, as well as in all higher forms of self-activity, say of thought and will.

"It is important to recognize the existence of discrimination in this lowest stage of blind feeling—the most rudimentary animal soul. Feeling, in the act of discriminating between the existing self and its possible self, is constructive ideally, for it repeats to itself its limitation. The limit to its organism exists, and it is in interaction with its environment. But the self-activity in this higher phase of feeling (higher than the vegetative function of digestion) constructs ideally the limit of the organism and changes the limit for other possible limits, comparing it therewith. This comparison of one limit with other possible ones is the element of discrimination in feeling.

"Sensation is an ideal reproduction of the actual limit to the organism. It involves also the simultaneous production of other possible limitations, and hence contains a reference to itself, a feeling of self in its total capacity. On a background, so to speak, of the general possibility of feeling is marked off this particular limit which reproduces or respresents the existent. The contrast between it and the general potentiality of feeling is the birth of purpose or design, and (glancing upward) of all the ideals that arise in the human soul, moral, æsthetic, and religious.

"Self-activity as assimilation or digestion (vegetative soul), as feeling and locomotion (animal soul), and as thinking (human soul), is to be studied as the fundamental unity of psychology and physiology.

"It is not in itself an object of external observation, although external observation offers us phenomena that we explain by assuming self-activity as the individuality which causes them. Self-activity itself we perceive in ourselves by introspection. When we look within we become aware of free energy which acts as subject and object under the forms of feeling, thought, and volition. Becoming acquainted with the characteristics of these activities within ourselves, we learn to recognize their manifestations in the external world." *

"Looking at the world, then, with the reason, we see mechanical beings—helpless and unconscious—impelled from without; aggregated and disintegrated by external forces; the lowest form of being in the world, being that can not determine its own form, but takes it as an impress from some other being. From mechanical being reason looks up along the line of progress and sees beings that possess some power of determining their own form; at the summit of the world it sees man gifted with the power of perfect self-determination. I say the *power* of perfect self-determination, and not the *full realization* of perfect self-determination. For man has the *power* to transform any *thing*, *fact* or *event*, or any idea of his mind, and hence is responsible for them all. If it is already perfect, he can make it imperfect; if imperfect he can make it perfect; or he can by his self-activity approximate perfection or imperfection.

---

* "Illinois School Journal," vol. vii, pp. 395-399.

"Reason sees that the essence or essential being of the world must be not a thing or a being devoid of activity, but self-activity. It recognizes in a man a being in whom is realized this self-activity as an energy or power, but not as a completely self-realized being.

"Thus there are possible two forms of self-activity: first, self-activity as the *power* to realize itself; second, the self-activity that has completely accomplished this self-realization.

"Now the insight of reason sees the necessity of self-activity as presupposed by all existence and change in the world. But what self-activity? the first or second form of self-activity—the complete self-realization or the power to realize itself? Certainly the former, the completed self-realization, is presupposed by a world of incomplete beings involved in a process of realization. Certainly a being must realize itself before it can realize others. A world reason, therefore, that furnishes the self-activity necessary to a universe of dependent and derivative beings must be a completed self-realization. Only a finite time can separate a being from the perfection toward which it is growing or developing, and for which it possesses capacity. But time does not and can not condition the growth of the universe. It must be as complete at one time as at another. The absolute is unconditional as to time. Time past is greater than any given time, and hence more than sufficient for any possible development that was in progress. As a whole the universe is complete or perfect, and always has been. Any development or progress that we see now—any self-activities that we may now trace out in a stage of becoming or development, prove therefore that there is perennial renewal or new creation of beings that possess the capacity of growth." *

"Self-activity has been distinguished into determining and determined, or active and passive, subject and object of activity. We identified the subject as universal, the antithesis between subject and object as the particular or special, and the total as individual. These were seen as the primordial forms of the categories of reason—the universal, the particular, and the individual.

"(1.) The self-determined as self is pure active. The self-active is vital and living and thinking, and essentially self-knowing.

"(2.) It is not adequately expressed as self-active or self-knowing, because this involves an activity that makes itself passive, and a knowing that knows itself not as subject, but as object.

"(3.) To act simply to produce passivity within itself, is the act of self-annihilation, or of self-contradiction. To know one's self as object, and not as subject, is also not to know one's self truly, but to know what one's self is not. We see, therefore, that the explication of self-activity, or self-knowledge, or pure, absolute self-consciousness, demands that the self active shall determine itself as self-active, or that the self-conscious shall know itself as self-conscious, and that the free shall know itself as a free being.

"(4.) It follows, therefore, that independence of persons arises in the primordial self-active one. In order to be self-active and self-knowing, it is creative, and creates another which is the same as itself. In our

---

* "Journal of the American Akademê," vol. v, pp. 261, 262.

finite knowing, our thoughts and fancies exists for us, but only subjectively. In the absolute, their existence as thoughts is absolute existence. Hence, knowing and willing are one in God. This, indeed, is the ground of explanation used again and again in Christian theology in treating the Trinity.

"(5.) A first absolute self-activity begets a second independent, free, perfect self-activity. The second, too, is creative—his will and knowing are one. In knowing himself, he creates a third equal in all respects to himself.

" But the Second is begotten, while the First Person is unbegotten. In knowing himself, therefore, the Second Person makes an object of himself, not only as he is, but he makes an object also of his relation to the First, which is that of being begotten, or derived from the First. In the idea of derivation and begetting there is the idea of passivity. If the Second were only derived and begotten, he were only passive. But he has made himself self-active from all eternity. The passivity which is implied in derivation has been eternally annulled, but it is nevertheless an element in the self-knowledge of the Son, and as an object known, comes to exist as created, because his knowing is creating.

"In thinking his relation to the First Person, he therefore creates a world of finite beings, extending from the most passive up to the most active. It is a world in which all is process or evolution—no finite existing absolutely, but only relatively to the development of a higher being. All below man pass away and do not retain individuality. Man is self-determining as individual, and hence includes his own development within himself as individual, and hence is immortal and free.

"(6.) It is the thought of a becoming from passivity to perfect activity that is involved in the recognition of the derivation of the Second from the First Person, and this thought is the basis of the creation of the world. All stages of finitude are passed through on the way to the creation of man. The thought of what is merely object—the thought of the mere passivity—is the thought of simple externality or space. Space is the thought of one point outside of every other—no participation——simple exclusion—mere objects outside the subject. Space is the first thought of the creation, the lowest thought in the self-knowing of the divine Second Person. (The mechanical, chemical, and organic phases of nature we shall discuss in another place.)" (See next topic.)

"(7.) The Second Person knows himself as eternally elevated above all finitude and passivity, although his derivation implies passivity as a logically prior condition. And as he knows his perfection as having this logical prior condition, he knows his perfect self as existing as the consummation and summit of creation. Theology calls this a procession, or a double procession. If the Second Person could not know the evolution or process out of the passive into the active—out of the finite and imperfect into the infinite and perfect—then he could not know his derivation from the First Person. Then, too, there could be no such elevation of the world, no salvation of any of its creatures." *

---

* Vol. 17, pp. 313–315.

Life, Individuality, Absolute Personality.—"We will now consider the orders of being in nature in the light of the idea of creation already developed. Science in our time interprets the phases of nature in the light of the principle of evolution. In the 'struggle for existence' one order develops into another. When we have seen how a species has arisen from a lower one, and how a higher has ascended from it in this struggle, we have explained it in the spirit of science in our day. Let us notice that this 'struggle for existence' is a manifestation of self-determination. The adoption of this point of view marks the arrival at an epoch in which the orders of being will be seen as a progressive revelation of the divine.*

"How does this idea of evolution agree with the idea of creation as we have found it in considering what follows from self-activity as the first principle? The self-active is self-determining and self-knowing, subject and object. But as object it is also self-knowing and self-determining. In this we can find as yet no necessity for creation of finite beings. The All-perfect knows himself as all-perfect, and his knowing is creating, because will and knowing are one in the Absolute, and knowing himself he creates what is self-knowing, self-willing, and hence pure self-activity like himself a creator. But the second self-activity, in

---

* "'A subtle chain of countless rings,
   The next unto the farthest brings;
   . . . .
   And striving to be man, the worm
   Mounts through all the spires of form.'
"This is Emerson's statement of the doctrine in 1836."

knowing itself, knows its relation to the first—a relation of derivation, and, in knowing it, creates it. It is in this contemplation by the second of his derivation from the first that we find the ground of creation of a world of finite beings. The second knows himself as pure self-activity, but as having made himself such from a state of mere passivity implied in derivation. The state of passivity has been transcended, must have been transcended ever since the first came to self-knowledge. But as absolute self-knowledge is necessary in the first principle, the same has been attained by the second from all eternity.

"Hence the passivity involved in a derivation from the first is only a logical presupposition, and not chronological. It being necessary that this logically prior state of passivity should be known by the second person in recognizing his derivation from the first, it follows that he creates a third, not simply like himself, but as eternally proceeding from the depths of passivity.

"The perfect, which is a procession, is eternally perfect, but the passive is an ascending series of orders of being in a state of becoming—an evolution from passivity to self-activity. The becoming or evolution has necessarily the form of time, because there are change and decay. It has the form of space, because passivity involves externality or exclusion; for it (passivity) arises only in what is self-active, but is its opposite, and hence excludes it. But as this evolution is as eternal as the self-knowledge of the second person, the world in time and space is eternal; although of necessity its individuals exist only in a state of transition and loss of individuality. Suns and planets have their youth and old age just as animals and plants. But just as sure as there is a realm of perishable individuals, the end of whose existence is evolution, just so sure there must be a realm of immortal individuals ascending out of the lower realm of evolution and belonging to a realm wherein self-evolution or education prevails.*

"Vanishing beings, such as belong to the realm of evolution, form together what may be called an 'appearance,' or manifestation of a process. The theory of evolution interprets the history of the individuals by the law of the process which is that of the struggle for existence or the struggle for freedom and self-determination. This struggle is the school of development of individuality. There is no individuality where there is no self-activity. Individuality rises higher in the scale as it approaches the form of knowledge and will. A compendious survey shows us three orders of being: (*a*) inorganic nature, (*b*) life realized in plant and animal, (*c*) self-conscious intelligence realized in man. There are three principles in the first of these realms, progressively realized. The first is *mechanism*, or externality which is void of an internal bond of unity—space and time, mere materiality, mere exclusion and impenetrability in so far as they appear in nature, characterize this realm of mechanism.

"In so far as there appears dependence of one being on another we have a principle which attains its typical form in chemical unity. Each manifests another. Gravitation, even, is such a manifestation. One body at-

---

* "Says Emerson: 'It is a sufficient account of that appearance we call the world that God will teach a human mind.'"

tracted toward another attracts that other body in turn. Hence it gains weight and gives weight in turn. But in the chemical aspect of being each being shows some special relation to complementary beings with which it enters into combination in order to realize an ideal unity. An acid or a base, for example, has an ideal unity in a salt, and its combination with its opposite realizes this ideal unity. In so far as one being makes another the means by which it realizes itself there is a manifestation of teleology.

"Teleology is the third phase of the inorganic, and points toward life as its presupposition. Life is that in which every part is alike the means and the end for all the other parts—such is Kant's definition. Life manifests the phases of universal, particular, and individual in a process in which there are species and individual, and self-determination is manifested. In the plant the species only manifests self-determination, each step being the evolution of a new individual out of the old one. But in animal life there come feeling and locomotion. On the scale of feeling there develops sense-perception as well as representation in its two phases of recollection and fancy.

"When the animal progresses beyond recollection and fancy to generalization, he becomes immortal as an individual.

"Evolution prevails in nature, but it is not evolution of the lower to the higher through the unaided might of the lower. There is no such unaided might of the lower. The lower order of being exists only in the process of evolution into the higher. It exists only *in transitu*, and its individuality is fleeting.

The Divine Thought of eternal derivation and eternal annulment of derivation creates a world of finite beings existing not absolutely, but only in a process of evolution. Hence each thing has phenomenal existence, and not absolute existence; it is relative and dependent, and manifests its dependence by change.

"If one conceives evolution even as growth of a living being, or, still higher, as the process of education of a conscious being, still the development does not take place unaided. Only the perfect or completely developed can exist in perfect independence. All growing individuals and all finite things exist because created and sustained by a Perfect Being. The question that has seemed insoluble is, How can a Perfect Being create an imperfect one, and for what purpose would he create and sustain such a being? It is answered by showing that the Second Divine Principle recognizes his relation to the First as a begotten, a derivation which, in so far as it involves passivity, He has eternally annulled, so that he is equal to the First by his own might of self-activity.

"Creation is a free act, though necessary. It is not compelled by any external necessity. It is only a logical necessity, and not an external necessity. It is a logical necessity that the first principle should be self-active or self-determining, and hence free intelligence. But such logical necessity does not imply or involve fate or external constraint. This is a dialectic circle: (1) The First is necessarily free, (2) but is therefore necessitated and is not free; (3) hence, not being free, it is not *necessitated* to be free, (4) and hence *is* free in spite of (2). Logical necessity is spoken of in (1); fatalistic necessity in (2) and (3); (2) and (3) cancel each other and leave (1) or (4)." *

"We have seen the grounds for our conclusion that time and space are not externally perceived as objects or learned by contact with them as individual examples—in short, we have seen that the ideas of time and space are not derived from sense-perception. From the nature of the case, sense-perception is limited to what is present (here and now), and can not furnish us objects that are infinite, like time and space.

"We have considered the idea of the infinite and noted the fact that it is a positive idea and not a negative idea. This is very important, and must be borne in mind constantly in the psychology of education, or else we can not rightly adjudge the value or worthlessness of ideas that lie at the bottom of so much that is offered us in literature, science, history, and philosophy in our day.

"Time and space are the conditions of existence of all things and events in the world. The ideas of time and space make experience possible.

"In thinking these ideas, we think the infinite in an affirmative manner. Through the mistake of Hamilton and Mansell, George Henry Lewes, and especially Herbert Spencer, have been led into agnosticism, and most of the men of science and literature have followed them. If their doctrine of the inconceivability of the infinite is based on false psychology, we may see at once how much literature needs correction. Herbert Spencer, in his 'First Principles,' denies the conceivability of all

---

* Vol. 17, pp. 347-351.

'ultimate religious ideas'—such, for example, as self-existence, self-creation, and creation by an external agency. Nor can we conceive (according to him) of First Cause as infinite and absolute. He quotes Mansell: 'The Absolute can not be conceived as conscious, neither can it be conceived as unconscious; it can not be conceived as complex, neither can it be conceived as simple; it can not be conceived by difference, neither can it be conceived by the absence of difference; it can not be identified with the universe, neither can it be distinguished from it.' 'The fundamental conceptions of rational theology,' according to Mansell and Spencer, 'are thus self-destructive.'

"All these negative conclusions are based on the false psychology exposed in the previous chapters. Spencer says (page 31, first edition of 'First Principles'): 'Self existence, therefore, necessarily means existence without a beginning; and to form a conception of self-existence is to form a conception of existence without a beginning. Now, by no mental effort can we do this. To conceive existence through infinite past time implies the conception of infinite past time, which is an impossibility.'

"To us this all rests on the confusion of mental images with logical thought. We can not image infinite time simply because it is infinite. That it is infinite we can know, however, by thinking on its nature. We can see that any limited time is limited by time previous and subsequent, and that these three times—present, past, and future—all are parts of the same time.

"In fact, had Spencer been acquainted with Kant's Kritik he would have noticed his own contradiction.

For while he denies the possibility of conceiving self-existence in the first chapters of his book he does not hesitate to set up 'persistent force' as the highest scientific truth in the latter part of his book. His 'persistent force,' for the reason that it 'implies the conception of infinite past time, which is an impossibility,' is a phrase that could have no idea corresponding to it, according to his philosophy.

"Now, if we really can know the infinity of space and time, and the absoluteness implied in causality, it is a matter of great concern in education. For science is coming to be written and taught with these agnostic assumptions explicitly stated at every turn. There is nothing about natural science that warrants such agnosticism. It is only the teachers and expounders of it who have adopted a false psychology, and who give science their own point of view.

"As we have seen, the true doctrine of causality leads to valid conceptions of self-activity. In Chapter IV, Section IV, we have described the three stages of thought. The second stage sets up relativity as a supreme principle, and is pantheistic. The lowest stage of thought is atheistic, because it makes all things alike independent realities. The second stage makes all things dependent and subordinate to an ultimate blind force which swallows up all special forms of existence. The third stage of thinking reaches the ideas of the infinite and the absolute, and comprehends and recognizes the attributes of life, moral freedom, immortality, and the divine.

"With a belief that the words 'infinite' and 'absolute' do not express anything to which we may think any meaning, all religious and all moral and all æsthetic ideas must be set aside altogether, or else explained physiologically, or perhaps shown up as 'survivals' of crude early epochs of development. Religious ideas have been explained as a 'disease of language.' The sun myths that have furnished the symbols and metaphors for religious ideas are looked upon rather as the substantial meaning, and the spiritual ideas which have found expression in those symbols are regarded by such agnostics as spurious and unwarranted outgrowths.

"So freedom and moral responsibility, the sheet-anchor of man's higher life in institutions, has been denied, and is still denied, by all who deny the true import of causality, and who set up in its place an 'invariable sequence.' Herbert Spencer, in the first American edition of his 'Data of Psychology' (page 220), says: 'Psychical changes either conform to law or they do not. If they do not conform to law, this work, in common with all works on the subject, is sheer nonsense; no science of psychology is possible. If they do conform to law there can not be any such thing as free will.'

"The physiological psychologists, instead of explaining the nerves and brain as servants of mind, are prone to make them the originating source and masters of mind.

"But, according to our explanation of time, space, and causality, we are bound to see the soul as a substantial self-activity and original cause which acts on its environment *really* in assimilation and digestion, taking up matter and converting it into living tissue—vegetable or animal cells; and it reacts *ideally* against its environment in sense-perception, representation, and thought. It constructs the ideas of objects, places them in space and time, and thereby perceives those objects—not destroying them by the operation as the process of digestion does." *

Truth.—" Creation reveals its creator. Self-activity can be revealed only in self-activities. The plant reveals self-activity in its growth. It acts upon its environment, changes it, stamps upon it its own nature, and adds it to its own structure, changing inorganic elements into vegetable cells. Plant life thus reveals the principle of self-activity. Animal life feels and moves itself; both feeling and locomotion are forms of self-activity. Feeling is a reproduction of the environment by the self-activity and within the self-activity. Locomotion is the origination of movement in a body by the self-activity that has caused it to grow. Human consciousness is self-activity in the form of free and immortal personality. Even the inorganic world assumes globular shape and revolves on its axis, and also in an orbit. Its movement in returning cycles symbolically points back to absolute self-activity as its creator.

" The phases of nature found in the revolving globe, the plant, the animal, reflect, but do not adequately reveal, the principle of self-activity. Man alone in his intelligence and will reveals it; for man possesses the capacity for infinite culture. He can grow in knowledge and wisdom, and he can grow in holiness forever, by the exercise of his self-activity." †

---

* "Illinois School Journal," vol. viii, pp. 107–109.
† "The Chautauquan," vol. vi, pp. 438, 439, May, 1886.

"The scientific view finds the general or universal. First it discovers classes; next, laws; then causal principles. Science inventories facts, identifying them as falling under classes. Then it goes back of the idea of class and regards the energy that produces a class of facts by continual action according to a fixed form. This fixed form of action is called law. It rises above the idea of law to the idea of purpose or adaptation to end. That is to say, it discovers evolution or progressive development. In the view of evolution there is a goal toward which relatively lower orders are progressing, and the facts, forces, and laws are seen as parts of a great world-process which explains all. At this point science rises into philosophy. Philosophy is science which investigates all facts and phenomena in view of a final or ultimate principle—the first principle of the universe. When science comes to study all objects in view of the principle of evolution it has transcended the stage of mind whose highest object is to discover classes; likewise the stage that makes law an ultimate. Besides efficient cause which makes or produces some new state or condition there is 'final cause' or purpose—design or 'end and aim.' The theory of evolution takes into consideration this idea of the 'end and aim' of changes in nature. It ranges or ranks all phenomena according to their development or realization of an ideal. Now it is evident that purpose, design, or 'final cause' is an ideal that can have existence for a being (i. e., conscious existence) only in so far as it is a soul or mind. A living being like a plant, which can grow but not feel, does not perceive or feel its ideal, and yet its ideal guides and directs the activity of its efficient cause or active force. The ideal is only 'law' to the plant. But in the lowest form of animal life there is a feeling of want—that is to say, the want of an ideal different from its real. We can observe even the lowest animals moving in order to adjust themselves to the environment, or to appropriate the environment for food. As an external phenomenon we should never be able to explain such movements, because we can not perceive ideals with our external senses. We interpret such movements through our own introspection. We can feel wants and be conscious of motives. We can therefore recognize in a being the existence of introspection in the form of feeling, or in some higher form, only because we exercise the activity of introspection ourselves.

"Strange as it may appear, therefore, we conduct even external observation by means of introspection. Natural science, in adopting the theory of evolution, advances to the stage wherein it makes it its chief object to recognize development from a lower stage toward a higher—the progressive realization of an ideal. The ideal is unconscious in the inorganic world and in the plant world, but acts only as law or as vitality. In the animal world it is conscious of this ideal, and feels it as appetite or represents it in the form of a mental image.

"The evolution theory recognizes introspection as existing in the objective world—it sees in Nature a tendency to develop such beings as possess internality and energize to realize their ideals. It is curious to note that this movement in science begins by the utter repudiation of what is called teleology—i. e., it sets aside the old doctrine of design which looked for marks of external adaptation of nature to ulterior spiritual uses—such external design as one finds in a watch where the various parts are artificially adapted to produce what they never would have produced naturally. Such external teleology ignored the immanent teleology of nature. By rejecting the old mechanical teleology, which makes nature a machine in the hand of God, evolution has come to see the teleology which God has breathed into nature—to see, in short, that nature is through and through teleological. Nature is, in every particle of it, governed by ideals, which, however, are not perceived except by introspection. Matter is heavy, and falls, for example, only because it obeys an ideal—an ideal of which it is entirely unconscious, and yet which is manifested in it in the form of weight. Gravity is the manifestation of the unity of one body with another. The unity is ideal or potential, but its manifestation is real force, real attraction.

"This subject of introspection thus leads out to the end of the world and reappears underneath the method of modern natural science which, studies all objects in their history—in their evolution. Strangely enough the scientists of the present day decry in psychology what they call the 'introspective method.' And just as in the case of the repudiation of teleology, they are bound to return to some other form of what they repudiate. Renounce teleology and you find nothing but teleology in everything. Renounce introspection and you are to find introspection the fundamental moving principle of all nature. All things have their explanation in a blind attempt on the part of nature to look at itself.

"One more remark: A blind tendency in nature to

develop some ideal implies as its logical condition a completely realized ideal in the absolute first principle in which nature is given its being. If nature is evolution —a process moving toward self-consciousness—it is no complete and independent process, but a means used by an absolute personal being—God—for the creation of living souls in his own image." *

"If the standpoint of reflection upon the facts and processes of the world is that of theism, the outlook is entirely different than from that of atheism or pantheism.

"Instead of a formless highest principle which is hostile to the permanence of all particular individuals, a highest principle is set up, whose nature is perfect form. Perfect form contains not only the forming principle, but also the formed; it is self-determined and self-active, and hence subject and object. For theism finds the ultimate and absolute to be personality or perfect form instead of the negation of all form. Hence the world-process is to be interpreted rather as the evolution of this perfect form or conscious being, rather than as a process of producing individualities with no purpose except to annul them. There is an ideal at the summit of the universe, perfect personality, the goal toward which creation moves. Hence with theism there is immortality for man, and infinite progress possible. The divine Being is perfect form, and its influence gives a tendency in the universe toward the survival of whatever reaches conscious personality. It is understood here that personality implies consciousness and free will. Personality, according to theism, is not *per*

---

* "Illinois School Journal," vol. vii, pp. 347–349, April, 1888.

se finite and limited, but in the true form of infinitudes because it is self-determination, self-activity, and not something which is originated and sustained by something else. Imperfect creatures, like men, participate in this self-activity, and have the possibility of infinitely growing into it by their own free activity." *

"Let us turn our attention to the aspect of modern science that is least identified with philosophical thinking—namely, its empirical method. If we can learn by our investigation what it presupposes, we shall find ourselves in a position to determine the answer to the objection made to all philosophical and theological conclusions whatever—the objection, namely, from the standpoint of 'positive' or empirical science, to the effect that we can not transcend experience, and that experience is only possible in regard to finite and relative objects, and in no wise possible in regard to an ultimate principle. On this ground it utterly repudiates what it calls 'introspection,' and the 'method of introspection.' Moreover, it declares against all generalizations not based on and derived from external experiment, claiming that all scientific knowledge is knowledge obtained through specialization and actual inventory of details. It thus rejects all inferences of a theological character and holds them to be unwarranted by science.

"It is not the necessity of specialization for purposes of making an inventory of nature that militates against philosophy or theology, for why should not both these exist as well as specialized inventorying? It is the attitude of the scientists against all general surveys.

---

* Vol. 19, pp. 411, 412.

They assume that these general surveys are not only unnecessary, but vicious in all science; hence they deny the existence of a scientific philosophy or theology. But this assumption of scientists can be shown to be wholly grounded on a misapprehension of their own procedure in scientific knowing. It is due, in other words, to an incorrect account of the processes involved in the scientific method itself. It is a simple matter to initiate and carry on some one of the scientific processes by which discoveries are made, but the system of science as a whole is presupposed as a sort of invisible guide or norm that makes possible the act of specialization. We have division of labor and the specialization of the work of the individual, because of the system of collection and distribution which commerce carries on, and by which it supplies each with the needed food, clothing, and shelter that he does not produce, for the reason that he is engaged in his special vocation that furnishes only one of the many required necessities.

"The special scientist can not confine his attention to one subject without definition and limitation effected by the collective labors of his fellows, not only in their special departments, lying contiguous to his own, but as well by their labors to state the relations of the special results to each other. . . . The specialist sometimes supposes that his industry is all that is required for the creation of science in its completeness. He condemns what is called the philosophy of his subject, as though it were premature generalization and unwarranted systematizing. On the other hand, it must be confessed, that the philosopher is apt to be impatient at the plodding toil and narrow gains of the specialist. But the fact that it needs both species of investigation becomes evident when we look to the practical field of human activity. Man must act as well as think.

"The will executes while the intellect surveys or analyzes. In the performance of a deed the will should act in view of all the circumstances, but this view of all the circumstances is an intellectual survey. Hence human action demands a general survey of the circumstances before it in order to act rationally. Suppose we omit the philosophical activity of the intellect—leave out the generalization consequent on a survey of the whole—and try to act with the aid of the specializing intellect alone? Then the will resolves and executes in view of a fragmentary circumstance, and does not weigh one particular motive with another. The result will be lame and impotent, because it lacks considerateness and looks neither before nor after, but acts from one motive, and a trivial one, because it is an intentionally special view and not a general survey.

"The necessity of practical activity in any province, therefore, demands the intellectual activity of forming a general survey, as well as the intellectual activity of analyzing and specializing. It is important to see how these co-ordinate.

"Rational will-power is the will under the guidance of directive intelligence. This intelligence surveys various objects of action and selects one of them as desirable; it surveys likewise various modes of action, and adopts what seems to be the best. Now, it is clear enough that analytical investigation may divide and subdivide objects and means forever; if the will waits for the completion of analytical investigation, it waits forever. The analytical intelligence can never arrive at a conclusion. Its analysis only serves to open up new vistas of further investigation. But at any point of its procedure it is possible for the intellect to stop its analytical investigation and unify its results by comparison, sum all up in a general conclusion, saying: 'In view of all that is thus far discovered, this conclusion will follow.' The trend is discoverable when only two facts are ascertained; a third fact may reveal a modification of the previously discovered trend, or, perhaps, only confirm it. The practical activity, whenever called upon to perform a deed demands a cessation of analytical investigation and the interposition of a general survey, in order to discover the trend that is revealed by the facts discovered; with this provisional view of the whole, it acts as rationally as is possible with its imperfect intelligence.

"Admitting that the increase of light by the further discovery of new facts by the aid of the analytical intellect is a never-ending process, we shall admit also that the will may act more and more rationally according to the quantity of analytical, specializing work of the intellect that has been performed. But there can be no direct step from the specializing activity to the will-activity of man. There must always supervene a summing up of those special results in a general survey before they become of any practical use. The jury must not permit themselves to decide until the case is closed. The case must be closed when only a part of the facts are in, because only a part of the facts can be ascertained. In any science the facts can never be all ascertained, because each fact is divisible by analysis into constituent facts, each process into constituent processes forever. This is evident from the infinite divisibility of time and space. Therefore we may affirm without contradiction that specializing science must admit the necessary intervention of the philosophic activity which takes general views or surveys before its results can become useful in human activity.

"But this is not all; if we examine what constitutes a science we shall be compelled to acknowledge that mere specializing analytical industry can never produce a science. Science is systematic knowledge. Facts are so united to other facts within a science that each fact sheds light upon all facts; and every fact upon each fact. From the special facts discovered by the analytical activity of the intellect, not only no practical use would ensue, but no theoretic use except through their synthesis by general surveys. A science results only after the particular facts obtained by analytic specialization are summed up. The case must be closed, and for the moment the assumption made that all the facts are in, if we are to discover the connecting link which binds the facts into a system. Without system no mutual illumination occurs among the facts; each is opaque and dark. So long as a fact in a science does not yet help explain other facts, and receive explanation from them, it is as yet no organic part of the science. It is itself an evidence of the imperfection of the science. The science appears only when the general survey has become possible. Facts are united into a system by principles—energies that include forces and laws.

"Studying more carefully the function of the synthetic activity of the mind as seen in the general survey, its difference from the analytic activity becomes clear. The analytic specializing divides and subdivides the fact or process before it, and goes from wholes to parts. The synthetic discovers unities of facts by means of relations of dependence. This phase or fact and that phase or fact are parts or results of one process, and so it concludes that they may be comprehended in one. Then, again, it steps back from the discovered unity and looks for relation to other unities and its dependence on a higher process, which unites it with coordinate processes. Each new generalization is only an element of a higher generalization.

"Science demands inventory, general survey, and experiment. Even in the matter of making an inventory, science avails itself of general survey under the form of definition. No definition can be made without such a survey, for it involves an attempt to grasp together a whole class under some common characteristic. Without the definition hovering in the mind, how shall one know which facts to include in its inventory and which to exclude? To take any and all facts without limiting the selection within a category, would be the purest futility. Inventory proceeds, therefore, by recognizing new individuals as belonging to a previously described class. Within this class new characteristics are to be recognized and new sub-classifications made. Experiment, too, starts from a principle already generalized or assumed as an hypothesis—thus grounded in a general survey, like the inventory-process, only far more explicit. A fact is to be found and identified by the inventory; but by the experiment it is to be constructed. The theory or hypothesis is derived from general survey, and it furnishes the rule for the construction of the fact. If it finds the reality to accord with it, there is verification of the theory or hypothesis —the principle is confirmed. If the reality does not result according to the theory, there is a refutation of it. The theory was simply an extension of the conclusion drawn from the general survey from what was before known.

"Analytical specialization is most successful in the form of experiment, and is guided by hypotheses. Witness the immense fertility of biological research in recent science when its industry is guided by the Darwinian hypothesis. That hypothesis is, of course, like all theories, the result of a general survey, the synthetical activity of the mind. This is what may be called the philosophical activity of the mind. It closes the case, stops the process of analysis and inventory of new facts, assumes that all facts are in, and asks in view of them: 'What unity, what principle is presupposed?' The answer to this question unites into a system what is known, and furnishes an hypothesis or provisional theory for further analysis and inventory of special facts. Thus the philosophical activity enters science as an indispensable factor, and alternates with the analytical activity that discovers new facts.

"But there is another phase of the synthetic activity of mind which transcends this hypothetic synthesis, this making of provisional theories. It is the *a priori* synthesis that underlies all mental activity. Intellect recognizes by an *a priori* act time and space as the logical condition of the existence of all nature—the entire totality of facts and events. What it knows of time and space is formulated in the science of mathematics as so much theory of nature that is known *a priori*. So much is not in need of experimental verification, because it is certain at the very outset that nothing can exist in the world unless it conforms to the mathematical laws of time and space. Besides the mathematical elements of theory there are other *a priori* elements equally sovereign in their sway over experience; such are the law of causality, the principles of excluded middle and contradiction, the ideas of quality and quantity, the idea of the conservation of energy. The mariner plows the sea, looking from wave to wave, passing from horizon to horizon, but he holds on his course only by the observations which he makes ever and anon of the eternal stars. So the specialist lifts his eyes from the multitudinous seas of facts through which he moves, to the fixed lights of mathematical truth, or to the planets of provisional theory, and is able to go forward to a desired haven.

"The synthetic activity of the intellect looks at the history of its object. It expects to find in the history of its growth and development a complete revelation of the nature of its object. That which offers itself to the senses as the object perceived is not the whole of the phenomenon, but only one of its manifestations. We may call the phenomenon the entire process of manifestation, including all the phases. In one moment some one phase is exhibited, in another moment some other phase.

"The acorn which we see lying on the ground is not the whole process of its manifestation—not the whole phenomenon. It is only a temporary phase in the growth of an oak. In the course of time this acorn would sprout from the soil and become, first, a sapling, then a great tree bearing acorns again. The acorn itself depends upon the whole process which forms the life of the oak, and is to be explained only by that process. So likewise any other phase or immediate manifestation in the life of the oak—its existence as a young sapling, or as a great tree, or as a crop of leaves, blossoms, or, indeed, a single leaf or blossom or bud. Science sees the acorn in the entire history of the life of the oak; it sees the oak in the entire history of all its species, in whatever climes they grow; it sees the history of the oak in the broader and more general history of the life of all trees, of all plants; and, finally, it considers plant life in its relations to the mineral below it, and to the animal above it.

"To see an object in its necessary relations to the rest of the world in time and space is to comprehend it scientifically.

"The object just before our senses now is only a partial revelation of some being that has a process or history, and we must investigate its history to gain a scientific knowledge of it. Its history will reveal what there is in it. No object is a complete revelation of itself at one and the same moment. The water which we lift to our lips to drink has two other forms; it may be solid, as ice, or an elastic fluid, as steam. It can be only one of these at a time. Science learns to know what water is by collecting all its phases—solid, liquid, and gaseous—and its properties as revealed in the history of its relations to all other objects in the world. So, likewise, the pebble which we pick up on the street is to be comprehended through its geological history—its upheaval as primitive granite, its crushing by the glaciers of the Drift Period, and its grinding and polishing under icebergs.

"We must trace whatever we see through its antecedent forms, and learn its cycle of birth, growth, and decay. This is the advice of modern science. We must learn to see each individual thing in the perspective of its history. All aspects of nature have been, or will be, brought under this method of treatment. Even the weather of to-day is found to be conditioned by antecedent weather, and the Signal Bureau now writes the history of each change in the weather here as a progress of an atmospheric wave from west to east. The realm which was thought a few years since to be hopelessly under the dominion of chance, or subject to incalculably various conditions and causes, is found to be capable of quite exact investigation. This is all due to the method of studying each particular thing as a part of a process. When the storm-signal stations extend all over the world we shall learn to trace the history of atmospheric waves and vortices back to the more general movements of the planet, diurnal and annual, and we shall find the connecting links which make a continuous history for the weather of to-day with the eternal process of exchange going on between the frigid and torrid air-zones, and trace the relation of this to the telluric process of earthquakes and the periodic variation of sun-spots and their dependence upon the orbital revolution of Jupiter and other planets. Doubtless we shall not see a science of astrology, predicting the fortune of the individual man by the foreordained aspects of the planets under which he was born ; but it is quite probable that, when the history of the meteorological process becomes better known, we shall be able to cast the horoscope of the weather for an entire season.

"This method of science, now consciously followed by our foremost men of science, is not an accidental discovery, but one which necessarily flows out of the course of human experience. For what is experience but the process of collecting the individual perceptions of the moment into one consistent whole? Does not experience correct the imperfection of first views and partial insights by subsequent and repeated observations? The present has to be adjusted to the past and to the future. Man can not choose; he must learn in the school of experience, and the process of experience blindly followed upon compulsion, when chosen by conscious insight as its method, becomes science.

"The difference, therefore, between the scientific activity of the mind and the ordinary common-sense activity lies in this difference of method and point of view. The ordinary habit of mind occupies itself with the objects of the senses as they are forced upon its attention by surrounding circumstances, and it does not seek and find their unity. The scientific habit of mind chooses its object, and persistently follows its thread of existence through all its changes and relations.

"Science has not been conscious of its method to such a degree that it could follow it without deviation until quite recent times.

"We might say that Darwin, of our own generation, is the first to bring about the use of the historical method as a conscious guide to investigation. And, indeed, although science has found the true method, it has not seen the ground of the method—its ultimate presupposition. It has much to say of evolution, and justifies its method by the doctrine of development of all that is from antecedent conditions. Homogeneity and simplicity characterize the first stages; complexity and difference of quality and function characterize the later stages. There is growth in a special direction. By survival we learn to know what is most in accord with the final purpose of nature. But we can not see this teleology or final purpose except by taking very large arcs of the total circle of development.

"The reason for this historical method, however, is to be found in the necessity already shown, to wit: all total or whole beings—that is to say, independent beings—are self-determined beings. Self activity is the basis of all causal action, all dependence, all transference of influence. Hence it follows that when we behold a manifestation, phase, or incomplete exhibition of something, we look further to see the whole of which it is a part. We look back to its antecedents, and forward to its consequents, and by these construct its history. We have not found it as a whole until we have found it as energy that initiates its own series of changes and guides them to a well-defined goal. The oak as a living organism thus initiates its series of reactions against its environment of earth and air, and converts the elements which it takes up from without into vegetable cells, and with these builds its organs and carries itself forward in a well-defined method of growth from acorn through sapling, tree, blossom, fruitage, to acorn again as the result. All inorganic processes, likewise, when traced into their history, exhibit the form of cycles, or revolutions, that return into the same form that they began with, thus repeating their beginning, or rather making a sort of spiral advance upon it. The energy that repeats again and again its cycle of activity is either life itself or an image or *simulacrum* of life. The annual round of the seasons, the daily succession of day and night, the cycle of growth of the planets themselves, or even of the solar systems—each of these is an image of life, as Plato long ago pointed out. All points back to an efficient energy somewhere that is its own cause in the sense that it originates its movements and changes and causes its own realization." *

"To the question whether modern natural science is pantheistic, therefore, we are constrained to answer, yes, in its middle stages of thought, because the second stage (see Chapter IV, Section IV) of thinking is in its very nature pantheistic. But modern natural science is likewise atheistic when we view it as reflected in minds that have not got beyond the first stage of thought. They do not reach a thought of a unity transcending all finite individuals, but rest in the idea of an indefinite multiplicity of atomic individuals. But science is theistic in all minds that see the trend of its method. The study of all things in the light of the history of their evolution discovers a progress toward 'perfect form' or conscious being. Stated in the law of survival of the fittest, the universe is so constituted as to place a premium on the development of intellect and will-power.

---

* Vol. 19, p. 414–423.

This would be impossible on the basis of pantheism. In proportion to the degree of self-activity reached by any individual, it achieves control over nature, and possesses ability to make social combinations with its fellows. By this capacity for social combination, man of all animals is able to move against nature in an aggregate as a race, and infinitely surpass his efforts as an individual or as a multitude of individuals detached from organization into a social whole. It follows that in proportion as science directs itself to the study of human institutions, it becomes impressed with the superiority of spiritual laws over the laws governing organic and inorganic bodies. By intelligence and will man can form institutions and make possible the division of labor and the collection and distribution of the aggregate productions of the entire race. Each individual is enabled by this to contribute to the good of the whole, and likewise to share in the aggregate of all the fruits of industry.

"While material bodies exclude each other and do not participate, spirits, endowed with intelligence and will, participate and share in such a manner as to raise the individual to the potency of the race. This amounts to making the individual a universal. When each receives the fruits of the physical labor of all, each fares as well as if he were sole master and all mankind were his slaves; but as master he would be charged with the supervision and direction of all—an infinite burden; this burden he avoids in free, social combination, wherein each for his own interest works at his best for the sake of the market of the world, and thus benefits all, though incited by selfish desire for gain. The material productions of the race are, however, of small moment compared with the fund of human experience, which is first lived and then collected and distributed to each man, so that each lives the life of all and profits by the experience of all. The scientific man inventories nature through the sense-perception of all his fellow-men, and assists his reflections by the aid of their ideas. The life of the whole is vicarious; the individual gets its results without having to render for them the equivalent of pain and labor incident to the original experience. Participation is the supreme principle of the life of spirit—of intelligent and volitional being. Experience has discovered, by the mistakes of myriads of lives, what human deeds are conducive to the life of participation which endows the individual with the fruits of the labor and the wisdom of this experience of the race. Hence the will acts in the channels marked out as co-operative with the whole. This is moral action.

"As science widens its domain and correlates one province with another, it comes to realize in consciousness the spiritual principle of participation which makes science itself possible as the accredited knowledge attained by the joint labors of the race. It comes to realize, moreover, that its method implies in another shape the same principle, because it makes each fact throw light on every other, while it explains each in the acccumulated light of all the rest. Using the symbol of society, and its principle of participation which is the essence of spiritual life, we may say that science spiritualizes nature by setting each of its individual facts in the light of all facts, and thus making it universal by the addition of the totality of its environment.

"Unless the universe were based on a spiritual basis, whence could come the significance of the universal as the illuminating and explaining principle? Just as the principle of the division of labor in the province of productive industry, so, too, the principle of specialization in the prosecution of scientific investigation is rendered possible by the spiritual principle of participation. It presupposes the collection and distribution of the results of all and to all. While material products diminish by distribution, spiritual products, in the shape of moral habits and intellectual insights, increase by being shared. The more a truth is reflected in the minds of others, the better it is defined and understood. The investigator may safely trust himself on his lonely journey into details, because he is sure that these details are fragments of the total process and organically related to the whole, so that he is bound to find the unity again when he has completed the discovery of the history of the fragment before him. The typical man of science, Cuvier, can see the whole animal in one of his bones; Agassiz can see the whole fish in one of his scales; Lyell can see the history of a pebble in its shape and composition; Winckelmann sees the whole statue of a Greek goddess in a fragment of the nose or the angle of the opening eyelids. 'All is in all,' as Jacotot used to say. But not the fulness of realization of the highest is in the lowest. The lowest presupposes the highest as its Creator, of which it is the manifestation, although not the *adequate revelation*. By so much as material bodies lack of self-activity, they lack of revealing the highest principle. According to the principle of evolution, all things are on the way toward the realization of the perfect form. The perfect form is self-activity, as personal intelligence and will. While in the lower orders of being the individual is furthest off from realizing the entire species within its singularity, yet in the higher orders that possess intelligence and will this becomes possible, and each may, by continued activity, enter into the heritage of the race in knowledge and ethical wisdom. The perfect form is that complete self-determination which constitutes Absolute Personality. Finite relativity is grounded on the self-relativity of such an Absolute. In the investigation of this field of relativity science is discovering the presupposition, and in this quest it is, therefore, on its way toward theism." *

"A precondition of divine revelation is the creation of beings who can think the idea of self-activity. The idea must be involved in knowing as logical condition, although it need not become explicit without special reflection. Philosophy is a special investigation directed to theological conditions of existence and experience, and so likewise theology and religion are special occupations of the soul. The soul must find within itself the idea of the divine before it can recognize the divine in any manifestation in the external world.

"In discovering and defining the *a priori* ideas in the mind philosophy renders essential service to religion, because it brings about certain conviction in regard to the objects which religion holds as divine, and conceives

---

* Vol. 19, pp. 425-428.

as transcending the world although it has not yet learned their logical necessity. It imagines, perhaps, that the mind can have experience without presupposing in its constitution the divine doctrines which it has received through tradition. But philosophy may arrive at certainty in regard to the first principle, and the origin and destiny of the world and man without making man religious. He must receive the doctrine into his heart, that is the special function of religion. To know the doctrine is necessary—that is philosophy and theology; to receive it into the heart and make it one's life is religion.

"Philosophy has suffered under the imputation of being too ambitious, aspiring to 'take all knowledge for its province' or to usurp the place of religion and destroy the Church. We have seen that the mind possesses *a priori* logical conditions which enter experience and render it possible; we have seen, likewise, that the mind, in its first stages of consciousness, does not separate these from experience and reflect on them as special objects. It does not perceive their regal aspect, nor recognize them as fundamental conditions of existence. Nevertheless, it sees what it sees by their means, and may, by special reflection, become conscious of their essential relation. But this higher form of reflection is preceded by many stages of spiritual education in which partial insight into these *a priori* ideas is attained. Special phases, particular aspects of them, are perceived. In the acquirement and use of language, in the formation of ethical habits, in the creation and appreciation of poetry and art, in the pursuit of science, and especially in the experience of the religious life, these *a priori* presuppositions appear again and again as essential objects under various guises—a sort of masquerade, in which these 'lords of life,' as Emerson (see Emerson's sublime essay on 'Experience,' in which he describes the soul's ascent through five stages of insight) calls them, pass before the soul.

"The knowledge of these *a priori* elements in experience, although a special one, is the most difficult of acquirement. It is not a field that can be exhausted any more than the field of mathematics, or the field of natural science, or that of social science. New acquisitions are new tools for greater and greater acquisition. We must expect, therefore, that the idea of self-activity, which we have found as the first principle, will yield us new insights into the being and destiny of nature and man, so long as we devote ourselves to its contemplation." *

Beauty: Its Elements.—"There is a theory that the primary function of art is amusement. What makes this degrading theory plausible is the fact that there is sensuous enjoyment in the contemplation of works of art, but this may be traced to something higher than sensuous sources. The sensuous elements in art are regularity and harmony. 1. Regularity is the recurrence of the same—mere repetition. A rude people scarcely reaches a higher stage of art. The desire for ornament is gratified by a string of beads or a fringe of some sort. It is a love of rhythm. The human form divine is not regular enough to suit the savage. It is not regular enough to suit his taste. He must accordingly make it beauti-

---

* Vol. 17, pp. 311, 312.

ful by regular ornaments, or by deforming it in some way—by tattooing it, for example. Why does regularity please? Why does recurrence or repetition gratify the taste of the child or savage? The answer to these questions is to be found in the generalization that the soul delights to behold itself, and that human nature is 'mimetic,' as Aristotle called it, signifying symbol-making. Man desires to know himself and to reveal himself in order that he may comprehend himself. Hence, he is an art-producing animal. Whatever suggests to him his deep, underlying spiritual nature gives him a strange pleasure. The nature of consciousness is partly revealed in types and symbols of the rudest art. Chinese music, like the music of very young children, delights in monotonous repetitions that almost drive frantic any one with a cultivated ear. But all rhythm is a symbol of the first and most obvious fact of conscious intelligence or reason.

"Consciousness is the knowing of the self by the self. There is subject and object and the activity of recognition. From subject to object there is distinction and difference, but with recognition, sameness, or identity is perceived, and the distinction or difference is retracted. What is this simple rhythm but regularity? It is, we answer, regularity, but it is much more than this. But the child or savage delights in monotonous repetition, not possessing the slightest insight into the cause of his delight. His delight is, however, explicable through this fact of the identity in form between the rhythm of his soul-activity and the sense-perception by which he perceives regularity.

"The sun-myth arises through the same feeling.

Wherever there is repetition, especially in the form of return to itself, there comes this conscious or unconscious satisfaction at beholding it. Hence especially circular movement, or movement in cycles, is the most wonderful of all the phenomena beheld by primitive man. Nature presents to his observation infinite differences. Out of the confused mass he traces some forms of recurrence; day and night, the phases of the moon, the seasons of the year, genus and species in animals and plants, the apparent revolutions of the fixed stars, and the orbits of planets. These phenomena furnish him symbols or types in which to express his ideas concerning the divine principle that he feels to be first cause. To the materialistic student of sociology all religions are merely transfigured sun-myths. But to the deeper student of psychology it becomes clear that the sun-myth itself rests on the perception of identity between regular cycles and the rhythm which characterizes the activity of self-consciousness. And self-consciousness is felt and seen to be a form of being not on a par with mere transient, individual existence, but the essential attribute of the Divine Being, Author of all.

"Here we see how deep-seated and significant is this blind instinct or feeling which is gratified by the seeing and hearing of mere regularity. The words which express the divine in all languages, root in this sense-perception and æsthetic pleasure attendant on it. Philology, discovering the sun-myth origin of religious expression, places the expression before the thing expressed, the symbol before the thing signified. It tells us that religions arise from a sort of disease in language which turns poetry into prose. But underneath the æsthetic feeling lies the perception of identity which makes possible the trope or metaphor.

"2. Symmetry. Regularity expresses only the superficial perception of the nature of self-consciousness and reason. There is, as we have seen, a subject opposed to itself as object. Antithesis is not simple repetition but opposition. The identity is therefore one of symmetry instead of regularity. Symmetry contains and expresses identity under difference. We can not put the left-hand glove on our right hand. The two hands correspond, but are not mere repetitions of the same.

"It is a mark of higher æsthetic culture to prefer symmetry to regularity. It indicates a deeper feeling of the nature of the divine. Nations that have reached this stage show their taste by emphasizing the symmetry in the human form by ornaments and symmetrical arrangement of clothing. They correct the lack of symmetry in the human form in the images of their gods. The face is on the front side of the head, but the god shall have a face on the back of his head, too, to complete the symmetry. The arms directed to the front of the body must also correspond to another pair of arms directed in the opposite direction. Perhaps perfect symmetry is still more exacting in its requirements, and demands faces with arms to match on the right and left sides of the body. To us the idols of the ancient Mexicans and Central Americans seem hideous. But it was the taste for symmetry that produced them.

3. "Harmony is the object of the highest culture of taste. Regularity and symmetry are so mechanical in their nature that they afford only remote symbols of

reason in its concreteness. They furnish the elements of art, but must be subordinated to a higher principle. Harmony is free from the mechanical suggestions of the lower principles, but it possesses in a greater degree the qualities which gave them their charm. Just as symmetry exhibits identity under a deeper difference than regularity, so harmony, again, presents us a still deeper unity underlying a wider difference. The unity of harmony is not a unity of sameness nor of correspondence merely, but a unity of adaptation to end or purpose. Mere symmetry suggests external constraint; but in art there must be freedom expressed. Regularity is still more suggestive of mechanical necessity. Harmony boldly discards regularity and symmetry, retaining them only in subordinate details, and makes all subservient to the expression of a conscious purpose. The divine is conceived as spiritual intelligence elevated above its material expression so far that the latter is only a means to an end. The Apollo Belvedere has no symmetry of arrangement in its limbs, and yet the disposition of each suggests a different disposition of another in order to accomplish some conscious act, upon which the mind of the god is bent. All are different, and yet all are united in harmony for the realization of one purpose.

"Here the human form with its lack of regularity and symmetry becomes beautiful. The nation has arrived at the perception of harmony, which is a higher symbolic expression of the divine than were the previous elements. The human body is adapted to the expression of conscious will, and this is freedom. The perfect subordination of the body to the will is gracefulness. It is this which constitutes the beauty of classic art; to have every muscle under perfect obedience to the will—unconscious obedience—so that the slightest inclination or desire of the soul, if made an act of the will, finds expression in the body. When the soul is not at ease in the body, but is conscious of it as something separate, gracefulness departs and awkwardness takes its place. The awkward person does not know what to do with his hands and arms; he can not think just how he should carry his body or fix the muscles of his face. He chews a stick or bites a cigar, in order to have something to do with the facial muscles, or twirls a cane or twists his watch-chain; folds his arms before or behind, or even thrusts his hands into his pockets, in order to have some use for them which will restore a feeling of ease in his body. The soul is at ease in the body only when it is using it as a means of expression or action.

"Harmony is this agreement of the inner and outer, of the will and the body, of the idea and its expression, so that the external leads us directly to the internal, of which it is the expression. Gracefulness then results, and gracefulness is the characteristic of classic or Greek art." *

Beauty: Mediums of Expression.—"Art is the presentation of reason to man through his senses. Such union of reason with sensuous forms constitutes the beautiful, and Plato called the beautiful 'the splendor of the true.' Like this, the good is the presence of reason in the will. A philosophy of art has to find

---

* "The Chautauquan," January, 1886, vol. vi, pp. 191, 192.

the rational element in the beautiful, and see how this rational element manifests itself in other provinces as the good and the true. It must also study the material side of expression, and learn the means used to render prose reality splendid with beauty. Highest philosophy always finds that reason is the supreme principle of the world. It is revealed in the world of nature and man as a Personal Creator. Philosophy undertakes to show reason as the ultimate presupposition in all existence and in all ideas. Art always assumes reason as this highest reality, and has nothing to do with proving it—it shows it. It takes some material—marble, pigments, tones, words, events—and shapes these so as to exhibit reason acting as the ground and mediation of what is finite. There are reckoned fine provinces of art—architecture, sculpture, painting, music, and poetry. In this ascending scale we find that elements of time and space become less and less important, while the manifestation of reason becomes more adequate.

"In architecture a rhythm is expressed as arising from the two forces—that of gravity pressing down, and that of the strength of the material which supports and constitutes the structure. A dim feeling in the soul recognizes its own strivings symbolized in the pillar or column or dome or spire or in the whole temple. The Egyptian felt the same feeling on looking at the pyramid which pierced the sky and rose into regions of light and clearness, as he did when he expressed his creed of transmigration of the soul. Even after the destroyer Death had done his worst, the soul should be born again, after three thousand years, in a new body. After gravitation has done its work, and the structures of men have crumbled to dust, there still remains the form of the tumulus, rising as a hill. The pyramid imitates the form of the tumulus.

"The poor Hindoo felt himself pressed down to the earth by the weight of ceremonies imposed by the doctrine of caste. He looked at one of his temples cut out of solid rock, and saw the symbol of himself standing there as one of the human columns supporting the roof and the mountain over it. The Greek, on the other hand, saw in his Parthenon, or in his Temple of Theseus, the perfect balance and proportion of upward and downward—of spirit and matter. His soul found complete bodily expression in the serene and cheerful statues of the gods, and those temples were the fitting abodes of such deities.

"On the other hand, in after times, when men had come to aspire after a nearer approach to the divine, by renunciation of the body and its pleasures, they felt the need for another expression, and found it in the cathedrals of Rouen and Tours, of Amiens and Cologne. The nothingness of earth, its dependence on what is above, is manifested by the architectural illusion that all lines aspire to what is above; the pillars seem to be fastened to the roof as the source of support, and to hold up the floor by tension, instead of supporting the roof by the thrust of the floor below. The pointed arch and the lofty pinnacles express this struggle of the finite to reach the spiritual point of repose above. In the domes of our American state-houses, we can see the tolerant principle of justice extending like the sky, over all alike, just as the Roman felt the potent principle of civil law, which articulates in words the forms of universal will, in which all men can act and not contradict themselves or each other. The pantheon extended over all nations' gods, just as the blue dome, its prototype, extended over all peoples.

"In sculpture, also, the Indian god, cross-legged on a lotus cup, the sitting statues of Memnon on the banks of the Nile; the Jupiter Olympus, of Phidias; the Moses of Michael Angelo, all utter their correspondences to the souls that made them and rejoiced in them.

"Painting, music, and poetry, likewise have their epochs of symbolic, classic, and romantic, the first belonging to those nations and times when, as in Egypt or in Asia, the mind of man could not perceive so clearly his likeness to the divine, nor lift himself so much above Nature. Classic art of Greece and Rome reaches the harmony of Nature and man, and portrays bodily freedom. Romantic or Christian art has found the spiritual truth which it is unable to express in sensuous forms, and therefore it offers the spectacle of a struggle against matter and what is earthy, and the possession of an invisible, immaterial support. The painting can represent breadth, depth, and height, on a surface of insignificant size, by perspective, and thus, with very small material means, create an appearance of vast extent of space, while architecture must have actual size in order to produce its desired effects. Color brings out the expression of feeling and emotion, and thus endows the painter with the means of representing human character in its minuter shades of development, and especially in its deepest internality. Music is thoroughly internal, and can go beyond painting in the respect in which painting first finds itself in advance of sculpture.

Poetry appeals through trope or metaphor and personification directly to the productive imagination, and can produce the spiritual effects of all arts, as well as other effects exclusively its own. Its material is not marble or color, but the word, a product of human reason, so that in poetry reason is not only form, but also its own material. Poetry, therefore, by means of the word, which it uses musically, appeals to the thinking reason, and produces direct effects upon the soul, peculiarly its own, while all other arts act mediately through the senses of sight or hearing upon the feelings and imagination, and then reach the intellect by this indirect road.

"Although each epoch of the world has its art, yet we can not afford to be very generous in conceding to all the principle of the realization of beauty. Only where freedom is conceived in the mind can there be produced beauty in art. Freedom in the body gives us the highest reach of plastic art—that of Greece and Rome; freedom from the body, the highest forms of romantic art. Art everywhere must presuppose a personal principle in the world as its lord. In poetry we have this recognized in the very elements of poetic expression, to wit, in trope and personification, which form the very brick and mortar of poetry. The whole world of Nature is viewed as instinct with spirit, and man looks upon each plant and animal, and even each thing and place, as having human personality. Thus what religion worships as the supreme, and thought recognizes as truth, art will insist upon seeing in the world of finite objects." *

---

* "Concord Lectures on Philosophy," Summer School of 1882, pp. 117, 118.

Interpretation of "Art." — "The infinite is not manifested *within* any particular sphere of finitude, but rather exhibits itself in the collision of a finite with another finite *without* it. For a finite must by its very nature be limited from without, and the infinite, therefore, not only includes any given finite sphere, but also its negation (or the other spheres which joined to it make up the whole).

"Art is the manifestation of the infinite in the finite, it is said. Therefore this must mean that art has for its province the treatment of the collisions that necessarily arise between one finite sphere and another. In proportion as the collision portrayed by art is comprehensive, and a type of all collisions in the universe, is it a high work of art. If, then, the collision is on a small scale, and between low spheres, it is not a high work of art.

"But whether the collision presented be of a high order or of a low order, it bears a general resemblance to every other collision—the infinite is always like itself in all its manifestation. The lower the collision, the more it becomes merely symbolical as a work of art, and the less it adequately represents the infinite.

"Thus the lofty mountain peaks of Bierstadt, which rise up into the regions of clearness and sunshine beyond the realms of change, do this only because of a force that contradicts gravitation, which continually abases them. The contrast of the high with the low, of the clear and untrammeled with the dark and impeded, symbolizes, in the most natural manner, to every one, the higher conflicts of spirit. It strikes a chord that vibrates, unconsciously perhaps, but, nevertheless, inevitably. On the other hand, when we take the other extreme of painting, and look at the 'Last Judgment' of Michael Angelo or the 'Transfiguration' of Raphael, we find comparatively no ambiguity; there the infinite is visibly portrayed, and the collision in which it is displayed is evidently of the highest order.

"Art, from its definition, must relate to time and space, and, in proportion as the grosser elements are subordinated and the spiritual adequately manifested, we find that we approach a form of art wherein the form and matter are both the products of spirit.

"Thus we have arts whose matter is taken from (*a*) space, (*b*) time, and (*c*) language (the product of spirit).

"Space is the grossest material. We have on its plane, 1, architecture; 2, sculpture; and, 3, painting. (In the latter, color and perspective give the artist power to represent distance and magnitude and internality without any one of them in fact. Upon a piece of ivory no larger than a man's hand a 'Heart of the Andes' might be painted.) In time we have 4, music; while in language, we have 5, poetry (in the three forms of epic, lyric, and dramatic), as the last and highest of the forms of art.

"An interpretation of a work of art should consist of a translation of it into the form of science. Hence, first, one must seize the general content of it—or the collision portrayed. Then, second, the form of art employed comes in, whether it be architecture, sculpture, painting, music, or poetry. Third, the relation which the content has to the form brings out the superior merits, or the limits and defects, of the work of art in question. Thus, at the end, we have universalized the piece of art—digested it, as it were. A true interpretation does not destroy a work of art, but rather furnishes a guide to its highest enjoyment. We have the double pleasure of immediate sensuous enjoyment produced by the artistic execution and the higher one of finding our rational nature mirrored therein, so that we recognize the eternal nature of spirit there manifested.

"The peculiar nature of music, as contrasted with other arts, will, if exhibited, best prepare us for what we are to expect from it. The less definitely the mode of art allows its content to be seized, the wider may be its application. Landscape-painting may have a very wide scope for its interpretation, while a drama of Goethe or Shakespeare definitely seizes the particulars of its collision, and leaves no doubt as to its sphere. So in the art of music, and especially instrumental music. Music does not portray an object directly, like the plastic arts, but it calls up the internal feeling which is caused by the object itself. It gives us, therefore, a reflection of our impressions excited in the immediate contemplation of the object. Thus we have a reflection of a reflection, as it were.

"Since its material is time rather than space, we have this contrast with the plastic arts; architecture, and more especially sculpture and painting, are obliged to select a special moment of time for the representation of the collision. As Goethe shows in the 'Laokoon,' it will not do to select a moment at random, but that point of time must be chosen in which the collision has reached its height, and in which there is a tension of all the elements that enter the contest on both sides. A moment earlier, or a moment later, some of these elements would be eliminated from the problem, and the comprehensiveness of the work destroyed. When this proper moment is seized in sculpture, as in the 'Laokoon,' we can see what has been before the present moment, and easily tell what will come later. In painting, through the fact that coloring enables more subtle effects to be wrought out and deeper internal movements to be brought to the surface, we are not so closely confined to the 'supreme moment' as in sculpture. But it is in music that we first get entirely free from that which confines the plastic arts. Since its form is time, it can convey the whole movement of the collision from its inception to its conclusion. Hence music is superior to the arts of space in that it can portray the internal creative process, rather than the dead results. It gives us the content, in its whole process of development, in a *fluid* form, while the sculptor must fix it in a *rigid* form at a certain stage. Goethe and others have compared music to architecture—the latter is 'frozen music,' but they have not compared it to sculpture nor painting, for the reason that in these two arts there is a possibility of seizing the form of the individual more definitely, while in architecture and music the point of repose does not appear as the human form, but only as the more general one of self-relation or harmony. Thus quantitative ratios—mathematical laws—pervade and govern these two forms of art.

"Music, more definitely considered, arises from vibrations, producing waves in the atmosphere. The cohesive attraction of some body is attacked, and successful resistance is made; if not, there is no vibration. Thus the feeling of victory over a foreign foe is conveyed in the most elementary tones, and this is the distinction of tone from noise, in which there is the irregularity of disruption, and not the regularity of self-equality.

"Again, in the obedience of the whole musical structure to its fundamental scale-note, we have something like the obedience of architecture to gravity. In order to make an exhibition of gravity, a column is necessary; for the solid wall does not isolate sufficiently the function of support. With the column we can have exhibited the effects of gravity drawing down to the earth, and of the support holding up the shelter. The column in classic art exhibits the equipoise of the two tendencies. In Romantic or Gothic architecture it exhibits a preponderance of the aspiring tendency—the soaring aloft like the plant to reach the light—a contempt for mere gravity—slender columns seeming to be let down from the roof, and to draw up something rather than to support anything. On the other hand, in symbolic architecture (as found in Egypt), we have the overwhelming power of gravity exhibited so as to crush out all humanity—the pyramid, in whose shape gravity has done its work. In music we have continually the conflict of these two tendencies, the upward and downward. The music that moves upward and shows its ground or point of repose in the octave above the scale-note of the basis corresponds to the Gothic architecture. This aspiring movement occurs again and again in chorals; it, like all Romantic art, expresses the Christian solution of the problem of life." *

---

* Vol. 1, pp. 122-124.

Historical Epochs of Art.—" At the commencement of the Western or European epoch of the world history, we have two nationalities sharply contrasted—the one, the Greek civilization, seizes upon and represents in the form of sensuous individuality its idea of the rational; the other, the Roman civilization, seizes the realized *will* as the highest goal, and accordingly exalts the interest of the state above all merely *individual interest.* The Greek Homer paints for us the beautiful individual— Achilles or Helen or Paris or Hector; so, throughout Grecian history we are always called upon to admire the individual—the graceful symmetry of character, whether it be of Theseus or Ulysses, of Pericles or Socrates, of Aristotle or Alexander. The general interest does not overshadow the individual; the 'Iliad' tells us how Achilles, by his wrath against the king Agamemnon, can thwart the purposes of the whole assembled army of the Greeks.

"With Rome, the interest is not this interest in individuals centered wholly in themselves. We admire Numa and the elder Brutus, Curtius and Cincinnatus, Fabius Maximus and Regulus, Scipio and Cæsar, not for individual perfection so much as for their devotion to the state—for their self-sacrifice, and hence for their *personality;* for man becomes a person when he subordinates his mere individual will to the general will of the state.

"Greece is comparatively external in her earlier civilization, Rome comparatively internal. The former prefers what pertains to bodily form and to urbane manners—in short, to the arbitrary side of humanity; while the latter prefers what belongs to the inner character, to the deeper, more mediated, and hence more substantial culture.

"Greece is the art nation and Rome the prosy nation of legal forms; art personifies all nature and makes every stream a river god, every fountain the dwelling of a nymph, every grove and mountain the haunt of dryads and oreads. Out of that land of childhood, peopled by fancy and imagination, we step into Italy as the land of manhood, wherein the spirit no longer dreams of air-castles, but plies the daily care, looks with sober eye upon the world and sees *things—prose facts* —and makes no more personifications.

"In the course of events, 'when the fullness of time had come,' Christianity came into the world and found in Rome the ripest field for its insition and growth. It found its way also into Greece. The Christian spirit was more akin to the Roman life than to the Greek life; its penances and mortifications of the flesh were all foolishness to the Greek, but the Roman was used to personal sacrifice for the state. Hence Christianity had many a hard conflict with the Eastern life that it did not encounter in the West. It had all the time a tendency to degenerate into image worship. How natural to pass from the worship of Venus or Diana or Juno to that of the Madonna! Toward the close of the fourth century this became very prevalent and increased until Leo III, the great iconoclast, effectually checked it. The strange inversion that then appeared is this: Greece, transformed by Christianity, goes to the opposite extreme and destroys all images, while Italy, whose prosy formality is broken up by the miraculous element in the Christian doctrine, goes over to the sensuous so far as to refuse to give up image worship, and to secede from the East. Their principle carries the day, and the Nicene Council makes it a Christian doctrine. Soon after, about A. D. 1000, the veneration for saints and sacred relics leads to the practice of canonization, somewhat after the style of deifying departed heroes in a remoter antiquity. This was the basis laid for a future period of art in the Christian Church. But the crusades had to come first, and fill all minds with lofty aspirations that must be realized in some way. First by knightly deeds, personal prowess; and next the faint aurora of modern art arose above the horizon with Cimabue, Arnolf di Lapo, and Giotto. Then, with Dante the new age began, Christianity had found poetic expression, and the Medici family a century after stimulated art to its career of greatest splendor. Perugino, founder of the Roman school of painting, is the precursor of Raphael, who finished his 'Transfiguration' two hundred years after the death of Dante; Leonardo da Vinci, that universal genius, is a fitting precursor to Michael Angelo, the man in whom that age reaches its climax, whether we consider him as architect of St. Peter's church, as sculptor of the statues in the church of San Lorenzo, as engineer of the fortifications about Florence, as writer of sonnets profound and subtle in thought, or as painter of the frescoes on the ceiling of the Sistine Chapel, and finally of the 'Last Judgment,' called the 'grandest picture that ever was painted' and 'the greatest effort of human skill as a creation of art.' In order to appreciate this great master-piece, we have to bear clearly in mind the antecedent phases of art and the limits of their achievements. We have symbolic art for the Orient, classic art for Greece, romantic art for modern times— this, if we take as our basis the generalizations of the best writers on the theme. In the symbolic art—the Egyptian architecture, for example, with its rows of sphinxes and huge pillars—we have a gigantic struggle —a vast upheaval—spirit struggling and upheaving matter to get free and say something. This something it can never quite say. It is a riddle to it, and hence the Sphinx looks inquiringly to the blue vault overhead —an eternal question. Or the Memnon statue sounds at the rising sun, but can articulate no oracle that shall break this spell. Truth to the Oriental peoples has not yet got separate from the mere symbol. In classic art, on the contrary, the statue of Apollo stands opposed to the Sphinx; it is the achievement of what in Egyptian art is only struggled after. Spirit stands revealed in the posture and mold of every limb. The beautiful divinities of Olympus offer us the realization of this complete union of form and matter, of spirit and sense. The completest 'repose' is the result — no struggle disfigures the placid seriousness, the flesh is completely plastic to the indwelling soul. Why is not this the highest that art can do? *It is*, if the highest goal of spirit is simply to live a sensuous existence. In all modern time we have those who defend classic art as the sole form of art worthy of imitation. But the Christian era brought in an idea that contradicts at once the basis of classic art. The soul shall be purified only through renunciation—the hair-cloth shirt, the knotted scourge, the hermit's cave, the monk's cell, plenty of fasting and watching, these shall fit the soul for divine life. But not so can one gain a beautiful physique. Haggard and lean and gaunt is Saint Anthony or Simeon Stylites—not at all like the Vatican Apollo or the boy Antinous.

"So modern art must leave the repose of Greek sensuousness and return again to the struggling of the soul. But this time it is not a vain struggle as in symbolic art, wherein no free expression is reached; but romantic art represents to us the overpowering predominance of the soul over the body. Everywhere the latter is degraded, the former exalted. There seems to be an aspiration for the beyond, *the supersensuous*, that which 'passeth show,' and hence there is a contradiction in it. You look to see—what it tells you distinctly that you can not see—the truly beautiful with the senses. But at the same time the soul is sent back to itself, and its inner spiritual sense is awakened to see the eternal verities themselves. Thus in the highest painting of this form of art—'The Transfiguration'—we are referred upward and beyond from the demoniac boy to the disciples—by them to Christ, who again, with upturned gaze, refers us to the invisible source of light beyond our ken. Aspiration—*infinite aspiration*—is the content of this art. But what shall we say? Does art stop here? Is there not a higher art than romantic art—an art in which we have presented to us the total—the aspiration and its fulfillment? Such a stage of art does indeed exist, and deserves to be called 'universal art.' It is cosmical, because it is so comprehensive as to exhaust all phases of the subject it treats. Inasmuch as it resembles the classic art in its reaching a point of repose, it may be called new classic art. Such art is exhibited in a few great masterpieces; they are, chiefly, Dante's 'Divina Commedia,' presenting the drama of human life as viewed from the Christian ideal; Goethe's 'Faust,' presenting the series of phases passed through by the individual who ascends from the abyss of skepticism to the complete appreciation of the spirit of modern civilization and what it presupposes; Beethoven's great symphonies and a few of his sonatas, like the great F minor, for example; Shakespeare's 'Tempest' and perhaps the 'Midsummer-Night's Dream'; Michael Angelo's plan of St. Peter's church and his 'Last Judgment.' The old classic art realizes its repose in the individual—this is true even in the Laocoön. But the romantic presents the individual, or series of individuals, aspiring for a beyond, hence as out of repose; but the new classic adds the goal of aspiration, and hence restores repose again. So the new classic—the Michael Angelo form of art—differs from that of Agesander and Praxiteles as the full grown oak does from the acorn. The acorn is complete as an acorn; but the full grown tree is cosmical in its completeness; romantic art is the sapling oak—neither the repose of the acorn nor of the tree." *

Religious Thought in Art.—" But could there be any religion in such art (Greek) as this? Can religion be expressed by gracefulness? Not *our* religion, not Christianity, nor, as we shall see, any of the other heathen religions; they did not recognize the beautiful as the chief attribute of the divine, if, indeed, as an attribute at all. But the Greek religion made beauty the essential feature of the idea of the divine, and

---

* Vol. 3, pp. 73-77.

hence Greek art is centered on the beautiful and represents the supreme attainment of the world in pure beauty because it is pure beauty and does not reach beyond.

"Christianity reaches beyond beauty to holiness. Other heathen religions fall short of the Greek ideal and lack an essential element which the Greek religion possessed.

"Perhaps we shall learn to appreciate our own religion better if we look a moment at what the Greeks worshiped as the divine. They believed that the divine is at the same time human; and human not in the sense that the essence of man, his purified intellect and will, is divine, but human in the corporeal sense as well. The gods of Olympus possess appetites and passions like men; they have bodies, and live in a special place. They form a society or large patriarchal family. The manifestation of the divine is celestial beauty. Moreover, the human being may, by becoming beautiful, become divine.

"Hence the Greek religion centers about gymnastic games. These are the Olympian, the Isthmian, the Nemean, and the Pythian games. Exercises that will give the soul sovereignty over the body and develop it into beauty are religious in this sense. Every village has its games for physical development; these are attended by the people who become in time judges of perfection in human form, just as a community that attends frequent horse-races, produces men who know critically the good points of a horse. It is known who is the best man at wrestling, boxing, throwing the discus, the spear, or the javelin; at running, at leaping, or at the chariot or horseback races. Then at less frequent intervals there is the contest at games between neighboring villages. The successful hero carries off the crown of wild-olive branches. Nearly every year there is a great national assembly of Greeks, and a contest open to all. The Olympian festival at Olympia and the Isthmian festival near Corinth are held the same summer; then at Argolis, in the winter of the second year afterward, is the Nemean festival; then the Pythian festival near Delphi and a second Isthmian festival occur in the spring of the third year; and again there is a second Nemean festival in the summer of the fourth year of the Olympiad. An entire people composed of independent states, united by ties of religion, assembled to celebrate this faith in the beautiful and to honor their successful youth. The results carried the national taste for the beautiful, as seen in the human body, to the highest degree.

"The next step after the development of the personal work of art, in the shape of beautiful youth, by means of the national games and the cultivation of the taste of the entire people through the spectacle of these games, is the art of sculpture by which these forms of beauty, realized in the athletes and existing in the minds of the people as ideals of correct taste, shall be fixed in stone and set up in the temples for worship. Thus Greek art was born. The statues at first were of gods and demi-gods exclusively. Those which have come down to us cause our unbounded astonishment at their perfection of form. It is not their resemblance to living bodies—not their anatomical exactness that interests us—not their so-called 'truth to Nature,' but their gracefulness and serenity, their 'classic repose.' Whether the statues represent gods and heroes in action, or in sitting and reclining postures, there is this 'repose' which means indwelling vital activity, and not mere rest as opposed to movement. In the greatest activity there is considerate purpose and perfect self-control manifested. The repose is of the soul, and not a physical repose. Even sitting and reclining figures—for example, the Theseus from the Parthenon, or the torso of the Belvedere—are filled with activity so that the repose is one of voluntary self-restraint, and not the repose of the absence of vital energy. They are gracefulness itself.

"What a surprising thought is this of a religion founded on beauty! How could it have arisen in the history of the world, and what became of it? Let us consider a few of the elements wherein the Greek religion was superior to other heathen religions.

"The Hindoo worshiped an abstract unity, devoid of all form, which he called Brahma. His idea of the divine is defined as the negation, not only of everything in nature, but also of everything human. Nothing that has form or shape or properties or qualities—nothing, in short, that can be distinguished from anything else, can be divine, according to the thought of the Hindoo. This is pantheism. It worships a negative might which destroys everything. If it admits that the world of finite things arises from Brahma, as creator, it hastens to explain that this creation is only a dream, and that all creatures will vanish when the dream fades. There can be no hope for any individuality according to this belief. Any art that grows up under such a religion will manifest only the nothingness of individuality and the impossibility of its salvation. Instead of beauty as the attribute of divinity, the Hindoo studied to mortify the flesh, to shrivel up the body, to paralyze rather than to develop his muscles. Instead of gymnastic festivals, he resorted to the severest penances, holding his arm over his head until it wasted away. If he could produce numbness in his body so that all feeling disappeared, he attained holiness. His divine was not divine human, but inhuman rather.

"The Egyptian laid all stress on death. In his art he celebrated death as the vestibule to the next world, and the life with Osiris. Art does not get beyond the symbolic phase with him. As in the hieroglyphic, the picture of a thing is employed at first to represent the thing, and by and by it becomes a conventional sign for a word, so the works of art at first represent men and gods, and afterward become conventional symbols to signify the ideas of the Egyptian religion. The great question to be determined is this, what destiny does it promise the individual, and what kind of life does it command him to lead? The Egyptian symbolizes his divine by the processes of Nature that represent birth, growth, death, and resurrection; and hence conceives life as belonging to it. The course of the sun, its rising and setting, its noonday splendor, and its nightly eclipse; the succession of the seasons; the germination, growth, and death of plants; the flooding and subsidence of the Nile—these and other phenomena are taken as symbols expressing the Egyptian conception of the divine living being. Finally, it rises out of the immediate artistic description by symbols, and tells us the myth of Osiris killed by his brother Typhon, and of his descent to the silent realm of the under-world, and of his there reigning king, and of his resurrection.

"The Hindoo art, on the contrary, dealt with symbols that were not analogous to human life. They reverenced mountains and rivers, the storm-winds, and great natural forces that were destructive to the individuality of man; but also reverenced life in animals. They founded asylums for aged cows, but not for decrepit humanity.

"Persian art adores light as the divine; it also adores the bodies that give light—the sun, moon, and stars; also fire; also whatever is purifying, especially water. The Persian religion conceives two deities, a god of light and goodness and a god of darkness and evil. The struggle between these two gods fills the universe, and makes all existence a contest. The art of the Persian portrays this struggle and does not let pure human individuality step forth for itself. In Assyria and Chaldea we have the worship of the sun, rather than of pure light. Hence, there were artificial hills or towers, constructed with ascending, inclined planes on the outside, rising to the flat top, crowned with a temple dedicated to Belus, or the sun-god. Images, partly human, partly animal, represented the divine. The lion, the eagle—the quadruped and bird—the human face, these were united to make the symbol of a divine being who could not be manifested in a purely human form.

"The Egyptian religion, though it surpassed the Persian in that it conceived the divine as much nearer the human life, still resorted to animal forms to obtain the peculiarly divine attributes. There were the sacred bulls Apis and Mnevis, the goat of Mendes, sacred hawks and ibises, and such divinities as Isis-Hathor, with a cow's head; Tonaris, with a crocodile's head; Thoth, with the head of an ibis; Horus, with the head of a hawk; but Ammon, Phthah, and Osiris, with human heads and bodies. Thus we see that the Egyptian wavered between the purely human and the animal form as the image of the divine. So long as it is possible for a religion to permit the representation of the divine by an animal form, that religion has not yet conceived God as pure self-consciousness or reason. As a consequence of this defect, it can not account for the origin and destiny of the world in such a way as to explain the problem of the human soul. It is an insoluble enigma, whose type is a Sphinx. The Sphinx is the rude rock out of which it rises, symbolizing inorganic nature; then the lion's body, typifying by the king of beasts the highest of organic beings below man; then the human face looking up inquiringly to the heavens. Its question seems to be, 'Thus far, what next?' Does the human break the continuity of the circle of nature, within which there goes on a perpetual revolution of birth, growth, and decay; or does the human perish with the animal and plant, and lose his individuality? How can his individuality be preserved without the body? The Egyptian's highest thought was this enigma. He combined the affirmative and negative elements of this problem, conceiving that man survives death, but will have a resurrection, and need his particular body again which, therefore, must be preserved by embalming it. The body of Osiris had to be embalmed by Isis. The sacred animals (bulls and others) were embalmed after death.

"They had not learned that the image of God is man and, more definitely, man's reason or self-consciousness. It was, therefore, a great step beyond the heathen religions of Asia and Africa for the Greek religion to conceive the divine as dwelling in human form, however defective it was in respect to its doctrine of the particular attributes of men that are the true image of God.

"Plato and Aristotle came to the thought that God is perfect, self-conscious reason, and created the world to reveal and manifest himself, and graciously (or as they express it 'without envy,') permits men to participate in the divine reason and thus survive mortality. Christianity has ever admitted so much of the Greek philosophy into its theology as true doctrine.

"Studied from this point of view it would seem that an interesting comparison may be made between some of the prominent works of Greek art and some of the Christian paintings. . . . For our purposes we must study the best known, or the most accessible, works of art. Let us first turn our attention to the Apollo Belvedere, perhaps the most generally known and most popular of all antique statues. . . .

"The statue of Apollo is the highest ideal of art among the works of antiquity which have escaped destruction. The artist has created this work entirely from an ideal, and has employed only so much material as was necessary to carry out and make visible his design. This Apollo surpasses all other statues of the same as much as the Apollo of Homer excels those of succeeding poets. His statue towers above that of mortals, and his attitude bears witness to the grandeur with which he is filled.

"'An eternal spring, as in the happy Elysium, clothes the noble manliness of mature years with pleasing youth, and plays with soft tenderness over the haughty structure of his limbs. Its author must have risen in spirit to the realm of immortal beauty, and thus have become the creator of a divine being possessed of beauty exalted above nature! For here there is nothing mortal, nor aught that appertains to human feebleness. No veins or nerves excite and rouse this body, but a divine spirit, which is diffused like a gentle stream, manifests itself, as it were, in every outline of the figure. Apollo has pursued the Python against which he first bent his bow, and has overtaken it with his powerful stride and slain it. From the height of his all sufficiency, his inspired glance pierces beyond his victory as if into the infinite; contempt sits on his lips, and the indignation which he suppresses expands his nostrils and rises to his proud forehead. But the peace which hovers around the brow in a holy calm remains undisturbed, and his eye is full of sweetness as if among the Muses who seek to embrace him. In all the statues of the father of the gods which remain to us, and which art reverses, he does not approach so near to the greatness with which the mind of the divine poet conceived him, as here in the face of his son; and the single beauties of the other gods are here united as in Pandora. A brow of Jupiter, when about to give birth to the goddess of wisdom, and eyebrows which by their movement explain his will; eyes of the queen of the gods, arched with greatness; and a mouth such as he formed who infused voluptuousness into the beloved Branchus. His soft hair plays round his godlike head like the flowing tendrils of the noble vine, moved as it were by a soft breeze. It seems anointed with the oil of the gods, and is bound by the Graces on the crown of his head with charming comeliness.' . . .

"Apollo was originally the sun-god; but in course of time the Greek conception of him became higher, and he represents finally the noblest and best of the Olympian gods. He is the god of purity, never yielding to lust like Zeus. He is the god of healing, and also the leader of the Muses, and the god of poetry and music. He is the god of divination and spiritual light. His oracle at Delphi governed for a thousand years the Greek tribes, and for most of that period kept them united. Most important and elevated of his attributes is that of the purifier, who cleansed from sin and the avenging Furies the guilty ones who sought his shrine. . . .

"Turning to a work of Christian art, we at once feel that we have entered a world profoundly different from that of classic art.

"Romantic or Christian art in a certain sense contradicts art itself, inasmuch as it points beyond the visible to an invisible which can not be adequately manifested in physical form.

"In the cathedral of St. Bavo (formerly St. John's Cathedral) in Ghent, is, or was, a very celebrated altarpiece painted by the brothers Hubert and Jan Van Eyck, both of Ghent. This picture was painted in oil colors and is regarded as the greatest work of painting in northern Europe. . . .

"The subject is well chosen from the book of Revelation, affording opportunity for the employment of the rich and vivid oil colors which had then become possible by Van Eyck's invention of a transparent varnish with which to dry the oils.

"The blotting out of sins and the reconciliation of man with God, through the sacrifice of the sinless Lamb of God, furnishes the theme—the highest theme of religion, although perhaps it is not well adapted for art in the form conceived by Van Eyck. We must not bring with us, however, ideas of the limits of sculpture and painting, but enter at once sympathetically into the work of art before us. We shall find this central religious thought reflected from all parts of this complex altar-piece. 'The celebration of this idea,' says one, 'runs through the whole like the theme of a symphony.' . . .

"In each part of this great picture we see reflected some phase of the great central thought of the sacrifice of the Lamb. The martyrs, the prophets, apostles, and Church fathers; the righteous judges, the crusaders, the pilgrims, the hermits, the instruments of the passion, the holy city, the prophets and sibyls, the fall of Adam and Eve, the sacrifice and murder of Abel, the Annunciation, Jehovah swearing to the new covenant, John the Baptist preaching Him who shall come, the angel choirs and orchestra celebrating the events, all carry us back to the one great theme—the redemption of man by the act of Divine condescension.

"In this work of art we do not see the gracefulness and beauty of form found in classic art, so much as the expression of deep religious feeling. The individuals have reached a state of inward reconciliation with the divine.

"In the Van Eyck altar-piece we recognize a work of art auxiliary to the Christian religion. Every part of it reflects in some significant way the great central theme of our faith—the redemption of man through an act of divine condescension. And yet we can not fail to find something to criticise in the painted representation. While the poetic imagination may conceive this relation of God to man under the figure of a sacrifice, and described in the book of Revelation the sinless Lamb of God slain for our sins, we are not shocked at the image of God in the form of an animal, because we go at once behind the image to its symbolic meaning and conceive, not the animal form, but the divine human form of Jesus. In poetry our fancy is left free, and we glide at once from the mental picture of the animal form to the divine significance that lies behind it. But when the animal form is fixed for us by plastic art in the shape of a statue or by graphic art in a picture, it occasions a shock to our æsthetic feelings, in proportion to our cultivated taste. A real sheep as an animal directly before our sight and touch is not beautiful nor sublime nor divine in any respect except that of harmlessness. But as a figure of speech which the mind entertains for a single moment before it passes on to contemplate the divine-human Son of God, it is a beautiful and even sublime suggestion.

"We see in the great altar-piece stately and solemn companies of saints and worshipers. Their faces are shining with the deep peace that comes from the reconciliation of the heart with God, a 'peace that passeth understanding.' It is this which re-enforces our religious feeling. On the other hand the realistic lamb on the altar does not assist, but requires assistance from, religious conviction. The spectator must refer it to the familiar and cherished figure of speech, and bring its tender associations to his aid while he gazes on the picture of a sheep upon the altar shedding his blood into the chalice.

" Altogether different from this is the great work of Michael Angelo in the Sistine Chapel. We feel ourselves elevated out of our narrow present environment and borne aloft into a higher world in which we behold our religious conceptions realized in worthy forms. The facts of religious history become transformed by Michael Angelo's genius into eternal types of human religious experience. The histories of the Old Testament, if taken by themselves in an isolated form, may have little to aid our religious sense; but when seized as eternal types of the history of the human individual and of human nature in general, they furnish fitting language in which to express our own religious experience or the religious experience of all men in all future ages of the world. Just as the mythology of Greece has given us the conventional language of art and poetry and is a sort of literary Bible, so the history of the Jewish nation has become for us the conventional language of religion —the Holy Bible of all future civilization. Works of art, therefore, that give emphasis to this conventional language by supplying worthy pictorial illustrations certainly aid the religious sense." *

---

* "The Chautauquan," vol. vi, pp. 192, 193, 255-258, 314, January, February, March, 1886.

Influence of Religion upon Art. — "That there should be a unity in man's higher endeavors is to be expected. His relation to the Absolute if threefold is still *one* relation. Thus art subserves the interests of religion, and in the form of speculative theology, religion and philosophy become one. The onward progress of each produces more and more a complete union of all in one. Art becomes religious, and religion uses æsthetic form, and philosophy comes to be at home in either of the two provinces as well as its own. But in the history of this progress there is likewise developed difference in manifold forms. Out of the germinating acorn pushes downward the root and upward the stalk in antithetic tension. Thus religion in its first distinction from art develops antitheses which are sharply in contrast with what is æsthetical. In a previous analysis we have traced out the element which religion adds to the art element (see next topic, 'Goodness'). The phase of creative power that destroys or subordinates the immediate sensuous existence is clearly perceived in religion, and religion accordingly feels *devotion* instead of *æsthetic* enjoyment. Devotion involves a subjective side, a perception of what a work of art does not possess. Every act of worship presupposes a conscious Being with which the worshiper seeks to commune. All subjectivity withdraws itself at once out of and beyond the sensuous.

"But from the lowest spheres up, there is an increase of adequateness on the part of art to present the content of religion. But art that should completely do this would vanish entirely beyond the appreciation of the senses, or would form a species of art like Browning's poetry, half æsthetic and half abstract, and addressed to the understanding. The paintings of Kaulbach belong to this order. There is, however, genuine art that accomplishes true miracles in this direction.

"Beethoven's 'Symphonies,' Michael Angelo's 'Last Judgment,' Dante's 'Divina Commedia,' Goethe's 'Faust,' these are some of the works that present us both the æsthetic and abstract or negative phases, and yet present us beautiful wholes. It is interesting to examine how this is accomplished, for in this we shall find the most profitable answer to our inquiry as to the reciprocal influence of religion upon art.

"It is foreign to the definition of art to attempt to portray the negative. The first attempts to do this are accordingly deeply impressed with this contradiction. It is romantic art that makes such attempts. After classic art had died and been buried for hundreds of years by the new religion—the Christian religion—there began again an aspiration to give sensuous realization to the divine—in this instance, the Christian form of the divine. There had been a hard fight indeed to root out the Greek sensuousness sufficiently to make the religion of Jesus of Nazareth flourish, and a race of iconoclasts had even to come first. But the West—Italy—where the internality of the conception of justice had developed with Roman power, there might with impunity develop an æsthetic tendency, one not hostile to the Christian idea. Painting could portray such meekness and holy resignation in the face, and such fortitude under bodily suffering that it should be employed first to represent our Lord in the events of his world-historical career, and second to do the same service for the saints and martyrs. Stiffness and awkwardness in the pose of the limbs of the body; emaciated forms, unkempt, unshorn, careless of raiment—as if purposely in contrast to the studied grace of classic forms—these saints invariably exhibited in their faces a perfect, implicit trust in the invisible. The visible which art portrayed said plainly, the visible is naught, the invisible is all. Utter neglect or contempt for worldly gratifications, and perfect repose in their faith, is seen in the early Italian paintings. Religious in a certain sense these paintings are, but in such a sense as to exclude æsthetic. When after a period Raphael came, we find very much that is æsthetic simply by itself, and yet every picture, even of his, admits the negative or ugly element as a *memento mori* at a feast. The 'Transfiguration' presents to us the grand 'contradiction' of this species of art. The family of the insane boy—whose figure is strangely non-æsthetic—look to the nine disciples supplicatingly, while the latter point up to Christ—the latter, in his highest moment, with transfigured face gazes with faith and trust longingly into the glories that hide the invisible source of all strength and power. Thus the family show or manifest dependence on the disciples, the disciples manifest dependence on Christ, and the latter on an invisible beyond. The whole picture is an index-finger pointing to an object that is not revealed. This and its class of paintings plainly say, 'I manifest that which can not be presented to the senses at all.' Here the negative side preponderates, and the chasm between the 'Transfiguration' and the 'Apollo Belvedere' or 'Venus of Milo' is enormous. In the latter is the perfect repose of attainment of utter freedom in the body; they triumph in their incarnation. In the former there is the ecstacy of repose in the freedom *from* the body, and incarnation is incarceration only to them. With Michael Angelo, indeed, we stop our flight to the beyond, and begin to realize that the sharp contradiction in romantic art may be surmounted. That daring genius everywhere unites the classic completeness and repose to the romantic striving and aspiration. In the 'Last Judgment' there is the totality of the finite mortal world placed *under the form of eternity*, and the infinite responsibility which attaches to the individual, portrayed in the looks with which each one meets the fruits of his actions. Each one sees his life through the perspective of his own deeds. Thus there is totality which gives the æsthetic again and does not by this omit the negative. The separate statue of Moses all will remember as the grandest and noblest form in stone. The 'Apollo Belvedere' is a beautiful child, but Michael Angelo's 'Moses' is a full-grown man, transfigured with the growth of noblest human experience.

"For the purposes of modern art as indicated by Michael Angelo, music is a far better instrumentality than painting or sculpture. Music already deals with the formless, with the phantasy, direct. It portrays by means of harmony and its opposite, and can represent an event in its inception, its progress, catastrophe, *denouement*, and final consummation. Thus it is exactly fitted to present the modern art which requires that not only the manifestation of the divine shall be made to the senses, but also the negative elevation of the same above the sensuous, shall likewise be portrayed in the same work of art, in order that the content of art may be adequate to that of religion. A work like Schumann's 'Pilgrimage of the Rose' portrays first a naïve infantile innocence and ignorance of life and its experience—an abstract, moonshiny music to which fairies dance and bathe in the dewdrops of the flowers. Second, the experience with human life, with its cares and trials, its discipline, turns the music to the expression of pain and the accompaniments of mockery and scorn. The experience with death brings in the solemn requiem, which in the presence of the nadir of human life lifts itself in trust and consolation to the invisible helper, and soothes the plaints of the disappointed soul which sought earthly pleasure alone. Lifted above the earthly and its pleasures as well as its torments, the soul gathers strength and attacks the real world with that independent spirit which is assured of an infinite refuge if obliged at any time to retreat from the battle. The *finale* gives us a complete and healthy conquest over the evils of life.

"Any one of Beethoven's symphonies or sonatas will give somewhat in the same form a collision between the sensuous and spiritual in human life and the victory of the latter, although frequently with very bitter struggles and plentiful self-sacrifice.

"In poetry we have at start far less of the sensuous to deal with, for it appeals only to the ear rhythmically and in romantic poetry with rhymes also; but relies for its sensuous effects chiefly upon the reproductive imagination to bring up such images as it will portray. Its form, therefore, permits it to hold the whole compass of the matter of art from its genesis to its complete annulment. It was to be expected that poetry should lend itself to religion from the very first, and that its content should generally involve religious collisions. Secularity, indeed, as in Shakespeare, when portrayed in its totality or entire extent, gives the Divine will, just as religion does, in its separate moments. For the spectacle of the will of the individual presents first its spontaneous, impulsive acts, colliding it may be with right, human and divine. In the end comes the reaction upon the individual from the social and religious worlds of humanity, and the result certainly is the annulment of the individual and of his one-sided strivings, or else a reduction of his deed and intention to harmony with the ethical and divine will, as made valid by the institutions of the Church and civil society. Thus Shakespeare may be said to be a religious poet, in the sense that he presents other than sensuous mediation in his plays. In his great essay on Dante's 'Divina Comedia,' Schelling has characterized the true province of modern art and its difference from the antique: 'The antique world is that of classes, the modern that of individuals; the law of modern art is that each individual shall give shape and unity to that portion of the world which is revealed to him, and out of the materials of his time, its history, and its science, create his own mythology.'

"That is to say, he shall make all the material of his time significant as type of the Divine purpose 'that moves at the bottom of the world.' Mythological figures are simply individual instances elevated to types, and thus transmuted from natural facts to spiritual facts and means of expression or portrayal — manifestation and revelation of the spiritual.

"'Into the struggle,' he continues, 'between science' (which creates abstractions and generalities) 'and religion and art' (which demand something definite and limited) 'must the individual enter; but with absolute freedom seek to rescue permanent shapes from the fluctuations of time, and within arbitrarily assumed forms to give to the structure of his poem, by its absolute peculiarity, internal necessity and external universality.' (This Dante has done, as he shows at length; this has Goethe done in the 'Faust.' No element of his own time or of the past history of humanity but is taken up into the work.) 'It unites the outermost extremes in the aspirations of the times by a very peculiar invention of a subordinate mythology in the character of Faust.' The action begins in heaven and passes through the world to hell and back again to heaven. In such works as 'Faust' and the 'Divine Comedy' is found the highest achievement of reconciliation between the realms of art and religion, and one feels that what was in its earliest germs indistinguishably art and religion, as in the Edda or Hymns of the Vedas, perhaps may yet become one in the final perfection of art, in spite of the incongruities which appear in the middle period of development.

"There is, however, another thought suggested by the consideration of Dante's 'Divina Commedia.' This first great Christian poem is regarded by Schelling as the archetype of all Christian poetry; its study in our time is to be regarded as a favorable sign. Of the thirty English translations of it, ten have been made within the past twenty years. The poem embodies the Catholic view of life, and for this reason is all the more wholesome for study by modern Protestants. The threefold future world—'inferno,' 'purgatorio,' 'paradiso'—presents us the exhaustive picture of man's relation to his deeds. The Protestant 'hereafter' omits the purgatory but includes the inferno and paradiso. What has become of this missing link in modern Protestant art? we may inquire, and our inquiry is a pertinent one; for there is no subject connected with the relation of religion to art which is so fertile in suggestive insights to the investigator.

"To conduct one through Dante's great poem, which, as Tieck said, 'is the voice of ten silent centuries,' is not to be attempted here. Only a few hints as to its significance will be ventured, and then some of the traces of the same insight in subsequent literature pointed out.

"One must reduce life to its lowest terms, and drop away all consideration of its adventitious surroundings. The deeds of man in their threefold aspect are judged in this 'mystic, unfathomable poem.' The great fact of human responsibility is the key-note. Whatever man does he does to himself. If he does violence he injures himself. If he works righteousness he creates a paradise for himself.

"Now, a deed has two aspects; first, its immediate relation to the doer. The mental atmosphere in which one does a deed is of first consideration. If a wrong or wicked deed, then is the atmosphere of the criminal close and stifling to the doer. The angry man is rolling about suffocating in putrid mud. The incontinent is driven about by violent winds of passion. Whatever deed a man shall do must be seen in the entire perspective of its effects to exhibit its relation to the doer. The inferno is filled with those whose acts and habits of life surround them with an atmosphere of torture.

"One does not predict that such punishment of each individual is eternal, but one thing is certain—that with the sins there punished there is special torture eternally connected.

> "'Through me ye pass into the city of woe.
> Through me ye pass into eternal pain.
> Justice the founder of my fabric moved
> To rear me was the task of power divine,
> Supremest wisdom, and primeval love.
> Before me things create were none save things
> Eternal, and eternal, I endure.'

"Wherever the sin shall be there shall be connected with it the atmosphere of the inferno, which is its punishment. The doer of the sinful deed plunges into the inferno on its commission.

"But Dante wrote the 'Purgatorio,' and in this portrays the secondary effect of sin. The inevitable punishment bound up with sin burns with purifying flames each sinner. The immediate effect of the deed is the inferno, but the secondary effect is purification. Struggling up the steep sides of purgatory, under their painful burdens, go sinners punished for incontinence—lust, gluttony, avarice, anger, and other sins that find their place of punishment also in the inferno.

"Each evil-doer shall plunge into the inferno, and shall scorch over the flames of his own deeds until he repents, and struggles up the mountain of purgatory.

"In the 'paradiso,' we have doers of those deeds

which, being thoroughly positive in their nature, do not come back as punishment upon their authors.

"The correspondence of sin and punishment is notable. Even our jurisprudence discovers a similar adaptation. If one steals and deprives his neighbor of property, we manage by our laws to make his deed glide off from society, and come back on the criminal, and thus he steals his own freedom and gets a cell in jail. If a murderer takes life his deed is brought back to him, and he takes his own.

"The depth of Dante's insight discovers to him all human life stripped of its wrappings, and every deed coming straight back upon the doer, inevitably fixing his place in the scale of happiness and misery. It is not so much a '*last*' judgment of individual men, as it is of deeds in the abstract. For the brave man who sacrifices his life for another dwells in paradise so far as he contemplates his participation in that deed, but writhes in the inferno, in so far as he has allowed himself to slip, through some act of incontinence.

"If we return now to our question, what has become of the purgatory in modern literature, a glance will show us that the fundamental idea of Dante's purgatory has formed the chief thought of Protestant 'humanitarian' works of art.

"The thought that the sinful and wretched live a life of reaction against the effects of their deeds, is the basis of most of our novels. Most notable are the works of Nathaniel Hawthorne in this respect. His whole art is devoted to the portrayal of the purgatorial effects of sin or crime upon its authors. The consciousness of the deed and the consciousness of the verdict of one's fellow-men continually burns at the heart, and with slow, eating fires, consumes the shreds of selfishness quite away. In the 'Marble Faun' we have the spectacle of an animal nature betrayed by sudden impulse into a crime, and the torture of this consciousness gradually purifies and elevates the semi-spiritual being into a refined humanity.

"The use of suffering, even if brought on by sin and error, is the burden of our best class of novels. George Eliot's 'Middlemarch,' 'Adam Bede,' 'Mill on the Floss,' and 'Romola'—with what intensity these portray the spiritual growth through error and pain.

"Thus, if Protestantism has omitted purgatory from its religion, certainly Protestant literature has taken it up and absorbed it entire." *

Goodness: Influence of Art upon Religion.—"The three forms in which man attains communion with the highest life, and enters independent spiritual existence, are art, religion, and philosophy. In art, as contradistinguished from the 'arts,' by which we understand the mechanic appliances and dexterities designed and employed for man's well-being—for ministration to his wants of food, clothing, and shelter, and social, secular necessities—in art, as thus contradistinguished, we include all realizations of the beautiful, all the diverse forms under which nations or peoples have endeavored to body forth in matter a manifestation of the highest in their consciousness. The divine, which in the consciousness of all peoples, is an invisible, for it represents the highest mediation, the completest gener-

---

* Vol. 10, pp. 208-215.

alization of which that consciousness is capable—shall become a *visible* somewhat. That which is far withdrawn from mere local and temporal existence, shall descend into time and space, and become embodied in a *thing* which we can perceive with our senses. Art makes the invisible visible.

"Religion has for its object a far higher function than art. It is not sufficient that some æsthetic feeling of the presence of the divine may be experienced—it is not sufficient that our outward senses alone shall give us intimations of the great ultimate fact of the world. We must be able to form conceptions which shall realize for us in the depths of our minds and hearts the divine. In what we see with the senses we are relatively passive recipients, and we are limited by external conditions, the time and the place, but in our power to call up images and conceptions we are in the exercise of greater freedom. We can call up the religious representations under any and all circumstances; they become, as it were, a present consolation which can not be taken away by external foes, but only forfeited through internal personal lapse from holiness.

"Not only is religion superior to art in this relation of freedom from the external limits of locality and time, but it has a more important prerogative in the fact that the portrayal of the divine is far more adequate than in art. Religious conceptions violate the demands of æsthetic truth, in order to present a deeper and truer idea of essential, spiritual existence. In the external form or shape we can have only the *effects* of spirit—its *manifestation*. But in religion we have *revelation*, and revelation is essential to all religion.

Revelation is superior to manifestation, in the fact that the latter gives us only the dead external results, while the former gives us the moving, creative causes. The self-active, spontaneous, *free*, can not be immediately presented to our senses. We can see or perceive only some disposition of matter so shaped and formed as to indicate the action of creative intelligence. The Apollo Belvedere has no limb or posture that does not seem fully possessed of the indwelling purpose of the grand personality that animates the figure before us. The classic beautiful achieves its triumph in incarnating the free soul so completely that no phase or outline of the sculptured block shall remain that seems to be in the way or not needed for the expression of the purpose of the divinity dwelling in the flesh. There is nothing more than this in classic art, and this is certainly enough. Ask yourself, in examining a work of classic art, is there an outline that looks as if it portrayed an external limitation which the individual had not been able to vanquish? If you find any such limitation you will find something anti-classic, something that is not quite up to the highest standard which the Greek spirit conceived. But with its highest realization—take the Apollo Belvedere—what is it more than an *intimation* of the free personal might? It is not a *revelation* of it, but a manifestation. The religious contemplation of Apollo would dwell upon his generic attributes, upon his spiritual disposition and character, and thus upon the creative cause of any or all of the moments which art might seize and portray. The religious conception may avail itself to a greater or less degree of artistic embodiment—thus it almost always uses allegory, but it always transcends the æsthetic limit and introduces a negative element that destroys and makes null any sensuous manifestation. Take the Hindoo art, essentially the portrayal of incessant incarnation of vitality. The Greeks reproduced the same thing under the myth of Proteus, but did not make statues of Proteus. The East Indian made a statue with four faces and eight arms, or the Egyptian made a compound of animal, mineral and human, a god Osiris or a Sphinx. In the corresponding religious conception there was not merely the creative descent into form, but the negative idea of desertion of that form—death, transmutation, change.

"An illustration of this thought occurs in the present aspect of natural science. In early attempts to construct a science of physics, men imagined the phenomena of heat, light, electricity, and sometimes even gravitation or attraction in general to be occasioned by fluids, or at a later period ethers or auræ were introduced to explain them. Still later these are explained by vibrations and vibratuncles. There is a passage from mere images of the fancy to a process of thinking the destruction of these images. The uncultivated thinker tries to conceive everything under the form of *thing* and its properties. When he has dissolved thing into an equilibrium of forces he has accomplished a great feat. Even the elevation from the thought of heat as a fluid to that of heat as a vibration of matter is the elevation from the thought of a thing—a dead result—to the thought of a *relation*. Heat as vibration is a relation—an activity of something. When we consider that heat is a relative term and that all bodies have some heat, we see at once that all bodies must be in a state of continual vibration, which vibration is in a continual process of interaction, every body through its vibration influencing every other body. Then again the form of bodies and their properties, whether solid, fluid, or gaseous, whether visible or invisible, whether luminous or opaque, tangible or intangible—all these depend on calorific vibrations directly or indirectly. Thus we see that by the mere change of the hypothetical conception under which we conceive an object in physics, we enable ourselves to penetrate far into the -essence of the material world about us. A thing is a fixed dead result, but a force is a pure relation, that which exists *in transitu* —in its passage from one manifestation to another. All forces are manifested in their activity—in their passage from one state to another. One force becomes another continually. All that seems fixed is really in transition, and the permanent is the *law* of forces and not the individual force—still less the temporary phase of the play of forces, the objects of our senses, what we call 'things.'

"Similar to this elevation of the understanding from the idea of things to that of forces, is the elevation of the reason from the sphere of art to that of religion. In art the divine is presented to the senses as a thing—but a thing moved and swayed by free spiritual might. In art our point of departure is the thing, and we are thence elevated toward the conception of free personality; the latter is intimated and not directly revealed. But in religion the Divine appears as creator and destroyer of natural things, as the dominant ruler elevated above nature, now manifesting Himself in the material as the beautiful or sublime, now manifesting Himself as the negative might that destroys the material form and reduces it to higher uses. These two phases combined make revelation, and hence it will be seen that revelation contains manifestation and its opposite or annulment. In the annulment of the beautiful the ugly reveals itself, and hence religion essentially contains the element (or moment) of the ugly. The phase of formation is followed by the phase of deformation, and this precedes the genesis of higher forms.

"The true essence revealed in religion has still another form of existence to man. In his pure thinking it may be cognized as the scientific truth of the universe. Philosophy includes the systematic unfolding of this knowledge. Thus we may say art sensuously perceives the absolute as the beautiful; religion conceives or imagines the absolute as revealed in its traditions and mode of worship, while philosophy comprehends the absolute as defined in pure thought. Thus in the language of religion the three may be defined as follows: Art is the piety of the senses, religion the piety of the heart, and philosophy the piety of the intellect. The impiety of these faculties is easily formulated; senses that can not discern the beautiful, but are content with what is ugly, have that form of impiety which we call bad taste; the heart which does not find its consolation in the great doctrines of religion, the intellect which sets up as its highest principle any other than absolute, self-conscious reason or personality—these are the other species of impieties.

"Looking again at the correlation of these three forms in which the individual communes with the highest, we see a frightful chasm between the last results of abstract thought and the facts that appeal to the senses. It is the whole which is beautiful. Thus matter as matter—as a system of gravity—must be beautiful as a solar system. But our senses can not perceive the universe, hence art strives to create a visible semblance of it in a convenient compass. The old mystics talked much of the macrocosm and the microcosm. The microcosm, or man, was the miniature universe, as indeed he possesses self-motion and the power of reflecting in his mind the macrocosm. It will be remembered that Leibnitz, in his system of monads, has each one possess the power of representing in and to itself the rest of the universe of monads, all existing ideally in each. To Liebnitz, then, the progress of the individual history of each monad was a progress in the clearness with which it represented the universe to itself. Very profound and suggestive is Leibnitz's system when applied to the world of souls, for souls only are true monads. The lowest monad, buried in itself, has only a dim capacity for feeling. Finally there is a monad that can sensuously perceive the beautiful—some Greek soul. Then a long distance beyond this soul is a soul that can represent to itself not only the beautiful, but also the causal process which makes it; here is a theistic, a Jewish soul. Another soul may in its representation be able to consciously mirror the conditions which lie at the basis of the two former stages of representation. In each stage of progress the soul adds, to the content of its representation, the counterpart which was lacking to its previous representation." *

---

* Vol. 10, pp. 204-208.

Philosophy of Religion.—" The philosophy of religion must be acknowledged on all hands as the most important work of the human intellect. In explaining religion as a phenomenon of human life, it is found necessary to expound the idea of the first principle of the world—the Absolute. In defining his idea of the absolute, man defines his idea of his own origin and destiny, and the idea of the relation which he holds to nature and to the Absolute. All practical activity of man is conditioned through this idea of the Absolute. Man's immortality and freedom are conditioned directly through the nature of God. If God is an unconscious natural power, man can have no other destiny than to be absorbed at some time into this unconscious power, and lose his individual being. Indeed, on the hypothesis of an unconscious first principle, it is impossible to explain how a conscious being ever came to exist at all. For consciousness is directive power, and the rationality which manifests itself in consciousness is an indefinitely growing potency in the control of the world, perpetually imposing its own forms on brute matter, and subordinating it to the service of man just as if man had made it originally for his own use. The hasty and general outlook is sufficient to give the presumption that the absolute is not only an all-powerful might, but an all-knowing might. The one most important truth of all is the truth in regard to the resemblance or difference of this first principle from man. If man, as consciousness, is in its image, then the trend of the universe is in the direction of the triumph of man's cause. His development will be an ascent toward the divine. In knowing himself, man will know with some degree of adequacy the divine.

"Another consideration of equal importance following from this is the doctrine that God is a revealed God, if he is a conscious being; his works reveal him. His creation is a manifestation of His will, and in the creation of intelligent beings He reveals His own intelligence. Hegel has laid great stress upon this thought in his 'Philosophy of Religion.' In the third part of that treatise he expounds the religion of the revealed God, calling it 'the absolute religion,' conceiving Christianity to be this absolute religion, and showing by strict analyses of the contents of the other religions that no one of them makes God a revealed God, and that the reason for this is that the idea of God in the pantheistic and polytheistic religions is the idea of a first principle which can not be revealed in a created world. Neither man nor nature can reveal Brahm, because Brahm is utterly transcendent, not only to the world, but to man in his highest development. Brahm has no form, but transcends consciousness as much as he does material form. With this we have the world of nature and the world of man, not as creations of Brahm, not as revelations of that principle, but as pure illusion—Maya. This illusion is to be accounted for on the hypothesis of the fall of man into individual consciousness, wherein he distinguishes himself from the all. It is 'the dream of the drop that hath withdrawn itself from the primal ocean of being,' and which colors all its seeing with the defect of its own finitude—consciousness being regarded as the origin of all division and particularity. Its form is that of subject-objectivity;

i. e., of a subject which is its own object, and yet a subject which looks upon the object as a world of alien existence—'It says "thou" to the rest of creation.' What momentous import this theory has for the people who believe it, we know through the history of the Oriental world—a history which Hegel prefers to exclude from the world-history as being a history that contains no principle of secular progress within it. For it looks upon all as negative to the divine, and hence as not being capable of improvement, but only fit for annihilation. The highest is Nirvana, or the rest of unconsciousness. Progress toward the annihilation of conscious being is progress toward the divine, as understood in the Orient. Such progress as that we call decay and decrease.

"With the idea of a revealed God we discover a radically different solution to the world. We find that man has a positive work to do; an active stage of civilization takes the place of Oriental quietism. Man has the vocation to render himself divine by learning the form of God's will as revealed, and then forming his own will in its pattern—adopting God's will as the form of his human will. He must learn the divine will, and make an utter sacrifice of his own will to it, so that his deeds shall be inspired through the divine, all finitude of the creature being offered up by renunciatory act to the divine, so that the conflict between the divine and human shall be ended by the self-devotion, the utter sacrifice of all selfishness on the part of the individual. The sacrifice of the Oriental devotee relates to the substance of his consciousness, and ends in annihilation, if he can achieve so much as he aspires for. The Christian renunciation does not go so far; it recognizes in God the absolute form, instead of an absolute formlessness. God has the form of consciousness, of personality. Hence, with this idea of the divine, the sacrifice of the individual for the divine is no annihilation of individuality, but rather the putting on the form of the freest and highest individuality. The sacrifice which the Christian devotee makes is no sacrifice of his human form, but only of its content; he takes into the form of his will and knowing a divine substance, the substance revealed as the will of God, and by this he preserves his individuality, and yet removes the barrier between himself and the divine through utter abandonment of self to the will of the divine will, which, being the will of a conscious personality, restores to man his sacrificed individuality in a transfigured form. Man, by his religious sacrifice, therefore, gains all and loses nothing but finitude and defect. The doctrine of grace, as the highest principle of divine action toward the world of man and nature, is the only doctrine in harmony with the idea of a revelation of God through creation. Were God any other than conscious personality, man and nature would reveal something essentially different from Him. A world which offers us a series of beings ascending from the inorganic to the organic, and crowns all with a human race, reveals a conscious first principle by pointing toward it as the final cause of its progressive series. It points toward such a divine principle, and only toward it." *

Goodness: Ethical Right.—" Man is born an ani-

---

* Vol. 15, pp. 207–209.

mal, but must become a spiritual being. He is limited to the present moment and to the present place, but he must conquer all places and all times. Man, therefore, has an ideal of culture which it is his destiny or vocation to achieve.

"He must lift himself above his mere particular existence toward universal existence. All peoples, no matter how degraded, recognize this duty. The South Sea Islander commences with his infant child and teaches him habits that conform to that phase of civilization—an ethical code fitting him to live in that community—and, above all, the mother-tongue, so that he may receive the results of the perceptions and reflections of his fellow-beings and communicate his own to them. The experience of the tribe, a slow accretion through years and ages, shall be preserved and communicated to each new-born child, vicariously saving him from endless labor and suffering. Through culture the individual shall acquire the experience of the species—shall live the life of the race, and be lifted above himself. Such a process as culture thus puts man above the accidents of time and place in so far as the tribe or race has accomplished this.

"Whatever lifts man above immediate existence, the wants and impulses of the present moment, and gives him self-control, is called ethical. The ethical grounds itself, therefore, in man's existence in the species and in the possibility of the realization of the species in the individual. Hence, too, the ethical points toward immortality as its presupposition. Death comes through the inadequacy of the individual organism to adjust itself to the environment; the conditions are too general, and the individual gets lost in the changes that come to it. Were the individual capable of adapting himself to all changes, there could be no death; the individual would be perfectly universal. This process of culture that distinguishes man from all other animals points toward the formation of an immortal individual distinct from the body within which it dwells—an individual who has the capacity to realize within himself the entire species.

"Immortality thus complements the ethical idea. In an infinite universe the process of realizing the experience of all beings by each being must itself be of infinite duration. The doctrine of immortality, therefore, places man's life under the form of eternity and ennobles mortal life to its highest potency.

"Since ethics rests on the idea of a social whole as the totality of man, and on the idea of an immortal life as the condition of realizing in each man the life of the whole, it lays great stress on the attitude of renunciation on the part of the individual. The special man must deny himself, sacrifice the present moment in order to attain the higher form of eternity. To act indifferently toward the present moment is to 'act disinterestedly,' as it is called. It is the preference of reflected good for immediate good—my good reflected from all humanity, my good after their good and through their good, and not my good before their good and instead of their good.

"This doctrine of disinterestedness has been perverted into a doctrine of annihilation of all interest by a school of ascetic moralists in our time—the school of the Positivists. According to them, it were a higher form of disinterestedness to forswear all interest, and to waive all return of good upon ourselves from others. In fact, the *ne plus ultra* of this disinterestedness is the renunciation, not only of mortal life, but of immortal life—the renunciation of selfhood itself.

"Such supreme renunciation is the irony of renunciation. It would renounce not only the pleasures of the flesh, but the blessedness of virtue and sainthood. It would renounce eternity as well as the present moment.

"The dialectic of such a position would force it into the next extreme of pure wickedness. For, see, is it not more disinterested to renounce eternal blessedness than the mere pleasure of the present moment? The more renunciation, the more ethical. Hence the denizens of the inferno—those plunged into all manner of mortal sins—are more virtuous than the saints in paradise. For the sinners, do they not renounce blessedness—the form of eternity—the infinite happiness, and in their self-denial take up with mere temporal pleasures that are sure to leave stings of pain? What nobleness to prefer hell with its darkness and fire and ice to paradise with its serenity and light and love! Is it not a step in advance even over such abstract ethical culture as rejects immortality from disinterestedness to plunge into positive pain, and thereby exhibit one's abstract freedom from all lures to happiness?

"But such 'ethical culture' is not true morality. Disinterestedness is only a relative matter in it—it is incidental, and not the essential element in virtue. It is of no use whatever except to eliminate the immediateness from life. The individual should become the species, and, instead of receiving good directly, should receive it as reflected from his fellow-men. Not to receive it as reflected from his fellow-men would paralyze the circulation which is necessary to the realization of the species, and man's ideal would vanish utterly. The principle of altruism implies receiving as well as giving. No giving can remain where no receiving is. Hence ethics vanish altogether with the paralysis of the return of good upon the individual from the whole of society. The individual is cut off from the species by absolute renunciation, and can not ascend into it by substituting mediated good for immediate, as all codes of morals demand. Humanity lapses into bestiality. Civilization is impossible without this ideal of the race as the goal of the individual. It is the object of language, literature, science, religion, and all human institutions.

"Thus, too, immortality is presupposed by all the instrumentalities of civilization. The completion of spiritual life in the communion of all souls is the final cause or purpose of immortal life." *

Ground of Ethical Right.—" Because the First Person knows the Second Person as self-knowing, he knows the self-knowing of the Second, and recognizes in the perfection of the Second his own perfection; also, in the creation of the Third Perfect Person by the self-knowing of the Second Person, the First Person recognizes his own perfection, so that the Third Person proceeds not only from the Second Person, but also from the First Person.

---

* Vol. 19, pp. 213–216.

"The Third perfect Personality is the Holy Spirit that lives in the Invisible Church. It is the archetype of all institutions. We recognize a sort of personality in institutions. The state, for example, has deliberative, executive, and administrative functions—an intellect and a will. What is imperfectly realized in historical institutions is perfectly realized in the Eternal and Invisible Church, which is composed of innumerable souls, collected from innumerable worlds, and all united, not by temporary devices of written compacts, or immemorial usages and formalities, but by the bond of love or the spirit of divine charity and self-sacrifice, for the true good of others. The Spirit of this infinite and Eternal Church is the Holy Spirit—'a procession but not a begotten,' because it arises or is an eternal involution from the manifold of creation through the self-knowledge of the First and Second Persons.

"Man as individual progresses or develops by social combination with his fellow-men, and thence arises institutions of civilizations—the family, civil society, the State, the Church. Historical institutions, being finite and having limitations incident to organization, are perishable, but their archetype is the Invisible Church, into which go, or may go, all souls after death. The principle of social combination or co-operation is altruism, charity, or love, the principle which sacrifices self for one's fellow-men. In that principle alone can perfect organization exist. The Spirit of the Invisible Church, the archetype of the Visible Church, and of all other institutions of civilizations, is the Third Person of the Divine Being, the Spirit of love and co-operation organized into the greatest reality of the universe. For it includes all souls that have lived in the universe from the timeless beginning of the consciousness of the Eternal Word. From this view we find the world to be the process of evolution of souls, so that this is the present, past, or future purpose of each and all stellar bodies.

"The first self-active being in its self-knowledge knows no passivity, no imperfection, and hence no finite being. The world is not to be explained from his self-knowledge except by mediation of the Second Person, called the Eternal Word. The relation of the First Person is, or may be, expressed, therefore, by Justice. Justice returns the deed upon the individual and gives each its due. The due of a finite or negative being, whose individuality exists through separation and exclusion and negation of others, is therefore self-annihilation, and such is the fate of all finitude in the thought of pure self-activity, except it is saved through the intervention of the thought of the Second Person, who thinks his relation to the First as derivation or sonship. But the Eternal Word thinks his origination from God eternally as an annulment of passivity and isolated material existence, and a rising into the perfect unity of the Church. Here we have the form of perfect grace. A perfect being, whose entire activity brings up from nothing finite beings, and gives them existence and progression in order to culminate in man, who can carry out this development by uniting with his fellow-men in social union, and ascend into the Invisible Church." *

---

* Vol. 17, pp. 315, 316.

SECTION VII.—THE EMOTIONS.

Duplication of Self-Activity in Emotions: Sentient, Psychical, Rational.

"Feeling, as it appears in the child, at first involves heredity, and its manifestations are in the form of instinct. It is immediate, and rules as a sort of nature. Whatever becomes a part of one's nature comes back to the form of feeling again; hence the way to educate feeling is to make over a new nature, by acting on the will and intellect. Take the youth who has a perverse emotional nature through heredity; make him form ethical habits by unceasing practice of what is right. Teach him to see the good view of the world as a rational and necessary view, and when the good habit has become formed, and the intellectual view is accordant with it, the problem is solved by the new habit and view becoming immediate again as a feeling. But the secondary feeling, inasmuch as it is based on what has been reasoned out, and is not habit following blind instinct, is not a blind feeling, but an enlightened feeling. The tendency of all education must be from all blind feelings into enlightened feelings." *

"Self-activity is in every new-born soul as a spontaneity—a possibility of unlimited action, good or bad. But its activity must take a certain direction or else it will cramp and fetter itself. By bad action it will curtail the limits of its freedom; by good action it will extend those limits. In other words, the ideal nature of self-activity is expressed by the ideas of truth, beauty, and goodness, and in these directions the individual

---

* "Education," vol. vi, p. 167.

may develop himself without wasting his energy in self-contradiction. The opposites of the true, the beautiful, and the good, are the false, the ugly, and the bad. To do or produce these things is to do or produce what is internally contradictory and self-nugatory, and what consequently reduces itself to a zero. Such use of self-activity fails to develop it; its endeavors do not build up anything; all its products are negative, and it is left in the end where it started—at the bottom of the ladder of human culture. But whereas it started at first with butterfly wings and mounting hopes, it now, after its wrong efforts, sits down in despair, with an ever-gnawing worm in its consciousness.

"Educate toward a knowledge of truth, a love of the beautiful, a habit of doing good, because only through these forms can the self-activity continue to develop progressively in this universe. These forms—the true, the beautiful, and the good—will bring the individual into union with his fellow-men through all eternity, and make him a participator in the divine-human work of civilization and culture and the perfecting of man in the image of God." *

"Educate the heart? Educate the character? Yes, these are the chief objects; but there is no immediate way of educating these. They must be educated by the two disciplines—that of the will in correct habit, and by that of the intellect in a correct view of the world. When the practical habit and the intellectual view coincide, then it becomes a matter of the heart, and character is the result. 'Character,' said Novalis,

---

* "Education," vol. vi, pp. 157, 158.

'is a completely developed will.' It is also a completely developed intellect. Because in God intellect and will are one; so in man the highest aim is to unite insight with moral will. Self-activity becomes intellect, self-activity becomes will. At first self-activity is mere spontaneity without reflection. The highest character is infinitely reflected self-activity." *

"Habit soon makes us familiar with subjects which seem remote from our personal interest, and they become agreeable to us. The objects, too, assume a new interest upon nearer approach, as being useful or injurious to us. That is useful which serves us as a means for the realization of a rational purpose; injurious, if it hinders such realization. It is a false and mechanical way of looking at the mind to suppose that a habit which has been formed by a certain number of repetitions can be broken by an equal number of denials. We can never renounce a habit which we decide to be pernicious, except through clearness of judgment and firmness of will. The passive habit is that which gives us the power to retain our equipoise of mind in the midst of a world of changes (pleasure and pain, grief and joy, etc.). The active habit gives us skill, presence of mind, tact in emergencies, etc.† By habit, the soul makes a second nature in place of its animal nature, controlling its body in accordance with customs, fashions, and ethical laws." ‡

In the process by which "the will makes objective its internal subjective form" there is reduplication in

---

* "Education," vol. vi, pp. 167, 168.
† "The Philosophy of Education," pp. 32, 34.
‡ Ibid., p. 3.

the "emotional nature of man, involving his feelings, passions, instincts, and desires"; and according as the emotions depend upon the sensuous ideas, abstract ideas, absolute idea, will the plane of the emotions be sentient, psychical, rational.

Sentient Emotions.—"The bond that unites a people is a natural, and not an artificial bond; it does not depend on leagues and treatises, but on community of descent and consequent identical race peculiarities, common language, manners and customs, and traditions. Each individual of a people finds himself living in this identity with his people just as he finds himself living in identity with a family. The family identity (called 'identity' because it is a common life the same for each, consisting of mutual relations and common possessions in which each owns an undivided share) is a 'natural' one in the fact that it, too, arises from the laws of nature, and not from free choice. The individual, e. g., can not choose his ancestry. This natural unity of people gradually gives place to the recognition of common humanity and an observance of humane duties toward all men.

"The spiritual nature of man (his will, intellect, and heart) is opposed to his animal nature. Matter is exclusive; animal gratifications are exclusive and selfish." *

"In the world we find, besides bodies or forces, also life, or self-manifestation. Life is emancipation, and *thought* is its consummation. The principle of life is synthesis, combination, participation. Thought or mind is the realization of this principle. Hence the problem

---

* "The Philosophy of Education," pp. 186, 187.

of life finds its solution in the law: Act for others; live through them; combine with them. For it recognizes itself in the others, and thereby cancels the alien element which belongs to matter. Hence in human history arise all the institutions or combinations which serve to remove fate from the life of man and substitute for it forms of *human help*. The individual, so far as he is a natural being and possessed of a body, has relations to the without, is dependent and under fate. But human combination in the form of trade and commerce, of special industries, and, above and beyond these, in the institutions of the family, the state, the Church, the civil corporation, shall make over man's externality into a human externality wherein his fate is only himself—is only the semblance of fate, but whose reality is his own self-determination.

"Thus the solution of fate for man, as a union of the natural and spiritual, is to make the race the shield of the individual, to surround the individual with the species. All culture means nothing more than this: that the individual, by means of his activity, study, and practice, avails himself of the experience of the race—acquires its wisdom, and gains its mode of acting." *

ILL.—Sensuous emotions include the many phases of pleasure and pain, hope and fear, arising from the supply or lack of the physical necessities, food, clothing, shelter, etc. The beggar who can barely "keep soul and body together" and the voluptuary or "leader of fashion," who spends time and money and thought to tempt an already satiated appetite or to get "the latest

---

* Vol. 11, p. 270.

in color or style," represent the extremes in this plane of emotions; for "they are as sick that surfeit with too much as they that starve with nothing."

As the thought and action of a large portion of humanity are concerned with the "things" of life, and do not arise out of the sensuous plane, so the emotions will necessarily be of the same order; the solemn truth of this fact is strongly brought out in Helen Campbell's "Prisoners of Poverty," in which she shows that one of the greatest needs of the so-called "wage-earners" is an awakening of new desires, that "contentment with their lot" is an emotion fatal to true growth and progress in any grade of society. Washington Gladden in "Applied Christianity" points out some of the ways that those of society more favored in ancestry and inheritance can assist the less fortunate to participate in the higher possessions of the race; thoughts that are concerned simply with the "daily round" must be modified and supplanted by the means of reading, music, amusements, social, and religious influences, by new thoughts, and then will the new thoughts and actions become immediate in a new and higher grade of emotions.

Owing to the complexity of man's nature in thought and action even in the merely temporal phases, any attempt to classify the countless emotions is for the most part arbitrary. Besides the legitimate emotions brought about by a wholesome regard for the needs of the body, there is not only the disproportionate care and anxiety for things fleeting and transitory, but also the degeneracy of the sensuous emotions into the sensual; all forms of amusements involving gambling, excessive indulgence of appetite, all kinds of questionable literature, and social and business dealings arousing petty envyings and jealousy of the possessions of another, beget emotions which have arisen from thoughts which are ugly and untrue.

Psychical Emotions.—"Spiritual life is participation; the intellect and the moral will develop through sharing all acquisitions with others. Wisdom is a product of the race, and not of one individual exclusively; the greater the number who participate in wisdom, the better for all." *

"Man is a being who can develop within himself— he can collect experience from the individuals of his species, and redistribute this experience to the individual—thus elevating the life of the individual into the life of the species, and without destroying the latter's individuality, but, on the contrary, increasing it. For in our human affairs the man goes for most who has taken up into himself the life and experience of his fellow-men most effectually. Shakespeare and Goethe, Homer and Dante—these are vast individualities, comprehending human nature almost entire within each. Man is great when he avails himself of the power of his species. Even the Cæsar or the Napoleon is great through his representative character—summing up in his will the will-power of his nation and distributing it again to them as directive power. Each humble individual, too, who serves under the Cæsar or the Napoleon participates to some extent in the greatness of individuality of the great leader, because he is led out of

---

* "The Philosophy of Education," p. 187.

and beyond himself to live for others and through others and in others. Thus each one gains individuality while he gives it to others. Here, in secular affairs, is the same principle which the doctrine of grace enunciates for the religious consciousness." *

Ill.—As it is the nature and general scope of the different planes of thought with which we are concerned in psychology, so any attempt to fix a sharp dividing line between the different grades of emotions is useless. Love, hate, joy, sorrow, fear, hope, envy, etc., come from the participation of man with man in the common interests of humanity; emotions which arise from the political, industrial, and social relations of mankind, may be called psychical. Emotions arising from the contemplation of man's relation to God are rational; reverence, godly fear, humility, true charity—" devotion to others "—and a love for the beautiful and true partake of the nature of the divine.

As thought in its nature is infinite, so emotions in the grades of psychical and rational are infinitely expansive. The institutions of society, family, school, civil society, state, and Church, are for the assistance of the individual in the development of thought and will and feelings. In all these institutions the individual learns to subordinate his will to the will of others, and in giving up his selfishness he is enabled to co-operate and combine with others, and in so doing he receives their thoughts and becomes a participator in their spiritual life.

In the family, the child begins the process of mak-

---

* Vol. 15, pp. 209, 210.

ing over the instinctive feelings into conscious enlightened feelings, or emotions; he receives from the family instruction which enables him to form habits of care, thoughtfulness for others, and obedience, which fit him for life in the other institutions of society; in this family life the child receives this help freely, without all the suffering and experience which it has cost the parents. The school is supposed to continue and supplement the training of the family.

In civil society the individual, even when working from self-interest, as a manufacturer in making the best cloth that it may sell better, really works for the good of society; and in turn the individual calls society to his aid and receives the products and experiences of others without the trouble of doing it all for himself. But when civil society generally recognizes, even in business transactions, that a reasonable "altruism" is a better principle of action than "self-interest," then will the emotions incident to industrial life be more akin to the heavenly!

The state further educates the individual in self-sacrifice. The state may demand the property, and even the life of the individual, and the state in turn protects and assists the individual. No more remarkable example of obedience to the state can be given than Socrates, who, when the sphere of the state was far less well defined than it is to-day, voluntarily gave himself to death rather than violate his duty to that "larger self" represented by the state authority; and our own century has as conspicuous an example in the heroic and self-sacrificing Abraham Lincoln.

But it is in the Church where the doctrine of grace

has its best exemplification. The Church is the institution which consciously adopts the principle of self-sacrifice as the rule of thought and action. The spirit of the Founder of Christianity, who freely gave up all things, but in so doing entered into the glory and power of the Father, can enter and uplift the life of every individual and every institution of society.

Rational Emotions.—" It is possible to seize the principle of grace in an abstract manner, and set it over against other principles, such as justice and free will. Or it is possible to misunderstand it altogether, as in the case of naturalistic theories which can think of no possible view of interrelation except the materialistic one, which admits of no participation, but only of exclusion. Justice is not a principle which is to be thought as limiting grace; grace itself assumes the form of justice in proportion as it meets the free responsibility of the individual. Without responsibility there can be no justice; for justice returns upon the individual only what he has uttered in freedom. But the principle of grace extends below the realm of free responsibility to the lowest manifestation of the creation. It is grace that draws up all creation toward the highest, and endows beings with progressive degrees of individuality and realization of the divine image. The animal, it is true, is not immortal, but so much life as it has is the life of the species, and is a gift of grace which gives him the light of life, not for his having a right to it, but for the sake of divine love which pours itself out in creation, from freedom and the desire of good. When the human being arrives, he progresses into knowledge and will-power, and this brings responsibility, and with it the principle of justice. Justice is the principle of grace applied to free beings, because justice is respect shown to the responsibility of the individual who acts. Justice assumes the actor to be self-determined and free and to own his deed; whatever his deed is it is returned to him. To return the deed of an irresponsible being upon it would be to annihilate it. To treat a free being as though it did not own its deeds would be to offer indignity to it and annihilate its freedom. But freedom is itself the last and highest gift of grace, and grace will preserve that before all else. Freedom is self-determination, but not the self-determination of a mere particular individual in its isolation, but rather as participation in the life of the species—in the life of God, rather. Freedom, which should energize to will only its particularity, apart from the divine and from the human race, would merely set up for itself a limit in the race and in God. This would be the hell which selfishness makes for itself. Even grace, which seeks to give to others, receiving naught in return, would be the highest pain to the isolated will that seeks to find itself alone in the universe. Dante makes his "Inferno" to be caused by the fall of Lucifer, through pride, he striking the earth and hollowing out the vortex with its terraces on which sinners are punished. Pride is the worst of mortal sins, because it loves only itself and repels God and man and all that is valued by them. Grace is the most repugnant to pride. Next to pride is the sin of envy. But envy is not so deadly as pride in that it does not hate all that is from others. It hates God and man, but it loves the temporal blessings which they possess, and desires to possess them exclusively itself. Next above envy is anger, or that which does violence to its fellows against God. Anger is not so deep a sin as envy or as pride; for it strikes the particular individual or special persons, but not the foundation of all society and of all union with God, while pride and envy are hostile to all association, whether with man or with God.

"Christianity defines the 'mortal sins' from this view of divine grace. Freedom is turned against itself for its own annihilation in these sins, because it wills against participation in the life of the species as well as in the divine life. It is the principle of grace which Goethe, in the second part of his 'Faust,' calls the eternal feminine 'Das Ewig-Weibliche,' which is the moving principle of all progress toward the goal. Goethe, like Dante, makes divine love or grace the very element that is most painful to the devils who undertake to seize Faust's soul. Association is the most destructive agency which fiendishness can come in contact with. The angels appear in the clouds strewing roses (of love), which the devils find to be the most exquisite torture when they are struck by them. Even the association of devils for a purpose is liable to undermine the absolute hate which is the ideal of the perfect devil. Slavery would undermine it, for the slave would be forced into submission of his will to another; and to toil for another is to sacrifice one's self for that other, and to some extent to realize the principle of grace. So, if Mephistopheles controls other devils he realizes his purposes in and through them, and they subordinate their individual wills to his will—thus simulating the principle of grace—thus deep is the principle of grace constitutive of the nature of the human world and of the forms of human life. Even slavery has a positive side to it, which is medicative toward those worst of spiritual ills—pride and envy. Goethe had come to this view of grace during his life, starting with the pantheistic theory, and finding its consequences inhuman; not even devils could live under such a theory. There was a glimpse of the true theory of the world in his mind quite early in life, and he tells us that he saw the Faust problem then in its entirety, first and second parts. He had seen that the universe is based in its deepest laws on the principle of 'saving grace.' The three phases of holiness in the Christian Church are portrayed by him in the last scene of 'Faust.' There comes first the Pater Ecstaticus, who calls upon arrows to transfix him (as they did St. Sebastian), and for lances, bludgeons, and lightnings to martyr him, so that his 'pining breast' may be rid of its 'vain unrealities, and see only the star of everlasting love.' This view is simply negative to the finite and earthly. Pater Profundus comes next as the representative of a more perfect state of holiness. He looks upon nature, and sees it as the spectacle of God's love forming and preserving created beings. Not only this, but he sees that even the lightning and the terrible mountain torrent are messengers of love, bringing fertility to the vale and purity to the air; he sees the world as instrument for the realization of spirit. There is next Pater Seraphicus, who is a higher saint, because he does not spurn the world and seek only his own bliss in ecstatic contemplation, nor see merely the mediatorial process in creation, like the Pater Profundus, but he 'takes up into himself the blessed boys . . . brought forth at midnight hour, with a soul and sense half shut, lost immediate to the parents, by the angels straightway gained'; lets them see the world through his eyes, and, by allowing them participation in his human experience, equalizes their fate which had denied them earthly life. Here we see that the soul is represented as gaining something positive from the earthly life which must be made up to it by the gracious aid of some Pater Seraphicus if too early death has deprived it of human experience. But Dr. Marianus ('in the highest, purest cell') sees the Virgin as the symbol of divine grace (as the feminine is especially the bearer of human tenderness and mercy on earth, so it becomes properly a symbol of divine grace), and thus celebrates divine grace as the deepest principle of the divine nature, and as containing all other principles within it.

"Milton, in representing the fallen angels as having society and combination, in the form of a hellish commonwealth, with a legislative assembly over which Satan 'exalted sat,' has painted the demoniac as possessing divine elements. It is Dante alone who has consistently presented to us the symbolic portraiture of the degrees of sin in its effects upon the soul, and has shown us Lucifer 'immersed to his midst in ice,' his pride repelling all the universe, and thus freezing him with isolation—for warmth is the symbol of association—even our clothing warms us by contact, and we warm our spiritual capacities into activity by association, contact, with other souls, so that love is regarded as spiritual warmth. The institution of the state and of civil society, of the family, and still more the institution of the Church, weave for human life a spiritual clothing—the universal enwrapping the particular—and preserve vital heat within it.

"If these views are correct, it is not wonderful that the great fathers of the Christian Church, who have seen this principle of grace revealed as the ground of true life and the solvent word that alone explains creation, have laid so much stress upon it as to make it seem often as the exclusive principle rather than the inclusive principle. Hence justice has been opposed to grace and stern legality made to stand over against grace, simply because the principle of grace was interpreted in a one-sided manner. Then, too, freedom has been thrust back as if it had been impossible with divine sovereignty; when, in fact, it is grace alone that makes freedom possible. For freedom is participation in the form of the absolute, and hence the realization of independence, which alone can be conceived through the idea of love or grace which freely imparts itself to others and lives in their living." *

Section VIII.—The Will.

Stage of Knowing presupposed in Contemplation of Freedom—Substantial Will: Self-activity: Totality: Freedom—Formal Will: Action—Change sometimes regarded as produced only by Environment: External Conditions; Motives.

Stage of Knowing presupposed in Contemplation of Freedom.—"The truth of freedom or free will can not be seen from the second stage of knowing, which gets no further in its consciousness than the thought of environment. To it, therefore, fate is the highest

---

* Vol. 15, pp. 210–213.

principle. Again, to the first stage of knowing what seems very clear to the second stage may be a dark enigma. The idea of fate is to it inconceivable, because it does not think objects as in a state of relativity to their environment. Although all experience contains the three elements already pointed out—object, environment, and logical presupposition—yet the first stage of knowing is distinctly conscious only of the object; the second stage notes chiefly the environment, and thinks things as conditioned by necessary relations of dependence, while the third stage of knowing looks especially to the logical presupposition.

"Notwithstanding these radically different views of the world and its existences, it is not difficult to pass from a lower stage to a higher. Any one whose point of view is so elementary as to include the immediate object as the most essential item may be led up to the insight that the environment is most essential by calling his attention, step by step, to the essential relations which condition the existence of the object. He will soon come to see that the object depends on the environment, and will concede that the totality of conditions makes that object to be what it is, and prevents it from being anything else. This is the standpoint of fate—external constraint in the form of the 'totality of conditions' environs all objects in the world, and makes them to be what they are. Any one habituated to observe the essential relations or environment of an object will adopt this as a final principle until he gets the third point of view—that of totality. The underlying logical condition, which is presupposed both by the object and its environment, is not a dependent being, nor a mere correlative of dependence. It is a totality, and self-determined.

"The conviction held by those in the first stage of knowing is that objects all possess self-existence in their immediateness, and that all relations are accidental and not essential. The conviction of those in the second stage is the relativity of all existence, and the omnipotence of fate. The third stage of knowing is the contemplation of the form of totality, which being self-determined is free. Its utterance therefore is: All beings are free beings, or else parts or products of free being."*

"The second stage of thinking leads up to a third stage which regards all things as manifestations of self-activity—as revelations of the supreme, divine self-activity. The second stage of thinking is pantheistic, in so far as it looks upon all objects in the world as mere dependent beings caused through others and as not possessed of self-existence. According to this view, it makes all beings necessitated by others, and these again, by others. The infinite progress of dependence upon others seems insurmountable. Pantheism denies true self-existence to all created beings. It makes them all shadows of an absolute which possesses no qualities or attributes. Quality and attribute are limitations, and hence incompatible with the absolute, says this second stage of thinking. But such an absolute is an empty void, for all activity is denied to it. If finite things are merely relative and dependent, they do not manifest or reveal 'the absolute' as conceived by pantheism, and, hence, they are in very truth vain shadows. But

---

* Vol. 17, pp. 342, 343.

an absolute that possesses no attributes and no self-activity is an absolute nothing. For it can not relate to the world as creator without activity of its own, nor can it relate to itself without self-activity. If it is a mere image or picture of some immense being occupying space but devoid of motion, then the fact of its filling space makes it an aggregate of parts—a gigantic thing composed of things, and we have only the first or elementary stage of thought. The first stage of thought conceives things and not forces. If it attempts to conceive forces, it pictures them as things—heat, light, and electricity, as 'fluids.' The second stage of thought conceives forces as the reality underlying things. Things are equilibria of forces. The first stage of thought is atheistic, because it refuses to think a true absolute, but insists on an image or picture of some limited thing, however great it may be. The second stage of thought is pantheistic, because it can not see any independence or self-existence except in the absolute: 'The absolute is all that truly is, and all created beings are mere shadows of it.' This is the principle of 'absolute relativity,' which we hear from the evolutionists. All things are what they are through their relation to others. The totality is what it is through its relation to the absolute. The absolute is conceived in this theory as that which has no relations, and this is the fallacy of pantheism.

"Pantheism is a true and valid thought, in so far as it perceives the necessity for a one absolute as the ground of a world of finite and transitory things. It is wrong, in so far as it denies self-activity to the absolute.

"But atheism is no philosophic basis for a view of

human and divine relations; nor is pantheism. Atheism logically sets up the principle of individual self-interest. Pantheism logically sets up (as Buddhism or Brahmanism) the absolute renunciation of the individual. To be like its absolute it must annul all finitude, all individualism, and even all personality.

"The third stage of thinking perceives self-activity as the first principle, as the absolute. Hence its absolute is not empty, but filled with self-relation which is thinking and willing. Its absolute is, therefore, creative. While pantheism conceives an absolute which does not create because it does not act at all, and, hence, the beings in the world are to be regarded as shadows possessing no real being; theism, on the other hand, conceives the absolute as Personal Creator, and it looks upon the beings in the world as possessing reality in various degrees." *

Substantial Will.—" Self-activity is freedom. Dependence on another and passive recipiency of influences from without signify fate and necessity. There can be no real individuality except in the form of self-activity or self-determination. That which belongs to something else, and exists through the activity of that other being, is only a manifestation or phenomenon. All that it is reveals the nature of the energy of that other. With only the idea of fate or external constraint, and no consciousness of self-activity as the ultimate presupposition, the mind is obliged to deny individuality even to human beings, and to regard all beings as phenomena. Phenomena are syntheses of effects, manifesta-

---

* "The Chautauquan," vol. vi, p. 438, May, 1886.

tions of energy or influence, that has originated in some source lying beyond the sphere of manifestation. But just as the thought of influence or causality involves self-separation or self activity, so, as a matter of course, every special instance of it has the same implication. A phenomenon as a manifestation posits or presupposes the existence of the pure energy or self-activity whose manifestation it is. Dependence, or any form of essential relation, presupposes self-existence as that on which the object depends and as that whose energy it manifests.

"It is impossible, therefore, to think fate or external necessity as a finality, or, in fact, as existing, except as a result of freedom. 'All things are necessitated by the totality of conditions' is the principle of fate; but its logical condition or presupposition is that the totality of conditions is self-conditioned. If the totality of conditions contains energy, that energy must be self-determining or free. Necessity or fate presupposes freedom as its ground or condition. Hence, if there is anything there is individuality. But whether we shall find many individuals in the world, or whether the world as a totality forms only one individual, is not evident from this principle alone. . . . But with the principle of fate as a finality, we should be obliged to deny freedom to all individualities, and explain persons as somehow products of fate.*

"* Rowland G. Hazard, in his book on 'The Freedom of the Mind in Willing,' concludes that every being that wills is a creative first cause.' He shows that self-activity is an essential presupposition of a conscious being possessing will. He has very acutely perceived that it is spontaneity or automatism that is denied by the

"The fundamental truth is that the first principle is free, and that whatever is a totality (or independent whole) is free. It is clear that the first principle can reveal or manifest itself only in free beings. It would follow, too, that creation exists for the development or evolution of free beings, and that free beings can exist in a state of development.

"There is change; change implies that what is real does not cover all the possibilities of being. Water, for example, is liquid at this moment; at another moment it may be solid, as ice; or an elastic fluid, as steam. It is only one of these states at a time; one state is real and the other two are potential. Were it possible to regard the total existence of water as exhausted in these three states, we might say that water is only one third real at any given instant of time. Were all possibilities or potentialities real at the same instant, there could be no change. Here we arrive at the conception of actuality or total being, including all potentialities, whether real or otherwise.

"One can get but little ways into the discussion of the great question of individuality without making this distinction between beings which are part real and part potential and those whose potentialities are all real. Self-activities are those which are all real; they are self-realizing beings. Their real side exists through their will. But it seems strange at first that there should be two kinds of self-activity—the one a perfect Creator, God, and the other an imperfect self-realizing

---

fatalists, and that they ignore a most obvious fact of consciousness and observation.

being. Actuality is individual, while reality may be only a phenomenal manifestation of an individuality. The individuality, as self-active, exists as wholly real, and gives existence to a product of his will which forms a second sphere of reality. This second sphere of reality may be a progressive realization, and it is here that we have the distinction between God and man, God being perfect also in the second sphere of realization, while man is only progressively so. It is man's vocation to make himself objective in a second sphere of reality —the external world. When he has accomplished this, then he is both subject and object the same.

"To this distinction of reality from·actuality we may give other names, as, for example, phenomenon and substance. Phenomenon is the reality which is subject to change through the activity of the totality of the process. The phenomenon manifests the nature of the energy, which makes the process, that energy being always a self-activity. Substance is another name given to self-activity to express the phase of abiding and continuance that it has.

"Freedom is the essential form of the total or self-activity because it is independent. But in its self-realization it makes a second sphere of reality, the products of its acts. In what we call the actual there is the entire potency, which is manifested in the fragmentary realities not only in their creation, but also in their destruction. Hence it has been said, 'What is actual is rational,' because the actual is a process that annuls all partial realities. The more potentialities that are real the nearer is the existence to a true individuality. A being in which the entire circle of possibilities is realized is an actuality or energy and a complete individuality. When but few of its potentialities are real, it possesses little individuality; for when new potentialities are realized the being is changed so much that it becomes another. A being with one of its potentialities real would be as unstable of individuality as a pyramid on its apex is unstable of position; a being with all real would be immortal, though it were ever so undeveloped and lacking in education and culture. Before actuality a being progresses through evolution in which its individualities are continually lost. After actuality, permanent individuality is attained, and it can progress only through self-determination, which shall make for itself a sphere of externality identical with its own actuality. In one sense we speak of the uncultured man (child or savage) as having unrealized potentialities. These potentialities belong to his sphere of second reality, which he must create for himself." *

Formal Will.—" A stronghold of fatalism is founded on a confusion of the different meanings of the word necessity. In logical necessity there is nothing to contradict freedom of the will. Only external necessity is incompatible with such freedom. It is a logical necessity that the totality must be self-active and free. An external necessity or constraint would destroy freedom; but a moral necessity confirms freedom.

"The most important distinction is here to be made —the distinction between spontaneity or mere self-activity in its first degree, and moral freedom or self-activity in accordance with its own nature.

---

* Vol. 17, pp. 344–347.

"It is clear that a self-active being may act in contradiction to itself, or in such a manner that its deeds are mutually destructive and reduced to zero. Or, again, it may act so that each act confirms and strengthens all others. The latter species of acts is said to be moral actions; it is in harmony with the nature of freedom or self-activity, while the former is immoral and tends to mutual destruction.

"Human institutions (family, society, state, Church) are founded in the interest of true freedom. The freedom of each individual acting according to moral laws, goes to the support of all individuals in the exercise of their freedom. The individual may insist upon his caprice and arbitrariness, and set himself against the moral framework of society. In this case he exhibits his formal freedom at the expense of his substantial freedom. For he obliges his fellow-men to conspire against the exercise of his powers, to realize his volitions, and to interpose prison bars or other constraint. His will can not be constrained, because it is absolutely self-active; but his control over the environment beyond the limits of his individuality is resisted by other free individuals whose environment he attacks. Formal freedom is the freedom to attempt whatever one chooses; substantial freedom is the freedom of the race, which one individual shares with the rest by willing what is in accordance with the nature of self-activity, and therefore co-operative with the moral will of all men.

"This capacity for substantial freedom through combination of the individual with the race points toward immortality. Since each individual learns the nature of pure self-activity through observing the mutual effects of human deeds, that is to say, learns what deeds are not self-contradictory but affirmative through the moral laws discovered by the race as its aggregate wisdom, it follows that the perfection of each individual is attained in proportion to his acquirement of this wisdom of the race, and his realization of it in his own life. The free being has the power of co-operating with his race in such a way as to avail himself by intercommunication of the experience of all. Each life is thus in part vicarious. Each lives for the benefit of all, and all for each. By sharing in the experience of others the individual is enabled to reap their wisdom, and at the same time to escape the pain ensuing from their mistakes. Thus infinite growth in knowledge and holiness becomes possible. The ideal of human life is revealed in this: Infinite combination of humanity extending through an infinite future of immortal life; growth in the image of the Personal God through membership in the infinite Invisible Church. The principle of grace is realized in human institutions. By social combination each gives his individual mite to the whole and receives in turn the aggregate gift of the social whole, thus making him rich by an infinite return." *

Ill.—The substantial will is thought, self-determination; the formal will is action. The substantial will is freedom; the formal will may not act in accordance with freedom. As a practical illustration, a person is determining what occupation he shall follow as his life-work. The substantial will freely creates the reasons for one course of action and then another, and then as

---

* "The Chautauquan," vol. vi, pp. 439, 440, May, 1886.

freely determines which of the ways considered, on the whole, is the best. In this thought, or will, the only restraint is in the mind itself, so that this very self-restraint is self-determination or freedom. But circumstances may arise to hinder the realization of the substantial will in external acts. The will of another person as freely determines a like course of action where there was opportunity for only one. The formal will or external acts of one collide with those of the other; and so the thought or substantial will of only one is rendered real in the formal will, or external acts. But the will of one was as free in his determinations as the other, and in the activity of the mind itself is the true freedom. For, could these two people have power of thought and knowledge sufficient to discover all the results that will arise from the fact that they both choose an occupation in which one of them can satisfy all the wants or demands of society in that line, one will freely determine some other course of action; so that the fact that the formal will of one is restrained by the formal will of another only shows that finiteness brings limitations in thought, but does not change the fact that the will in its nature, in its determinations, is free. And it also shows that the more an individual realizes the thought of the race, or enters into the life of the species, the more will his determinations be in accordance with the substantial freedom of society, and fewer will be the collisions between his formal will and the formal will of others; for society, past, present, and future, reflects the will of God, and in God is perfect knowledge and perfect will, for "knowing and willing are one" with Him.

And further, in his chosen occupation, as an owner of a distillery, the individual may freely determine his deeds in such a manner that his substantial will is not in harmony with the substantial freedom of society. By so determining, the individual cuts himself off from the true unity of thought and will of society; and, if the substantial will of the individual becomes externalized, what had been already done in the determination of the individual becomes known to society through the formal will; but the formal will or deeds of the individual may contradict or destroy other deeds that were in the interest of true freedom. The individual freely destroys himself by his own determinations, which, as thought or substantial will, remain as sin which must be met with punishment or repentance, but which, rendered real through the formal will, become crime, and the state may, by a penalty which in a manner measures the deed, make known the fact that the individual has by his own determination cut himself off from society.

Society may restrain the formal will, but not the substantial will, for that is individual. John Bunyan and Savonarola, although prison bars for years restrained the formal will of each, were, notwithstanding, free beings.

Change sometimes regarded as caused only by Environment: External Conditions.—" 'Freedom of the will' seems an impossible thought to all persons on the second stage of culture in thinking, and who, consequently, have not reached the idea of self-activity. To them, fate seems the only logical outcome in the universe. Their principle reads thus: 'All things are necessitated; each thing is necessitated by the totality of its conditions to be as it is, and whatever is must be as it is, and under the conditions can not be otherwise.'

"Nothing seems clearer to the thinker who has advanced beyond the first stage of thought, which regards all reality as made up of things without relations. The second stage of thought, which sees the essentiality of relations and dependence, has fate or necessity as its supreme principle. To it all movement and change seem to originate through some external cause. According to it, therefore, there is no internal cause, no self-activity; everything is necessitated by its environment of outside circumstances. The difficulty with this view is that it confines its attention to dependent beings, and refuses to think of independent beings; it thinks parts, but will not think the whole or totality. If the part is dependent and relative, certainly the whole or totality can not be dependent and relative. The totality can not be necessitated by something outside of it, precisely because the totality has nothing outside of it.

"The totality must be self-necessitated or free. If the parts are necessitated by what is outside of them, yet the constraint is within the whole, and must arise in the self-activity of the whole.

"The idea of change is inconceivable on this basis of universal necessity. If one admits the fact of change, he is bound logically to admit self-activity in the totality. Let us look at this logic. According to the doctrine of fate, all things are necessitated by the totality of conditions. If things change, then something new begins and something old ceases to be. The thing before the change was necessitated to be what it was by the totality of conditions; and the new thing that has come to be after the change is also necessitated to be what it is by the totality of conditions. Under the same totality of conditions, however, there can not be two different states or conditions of a thing, for that would contradict the law of necessity and establish chance in it place. Under the same conditions, a thing must always remain as it is and can not change. Only a change in the conditions, therefore, will make possible a change in the thing. For, as the two states of the thing, the one before, the other after the change, are different, they require two different totalities of conditions to make them possible, according to the law of necessity or fate.

"By this process we have simply shifted the problem of change from the thing to the totality of conditions. Having explained the change of the thing by the change of the totality of conditions, we are called upon to explain the change in the latter. Since it is the totality of conditions, there is no environment of conditions outside of it, and hence it is its own necessity. If it moves or changes it must move or change itself. Here we have arrived again at self-activity as the presupposition of necessity. In other words, necessity can not be the supreme principle, for it presupposes self-activity or freedom in the necessitating totality, as the source from which the constraint proceeds.

"Thus the second stage of thinking is forced to contradict its principle of relativity and dependence on external necessity, and admit the principle of freedom, although only in the totality.

Motives.—" Since the objections to freedom of the will are based, for the most part, on the impossibility of self-activity, it follows that with the admission of its reality the chief difficulty is overcome. But it is surprising to see how many devices the second stage of thinking will invent to defend its position. A favorite argument with it is based on the necessity of the strongest motive. The environment is conceived to be a list of motives which furnish alternatives of action. The strongest motive, however, is supposed to constrain the will and render freedom impossible.

" Those fatalists who assert that the will is necessitated because it yields to the strongest motive, overlook the distinction between reality and potentiality, and do not consider that motives are possibilities and not realities. A reality is not a motive; a motive is only the conception of a desirable possibility. A potentiality or possibility is not an existence, but only an idea in the mind, which the mind originates by its own activity. After creating the idea of a possible existence the mind may make it real by an action of the will, or it may leave it a mere possibility. The mind creates the motive by its thinking activity, and creates also its realization by its will-activity, and, hence, is doubly creative, doubly free. It is the grossest of errors, therefore, to conceive the mind as a mere agent that transmits the causality of the motive to the deed, when, in point of fact, it is the cause of both the motive and the deed. To say that a motive constrains the will is the same as to say that something acts before it exists. According to this view, the motive—a mere idea without reality, acts upon the will and causes it to produce a reality for it—a possibility constrains a reality (the will) to change it (the possibility, the motive) into a reality." *

Ill.—As in the above example, it might be said that the person did not freely determine his occupation in life, that his friends, relatives, family, or "circumstances" determined what his occupation should be. In such a case, the freedom, the self-determination, has been removed from the individual to his environment, and the true substantial will or energizing remains, although transferred from the individual to the "totality of conditions"; but in placing the freedom, the self-determination in "circumstances" rather than in the individual, the individual becomes a product of fate, and it is in fact granting that "things" have more self-activity, more self-determination, than personality.

Or, it might be said, that the strongest motive of the individual, as "money-making," determined his occupation. Such a thought considers "motives" as ready made in the mind in a series from low to high, or weak to strong, and any one governing the mind as the occasion may demand. The true thought is—the mind creates the motives as well as the action, and thus, instead of being impelled by the motive, is doubly creative. An instinctive inherited desire for making money is not a motive until the individual has consciously made it a thought, and in that very thought the mind was creative or free.

---

* "The Chautauquan," vol. vi, p. 439, May, 1886.

CHAPTER V.

IMMORTALITY OF MAN.

"We come now to consider the question of the individual immortality of man in the light of the principles which we have discussed in the previous chapters. Our subject has two phases: First, we must inquire what are the conditions of immortality, and what beings in the world, if any, possess such conditions. Second, we must consider the question in the light of the first principle of the world, as we have found it revealed as the supreme condition of existence and experience.

"How is it possible that in this world of perishable beings there can exist an immortal and ever-progressing being? Without the personality of God it would be impossible, because an unconscious first principle would be incapable of producing conscious beings, or, if they were produced, it would overcome them as incongruous and inharmonious elements in its world. It would finally draw all back into its image and reduce conscious individuality to unconsciousness. In our investigation of the presuppositions of experience, we have found *causa sui*, or self-activity, as the ultimate principle, and we find in the human intellect and will what is harmonious with that principle. Let us note that science, in teaching the doctrine of evolution and that of the struggle for existence, favors the doctrine that intelligence and will are the surviving and permanent substance. For intelligence and will triumph in the struggle for existence, and prove themselves the goal to which the creation moves.

"Space and time and inorganic matter are pervaded by the principles of mechanism and chemism. Organic being, whether plant or animal, manifests self-activity in various degrees.

"The plant possesses assimilation, or the nutritive process. It reacts on its environment. It is a real manifestation of individuality. Perhaps one would say that the rock, or the waves, or the wind has individuality and reacts on its environment. Certainly the plant possesses individuality in a less questionable form. The action of water, air, and mineral does not avail to assimilate other substances into its own form. The plant takes up some portion of its environment into itself and stamps on it its own form, making it a vegetable cell, and adding it to its own structure. It strives to become infinite by absorbing its environment into itself. But it can not conquer *all* of its environment in this way; it would have to become some world-tree (*Yggdrasil*) to succeed in conquering all of its environment. The infinite, the absolute, the self-active, must be its own environment.

"The plant form of existence can not realize self-activity except to a limited degree. The portions of its environment which it takes up and assimilates, moreover, produce growth or expansion in space. This expansion implies separation of parts. The individuality of plants is rather of the species than of the particular plant. The individuality is in transition, being manifested by the growth of new limbs, twigs, leaves, or fruit, sprouting out from the old as the first did from the earth. Because the plant is a constant transition from one individual to another it can not manifest identity except in the species. In the animal we have feeling and locomotion, and the unity is found in the particular animal as well as in the species. Feeling implies self-activity, not only in reaction on the environment as in the case of nutrition, but in reproducing the impression made by the environment within the soul of the animal. Unless the animal reproduces for himself the limitation caused by the environment there is no perception. The reproduction is accompanied by an unconscious judgment or inference that transfers the occasion of the feeling to an external world. Thus, time, space, and causality, function in feeling or sense-perception, but the subject is unconscious of them. The animal sees, hears, tastes, smells, or touches the objects of his environment, unconscious that he does this by reproducing within himself the shocks made upon his senses by them.

"This activity of reproduction (sense-perception) is only in the presence of the objects. But there is a higher order of reproduction which is free from the presence of impressions on the senses; this is called *representation*, and is in two forms—(*a*) recollection of former perceptions, and (*b*) free fancy, in which the soul causes to arise within itself by limitation new combinations of perceptions recalled, or entirely new objects. Although the activity of representation is a higher form of manifestation of individuality, and seems to be quite free from time and place, because any former perception may be recalled at pleasure, yet it is still inadequate, because the object is a particular image, just as much as the perception of any particular object in the world.

"The being which perceives or feels is a self-activity in a higher sense than is manifested in plant life, but it is not its own object in the forms of mere feeling, or sense-perception, or recollection, or fancy. Individuality is persistence under change, self-preservation in the presence of alien forces, and self-objectivity. It is self-determination, or free causal energy, *causa sui*. To have as object a particular thing, therefore, is not to be conscious of individuality, either of one's own or of another's. An individuality that does not exist for itself has no personal identity, and hence is indifferent to immortality. When the self-activity in reproducing an impression perceives at the same time its own freedom or causal energy, then it becomes conscious of self. This takes place in the recognition of objects as belonging to classes or species. Here begins the immortality of the individual. Not before this, because the individual is and can be only a self-activity, and can not know himself except as generic. An individual that does not recognize individuality is not for itself, and its continuance of existence is only for the species and not for its particular self. But with the recognition of species and genera there is the recognition of self as persistent, although, at first, only in the form of recognizing the objects of the world as being specimens of classes and genera.

"Here begins immortality of the individual with

the recognition of individuality in the form of species, and directly it manifests itself in the formation of language or the adoption of conventional signs to represent classes, processes, and species. If any of the higher animals shall be discovered to accompany the act of sense-perception by recognition of the objects as examples of classes, and to possess conventional means of expressing, not particular objects, but general processes and species, then it will become necessary to admit the immortality of such individual animals.

"Above this form of recognition of species the conscious mind rises to the stage of reflection and the stage of insight. We have already discussed these stadia as (*a*) the perception of objects (*b*) their environment, and (*c*) their underlying presuppositions. It is only in this latter species of knowing that the soul comes to recognize itself in its true nature, and it celebrates this fact first in religion as a knowledge of God as Creator and Redeemer of the world.

"In our study of the idea of self-activity as the highest principle we found the explanation of the world and its destiny, and this explanation is the necessary complement to the psychological investigation of the question of immortality. The Divine Self-activity in whom knowing and willing are identical, so that His knowing is at the same time a creating of His object, knows Himself, but this knowing does not create directly a world of finite beings. He knows only Himself and creates or begets His own likeness, a perfect being equal to himself, the Second Self-activity or Person.

"The Second Person, equal in knowing and willing to the First, creates a Third equal to Himself, but also creates a world of finite creatures in a process of evolution. Because the Second knows his own derivation from the First, which is only a logical precondition and not an event in time antedating his perfection (for He is eternally begotten), in knowing it He creates it, and it appears as a stream of creation rising in a scale of beings from pure passivity up to pure activity.

"The inorganic nature, the plant, and the animal do not attain true individuality, but man does. Man makes his environment into the image of his true self when he puts on the form of the divine Second Person, as the one who gives Himself freely to lift up imperfect beings. As that form is the elevation of the finite into participation with Himself, so man's spiritual function is the realization of higher selves through institutions—the Invisible Church, which is formed of all the intelligent beings collected from all worlds in the universe. The social combination of man with man is thus the means of realizing the divine. The principle of the absolute institution which we call the Invisible Church is called divine charity or love. It is the missionary spirit, or the spirit of self-sacrifice for the good of others. This is the realization in man of the occupation of the Creator, and is, therefore, the eternal vocation of man.

"If man were not immortal there would be a break in the chain of beings that reaches from the pure external and passive up to the pure active, and hence the eternal elevation of the Second Person into equality with the First Person would be impossible, and, therefore, the First Person would not know himself in the Second, and hence there would be no self-activity at all, and consequently, also, there would be no derivative or finite being. But this is impossible. The immortality of man and the necessity of intelligent beings on all worlds at some stage of their process is manifest from this.

"The First Divine Knowing creates or begets the Second, and sees in it the world of evolution and also the Third divine unity of blessed spirits in the Invisible Church as the Holy Spirit. The creation of the world is the result of the knowing of the relation of the Second to the First Person; and as all this is within the self-knowing of the First, its origin is called a 'double procession.' It is not a genesis like that of the Second which is that of one person from another; but a procession inasmuch as it proceeds from the free union of infinitely numerous blessed spirits assuming the form of the divine life of the Second Person.

"Let one remember that even our finite temporal institutions possess in some sort a personality—deliberative and executive functions. It could be said that the state possesses a higher personality than the individual citizen, for it is not subject to his vicissitudes of sleeping and waking, youth and old age, sex, etc. But the Invisible Church is the perfect archetype of institutions, eternal in duration and infinite in extent, and complete and absolute in its personality. Space and matter exist only that worlds may become theatres for the birth and probation of souls.

"The social life of man as it is realized in institutions—family, civil society, state, and especially in the Church—is his higher spiritual life. Were not human souls immortal as individuals, however, there could be no perfection resulting from the creation of the world, and hence the Second Divine Person could not contemplate in creation his own logical precondition of rising from passivity to pure activity; or, what is the same thing, He could not recognize his own derivation from the First; and this would involve also the impossibility of his own ascent to equality with the First; and this, too, the impossibility of the perfect self-knowledge or self-determination of the First; and this the denial of independent being, and of any being whatsoever. Again, if we apply the principle of creation—self-knowing of the Absolute is creating—we may say that a world of imperfect beings implies the self-recognition of passivity or derivation on the part of the Creator. If there were actual present passivity and derivation, He could not be a Creator by reason of imperfection which would appear as a separation of will from intellect, as in man. But his logical precondition of derivation and passivity would imply a First Person. Again, these two would imply a perfect final cause or end for the creation of imperfect beings which could only be reached by the tuition and education of these into a perfect institution possessing perfect personality, and through immortal life." *

---

* Vol. 17, pp. 351-356.

THE END.

INTERNATIONAL EDUCATION SERIES.
Edited by WILLIAM T. HARRIS, LL. D.

A library for teachers and school-managers, and text-books for normal classes—including works on *Historical, Critical, Theoretical,* and *Practical Education.*

VOLUMES NOW READY.

Vol. I.—**The Philosophy of Education.** By JOHANN KARL FRIEDRICH ROSENKRANZ, Doctor of Theology and Professor of Philosophy at the University of Königsberg. Translated from the German by ANNA C. BRACKETT. Price, $1.50.

Vol. II.—**A History of Education.** By Professor F. V. N. PAINTER, of Roanoke College, Virginia. Price, $1.50.

Vol. III.—**The Rise and Early Constitution of Universities.** WITH A SURVEY OF MEDIÆVAL EDUCATION. By S. S. LAURIE, LL. D., Professor of the Institutes and History of Education in the University of Edinburgh. Price, $1.50.

Vol. IV.—**The Ventilation and Warming of School Buildings.** By GILBERT B. MORRISON, Teacher of Physics and Chemistry in Kansas City High-School. Price, 75 cents.

Vol. V.—**The Education of Man.** By FRIEDRICH FROEBEL. Translated from the German by W. N. HAILMAN, Ph. D., Superintendent of Public Schools at La Porte, Indiana. Price, $1.50.

Vol. VI.—**Elementary Psychology and Education.** By Dr. J. BALDWIN, author of "Art of School Management," etc. Price, $1.50.

Vol. VII.—**The Senses and the Will.** By W. PREYER, Professor of Physiology in Jena. Translated from the original German by H. W. BROWN, Teacher in the State Normal School at Worcester, Mass. Part I of THE MIND OF THE CHILD. Price, $1.50.

Vol. VIII.—**Memory.** By DAVID KAY, F. R. G. S. Price, $1.50.

Vol. IX.—**The Development of the Intellect.** By W. PREYER, Professor of Physiology in Jena. Part II of THE MIND OF THE CHILD. Price, $1.50.

Vol. X.—**How to Study Geography.** By FRANCIS W. PARKER, Principal of the Cook Co. (Ill.) Normal School. Price, $1.50.

Vol. XI.—**Education in the United States. A History from the Earliest Settlements.** By RICHARD A. BOONE, Professor of Pedagogy, Indiana University.

Vol. XII.—**European Schools; or What I saw in the Schools of Germany, France, Austria, and Switzerland.** By L. R. KLEMM, Ph. D., Principal of the Cincinnati (Ohio) Technical School.

Vol. XIII.—**Practical Hints for the Teachers of Public Schools.** By GEORGE HOWLAND, Superintendent of the Chicago Schools. Price, $1.00.

New York: D. APPLETON & CO., 1, 3, & 5 Bond Street.

BOOKS FOR TEACHERS.

Spencer's Education:
INTELLECTUAL, MORAL, AND PHYSICAL. Divided into four chapters: What Knowledge is of most Worth?—Intellectual Education—Moral Education—Physical Education. Price, $1.25.

Bain's Education as a Science.
The author views the "teaching art" from a scientific point of view, and tests ordinary experiences by bringing them to the criterion of psychological law. Price, $1.75.

Bain's On Teaching English,
WITH DETAILED EXAMPLES, AND AN INQUIRY INTO THE DEFINITION OF POETRY. Price, $1.25.

Johonnot's Principles and Practice of Teaching.
This is a practical book by an experienced teacher. The subject of education is treated in a systematic and comprehensive manner, and shows how rational processes may be substituted for school-room routine. Price, $1.50.

Baldwin's Art of School Management.
This is a very helpful hand-book for the teacher. He will find it full of practical suggestions in regard to all the details of school-room work, and how to manage it to best advantage. Price, $1.50.

Greenwood's Principles of Education Practically Applied.
The object of this work throughout is to impress this important question upon the mind of the teacher: "*How shall I teach so as to have my pupils become self-reliant, independent, manly men and womanly women?*" Price, $1.00.

Sully's Outlines of Psychology,
WITH SPECIAL REFERENCE TO THE THEORY OF EDUCATION. Price, $3.00.

Sully's Hand-Book of Psychology,
ON THE BASIS OF OUTLINES OF PSYCHOLOGY. A practical exposition of the elements of Mental Science, with special applications to the Art of Teaching, designed for the use of Schools, Teachers, Reading Circles, and Students generally. Price, $1.50.

Bain's Moral Science.
A COMPENDIUM OF ETHICS. Divided into two divisions. The first—the Theory of Ethics—treats at length of the two great questions, the ethical standard and the moral faculty; the second division—on the Ethical Systems—is a full detail of all the systems, ancient and modern, by conjoined abstract and summary. Price, $1.50.

McArthur's Education,
IN ITS RELATION TO MANUAL INDUSTRY. The important subject of manual education is thoroughly and clearly treated. Price, $1.50.

Hodgson's Errors in the Use of English.
A work for the teacher's table, and invaluable for classes in grammar and literature. Price, $1.50.

Descriptive Catalogue sent free on application. *Special prices will be made on class supplies.*

D. APPLETON & CO., Publishers,
New York, Boston, Chicago, Atlanta, San Francisco.

SULLY'S TWO GREAT WORKS.

Outlines of Psychology, with Special Reference to the Theory of Education.

A Text-Book for Colleges. By JAMES SULLY, A. M., Examiner for the Moral Sciences Tripos in the University of Cambridge, etc., etc.

"A book that has been long wanted by all who are engaged in the business of teaching and desire to master its principles. In the first place, it is an elaborate treatise on the human mind, of independent merit as representing the latest and best work of all schools of psychological inquiry. But of equal importance, and what will be prized as a new and most desirable feature of a work on mental science, are the educational applications that are made throughout in separate text and type, so that, with the explication of mental phenomena, there comes at once the application to the art of education."

Crown 8vo. Price, $3.00.

Teacher's Hand-Book of Psychology.

On the Basis of "Outlines of Psychology." By JAMES SULLY, M. A.

A practical exposition of the elements of Mental Science, with special applications to the Art of Teaching, designed for the use of Schools, Teachers, Reading Circles, and Students generally. This book is not a mere abridgment of the author's "Outlines," but has been mainly rewritten for a more direct educational purpose, and is essentially a new work. It has been heretofore announced as "Elements of Psychology."

NOTE.—No American abridgments or editions of Mr. Sully's works are authorized except those published by the undersigned.

12mo, 414 pages. Price, $1.50.

D. APPLETON & CO., PUBLISHERS,
New York, Boston, Chicago, Atlanta, San Francisco.

WORKS OF ALEXANDER BAIN, LL.D.,
PROFESSOR OF LOGIC IN THE UNIVERSITY OF ABERDEEN.

LOGIC, DEDUCTIVE AND INDUCTIVE. New revised edition. 12mo. Cloth, $2.00.

MENTAL SCIENCE: A Compendium of Psychology and History of Philosophy. 12mo. Cloth, $1.50.

MORAL SCIENCE: A Compendium of Ethics. 12mo. Cloth, $1.50.

MIND AND BODY. The Theories of their Relations. (Forming a volume of "The International Scientific Series.") 12mo. Cloth, $1.50.

THE SENSES AND THE INTELLECT. New edition. 8vo. Cloth, $5.00.

THE EMOTIONS AND THE WILL. Third edition. 8vo. Cloth, $5.00.

EDUCATION AS A SCIENCE. (Forming a volume of "The International Scientific Series.") 12mo. Cloth, $1.75.

ENGLISH COMPOSITION AND RHETORIC. Enlarged edition. Part I. Intellectual Elements of Style. Part II. The Emotional Qualities of Style. 12mo.

ON TEACHING ENGLISH, with Detailed Examples and an Inquiry into the Definition of Poetry. 12mo.

New York: D. APPLETON & CO., 1, 3, & 5 Bond Street.

www.ingramcontent.com/pod-product-compliance
Lightning Source LLC
Chambersburg PA
CBHW022109230426
43672CB00008B/1325